Looking for De Soto

LOOKING FOR

De Soto

A Search Through the South
for the Spaniard's
Trail

Joyce Rockwood Hudson

The University of Georgia Press

Athens & London

Paperback edition, 2012
© 1993 by the University of Georgia Press
Athens, Georgia 30602
www.ugapress.org
Designed by Louise OFarrell
Set in 11.5/13 Garamond #3 by Tseng Information, Inc.

Printed digitally in the United States of America

The Library of Congress has cataloged the hardcover edition
of this book as follows:

Hudson, Joyce Rockwood.
Looking for De Soto : a search through the South for the
Spaniard's trail / Joyce Rockwood Hudson.
xviii, 230 p. : ill. ; 24 cm.
Includes bibliographical references (p. 229–230).
ISBN 0-8203-1497-8 (alk. paper)
1. Soto, Hernando de, ca. 1500–1542. 2. Indians of North America—
First contact with Europeans—Southern States. 3. Southern States—
Discovery and exploration—Spanish. I. Title.
E125.S7 H87   1993
970.01'6'092—dc20   92-17252

Paperback ISBN-13: 978-0-8203-4100-2
ISBN-10: 0-8203-4100-2

British Library Cataloging-in-Publication Data available

Maps by Julie Barnes Smith

To our firstborn grandson, Chris,
and our second, Nick, who was
born while we were
looking for De Soto

CONTENTS

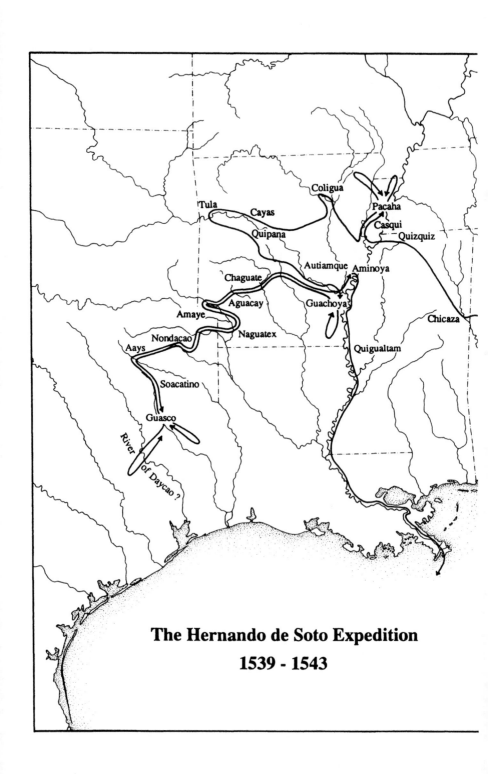

The Hernando de Soto Expedition

1539 - 1543

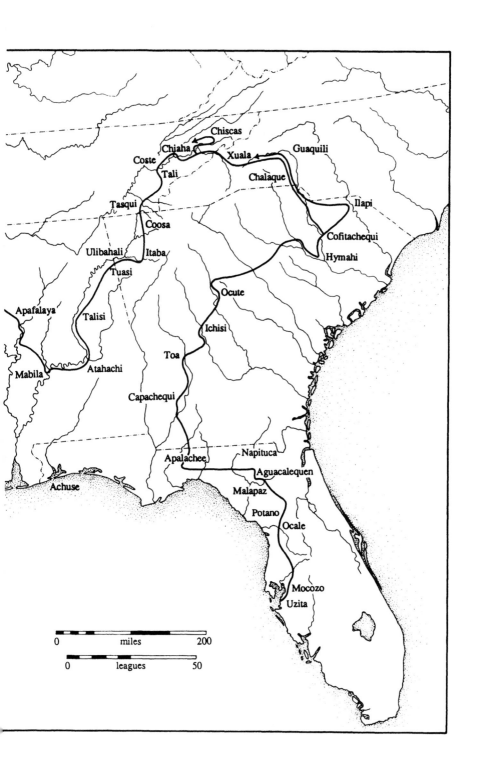

Chiscas

Chiaha

Coste

Tali

Xuala

Guaquili

Chalaque

Tasqui

Coosa

Ilapi

Ulibahali

Itaba

Cofitachequi

Hymahi

Tuasi

Apafalaya

Talisi

Ocute

Ichisi

Toa

Mabila

Atahachi

Capachequi

Napituca

Apalachee

Aguacalequen

Achuse

Malapaz

Potano

Ocale

Mocozo

Uzita

| 0 | miles | 200 |

| 0 | leagues | 50 |

INTRODUCTION

In the six weeks before Christmas 1984, my husband and I took a long drive through the American South. We were on a detective's mission—Charlie was Holmes, and I was Watson. The trail we were following was cold indeed: four hundred and fifty years since the perpetrators of the affair we were investigating had left the scene. There was little for us to go on except some scant written accounts that these perpetrators themselves had left us. Neither they nor we considered the affair a criminal matter. It was undoubtedly brutal, even murderous at times, but that was the nature of conquest in the sixteenth century.

Our mission, therefore, was not to solve a crime, but to solve a scholarly problem, one upon which Charlie had been hard at work for the past five years. Where exactly on the land surface of North America had the feet of Hernando de Soto trod? Although Charlie was consumed by the question, he was not seeking the answer for its own sake. The route of De Soto was something he had to know in order to make use of the information given by the chroniclers of the expedition about the Indians through whose territory they had passed. Charlie is an anthropologist whose special interest is the Indians of the southeastern United States. His concern is more with the aboriginal culture of the Indians than with their later condition as they adapted to the presence of Europeans. Hernando de Soto and his army of six hundred conquistadors were the first Europeans to encounter the Indians in the heartland of the American South. A handful of them wrote down a little of what they saw, leaving us the only relatively comprehensive picture we have of the aboriginal scene in the sixteenth century. Everything else that we know about the Indians at the dawn of European contact comes from archaeological investigations.

Charlie is not an archaeologist, but he spends a lot of time in conversation with archaeologists, and this record of our journey is as much about archaeology as it is about Spaniards and aboriginal Americans. The story of prehistory belongs exclusively to archaeology. History proper, in its technical definition, begins when written documentation begins, which in North America was with the arrival of the Europeans. An archaeological site can be prehistoric, which means that it was occupied before European contact; or it can be historic, meaning it was occupied after European contact and might therefore be mentioned in historical documents. Or it can be protohistoric, meaning it was occupied during the somewhat extended period of time when prehistory was merging into history. In southeastern archaeology, protohistoric generally means the sixteenth century. It is common for a site to have more than one of these components—prehistoric at the deepest levels, protohistoric above that, and a historic component closest to the surface.

The native peoples of the American South that are most widely known are the historic Indians of the eighteenth and nineteenth centuries: the Cherokees of the southern Appalachians; the Creeks of Georgia and Alabama; the Seminoles of Florida; the Chickasaws and Choctaws of Mississippi; and the Quapaws of Arkansas, to name only some of the most prominent. Although these people were descendants of the prehistoric inhabitants of the land, there are great differences between their way of life as we know it from the historical and archaeological records and the way of life of their ancestors, which we know almost entirely through archaeology—with a little help from the chronicles of the Spanish conquistadors.

The difference between the historic and prehistoric Indians is epitomized in one cultural feature: mounds. The prehistoric peoples of the South built flat-topped pyramids similar in form and function to the ones in Mexico. They were, however, smaller and were always made of earth, never of stone. Although the Indians of the South never reached the level of civilization of the Indians of Mexico, their mounds did serve as platforms for temples and for residences of the highest-ranking persons of chiefly lineages, just as the Aztec and Mayan pyramids did. It was this elevated status of persons claiming rank by birth that made the prehistoric southern Indians distinctive from the Indians in the rest of North America, and from their own descendants. When De Soto made his journey through the South, the mounds were in full use. The highest chiefs were living on them, and when these chiefs came down from atop the mounds and went abroad among their people, they were carried on litters on the shoulders of retainers, accompanied by much ceremony. The Spaniards report, and the archaeologists confirm, that the people in the chiefly lineages were sometimes of a larger size than the "commoners," often six feet or taller, which was also considerably taller than Spaniards of the time. This difference in height implies that from the day they were born the chief and his family were better fed than everyone else—evidence again of inherited rank.

In the seventeenth and eighteenth centuries, the old mounds still dotted the landscape, but few of them were being used anymore. Most of the Indians had lost all memory of who had built them and why. Their societies were largely egalitarian, and their chiefs gained their positions through personal achievement. Anthropologists have technical terms for these two kinds of societies. They would say that the ancestors on the mounds were organized into *chiefdoms*, and their egalitarian descendants into *tribes*. The chiefdom level of social organization is more complex than the tribe.

Why the discrepancy between the earlier and the later people? A large part of the answer is De Soto himself. He was a kind of holocaust sweeping through the land. There were around six hundred soldiers in the expedition, half of them mounted, and besides the soldiers there were several hundred servants, campfollowers, and Indian slaves who had been taken along the way: an army of a thousand, more or less. There were also war dogs—great greyhounds and mastiffs fitted out in armor—and a herd of several hundred pigs. Imagine such a sight to people who had never before seen anything like it. The Indians had never seen Europeans, horses, or pigs, nor heard the sound of firearms or felt their power. They knew dogs, but not of such horrific size, and not armored and trained to attack and disembowel humans. And they had never experienced the audacity of conquistadors, who seemed to be afraid of no one, not even the representatives on earth of the divine power of the Sun.

The high chiefs on the mounds believed themselves to be such representatives, and so did their people believe it, paying them tribute in corn, mainly, but also in deerskins, salt, and other valued commodities. The corn was put in public storehouses and later redistributed by the chiefs, who were regarded in their generosity as magnanimous givers of life. Not only was De Soto unafraid of the high chiefs, but he searched them out precisely because of the public granaries. His army needed food. The Spaniards were not skilled at hunting and gathering wild food from the forest, and even if they had been, there were too many of them for the forest to support. They needed large stores of corn.

Upon entering a chief's territory, De Soto would go directly to the chief and take him hostage, demanding from him corn, burden bearers, and women. Usually the Spaniards would keep the chief a prisoner until they had reached the far side of his territory, having used him to obtain what they wanted from his people along the way. Then as they crossed into new territory they would release the chief, who would now be free to return to his ravaged land to try to reestablish his authority. But the foundation of the chiefly claim to power was now in question. Could a true representative of the Sun be so easily overrun? Was there another god greater than the Sun? Should the people pay tribute to a chief who was powerless to protect them? There is evidence that some chiefs did reestablish some authority, but we can assume that their power was never again as great as it had been before De Soto came.

What De Soto began, European diseases finished. The De Soto army itself probably left diseases behind, though we do not know this with certainty. Other epidemics spread inland from the repeated contacts between European sailors and Indians on the Gulf and Atlantic coasts, and from the tiny missions the Spaniards founded along the southern Atlantic coast at the end of the sixteenth century. The Indians had no resistance at all to any European diseases—measles and influenza could be as deadly as smallpox and typhus. An epidemic of smallpox in an Indian town might kill more than 80 percent of the people living there. In the century and a half after De Soto, the aboriginal population of the South plummeted, and the power of the chiefs disintegrated once and for all. Remnant bands coalesced into simpler, egalitarian tribes. When the British arrived to colonize the Carolinas in the late seventeenth century, they were the first Europeans since De Soto to make the journey into the heartland of the South. The Indian societies they encountered were far different from the ones De Soto had seen.

Without the De Soto chroniclers we would know nothing of those people on the mounds except what archaeology can tell us. Archaeology is a wonderful science. From stains in the earth and the distribution of fragments of imperishable material left behind by a people, houses and towns can be reconstructed and inferences made about social and political life. But if the site is prehistoric, if no written documents exist anywhere that allude to it, then the inferences remain inferences, and the people whose traces have been unearthed remain in shadow. We cannot be certain of their name, or what language they spoke, or what their system of kinship was, or how far their political ties extended, or what was the true nature of their religion.

This is why the De Soto chronicles are so important. De Soto and his army spent four years traveling through the South. They trekked thirty-five hundred miles and visited Indian towns in every present-day southern state except Louisiana, which they traversed by boat down the Mississippi River without stopping. The chroniclers of the expedition tell us the names of the people they visited and what their societies were like. They tell us who was politically aligned with whom, and what were their warfare practices. They describe activity on the mounds, and tell us about the principal officials, and sometimes even make references to a chief's mother or sister or tell who his successor would be. This is the kind of information that can infuse archaeological information with new life. The Spaniards cared little about Indian culture for its own sake and did not go out of their way to give us these kinds of details. There is much they did not bother to tell us at all. But when their reported activities and passing comments are put together with information from specific archaeological sites, great amounts of light are shed. It is this need to match the information given in the chronicles with specific archaeological sites that makes it important to know exactly where De Soto went. This is what drew Charlie into the case and set him forward on this detective work.

He began the work with two archaeologists, Marvin Smith and Chester DePratter, who were graduate students at the time. For many years there had been an official De Soto route, the result of a federal commission set up in 1936 to mark the route for the four-hundredth anniversary of the expedition in 1939. This is the U.S. De Soto Commission route—or the Swanton route, as it is informally known in recognition of the anthropologist who spearheaded the effort. Few archaeologists were ever satisfied with the Swanton route. Very little archaeology had been done in the South in the 1930s, and the crucial test of the route—that the towns De Soto visited must coincide with archaeological sites of the right time period—could seldom be made. Now, almost fifty years later, there was much more archaeological evidence at hand, and Charlie and Chester and Marvin felt it was time to make a new effort.

The archaeological evidence is nothing, of course, without the De Soto chronicles. There are four of these, only three of which were written by persons who actually made the trip. One of those three was the work of Rodrigo Ranjel, De Soto's secretary, an intelligent and observant man who kept a daily record of events. His account is the most useful for details of time and place. The factor of the expedition, the king's representative, was a man named Luys Hernandez de Biedma, who wrote a shorter chronicle. Biedma often condensed events and omitted the names of less important towns, but he was the only one who gave compass directions, usually for several days travel at a time. The third chronicler who wrote firsthand was a man whom scholars usually refer to as Elvas, although that was not his actual name but the name of the province in Portugal from which he came. He wrote anonymously as "A Gentleman of Elvas." He gives a full and highly readable account, adding details not mentioned by the other two.

The fourth chronicle was written by a man who was not there at all, but who had an ear for a good story. His name was Garcilaso de la Vega, and he was from Peru, his mother an Inca and his father a Spaniard. He grew up in his father's household and was personally acquainted with men who had been with De Soto in "La Florida." Later in his life Garcilaso moved to Spain, where he became an important literary figure. There was one adventurer in particular who had spent long hours with Garcilaso telling stories of the De Soto expedition, and it is this man's story primarily that Garcilaso wrote down in the romantic style of the time and published as a major literary work. It is the most interesting of the four chronicles but the least reliable for reconstructing De Soto's route.

As it turns out, one of the most important documents used to reconstruct the route had nothing to do with De Soto at all, but with another Spanish explorer who covered some of the same ground thirty years later. Setting out from a Spanish outpost on what is now Parris Island near Beaufort, South Carolina, a Spanish captain named Juan Pardo led a small army up through the Carolinas and into the Tennessee Valley, then turned around and came back again. He visited some of the same towns De Soto visited, and he had a scribe with him who recorded his army's movements in much more detail than anyone did for the De Soto expedition. The Pardo document is a kind of Rosetta stone for the unlocking of the De Soto route, although no one had ever used it that way before. Charlie, Chester, and Marvin started with Pardo's route, plotting the wealth of information in that document against the geography and known archaeology of the country inland from coastal South Carolina. They produced a good route for Pardo, one that has since stood up to close scrutiny by other scholars. Since De Soto had covered most of the same territory as Pardo, visiting many of the same towns in the same order, Charlie, Chester, and Marvin now had a secure segment of the De Soto route upon which to anchor further efforts. From the Pardo segment they traced De Soto forward and backward and in a short time had brainstormed the route from the landing at Tampa, Florida, to the crossing of the Mississippi River near Memphis, Tennessee.

Charlie spent the next few years testing and refining this eastern portion of the route, leaving the route west of the Mississippi for later attention. He worked not only with Marvin and Chester but with any other archaeologist who showed an interest. Papers presented at archaeological conferences began attracting attention. Scholars who had thought De Soto an insoluble problem began pricking up their ears. Once the eastern route was fairly secure, at least in broad outline, Charlie turned his efforts to the western route. He was less familiar with the archaeology west of the Mississippi, but he read as much as he could and sketched out a route for Arkansas and Texas, which he then sent for comment to those archaeologists through whose territories it passed. One great asset in laying out the western route was the work of Dan and Phyllis Morse, Arkansas archaeologists who had already worked out a crucial segment of the route just west of the Mississippi River.

By this time Charlie had been at work on the route for five years. In the early, Pardo days the two of us had gone out several times to spend weekends driving segments of the Pardo route, checking to see if the proposed solution fit the actual lay of the land as well as it seemed to fit the maps. Sometimes it did and sometimes it did not. Adjustments were made on the basis of these trips, and Charlie came to see this as a necessary step in working out the route. This had been easy for us to do with Pardo, since we live in northern Georgia and did not have to drive far to pick up Pardo's trail. But most of De Soto's route lay further afield for us. We had at one time, while in Florida on other business, driven the first segment of the De Soto route from Tampa to Gainesville. But now the time had come for a more extensive effort.

In early November 1984 we packed our red 1965 Karmann Ghia full to the brim with books, maps, and luggage and headed down to Gainesville, intending to drive the entire remaining route and be home in time for Christmas. This book is the journal that I kept on that journey.

Although this is not a scholarly account, there are a few archaeological terms with which the reader needs to be familiar. Archaeologists use the term *Mississippian* to refer to that broad sweep of time during which the prehistoric peoples of the South lived in chiefdom societies, growing corn and building mounds. The Mississippian culture arose around A. D. 900 and lasted until European contact. It is generally broken temporally into early, middle, and late Mississippian. De Soto visited late Mississippian sites.

Mississippian culture was not everywhere the same. There were regional variants that are recognizable archaeologically, usually on the basis of pottery manufacture and design. These local variants are known as *phases,* which are usually named for the archaeological sites at which their distinctive characteristics were first noted and described. Thus, late Mississippian sites in central Georgia belong to the Lamar phase. In western Alabama and eastern Mississippi, Moundville III is the prominent phase of the late Mississippian period. In central Arkansas it is the Carden Bottoms phase. And so on. To know this is to know enough to follow our line of inquiry along the route.

This book is not the last word on the De Soto route. Far from it. It is the most transitory of documents, recording the ideas we were exploring at that particular time, for those few weeks. Many parts of the route that Charlie hammered out on this trip have stood the test of time and are still considered to be valid. Others have fallen away in light of further evidence. That is the nature of intellectual inquiry. Except for the maps at the beginning of each chapter (which depict the most current version of the De Soto route at the time of publication) and the brief epilogue with which I end the book, I have not attempted to update any of the ideas entertained by ourselves or by the scholars with whom we talked. This is a record of those days of our journey in 1984 and of those conversations we enjoyed so much.

CHAPTER ONE

Florida Springs

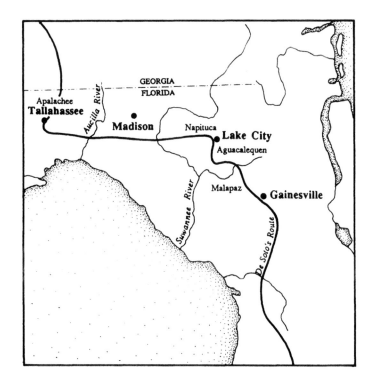

Near the village lay a large river which carried a great amount of water and which the Spaniards could not ford even though it was now summer. On both sides of this stream there were banks twenty-eight feet in height which were as sheer as a wall. In all of Florida, since there is little or almost no rock in the soil, the rivers cut away much earth and leave deep ravines. . . . It being necessary to construct a wooden bridge before this river could be crossed, the Governor {De Soto} brought up the matter with the Curaca {the native chief}, who thereupon commanded his vassals to build it. Then one day he and the Curaca . . . were strolling along and planning the bridge {when} more than five hundred native archers rushed out from the bushes growing on the opposite bank and shouted: "So you thieves, vagabonds, and foreign immigrants want a bridge. You will not see it built with our hands." And with these taunts they cast a sprinkling of arrows toward where the Governor and the Cacique Ocali stood. Thereupon the Governor asked his companion how he could permit this shameful behavior. . . . At that the Indian replied that he was powerless to remedy the situation, . . . for many of his vassals on seeing him inclined to the friendship and service of the Spaniards had refused him further obedience. . . .

On firing their arrows the Indians had raised a shout which provoked a greyhound to dash forward. Dragging to the ground one of the Governor's pages who was holding it by the collar, the dog now freed itself and plunged into the water. . . . Then as the animal swam the stream the Indians hurled their arrows so skillfully that more than fifty of them penetrated its head and shoulders. . . . Even so, the dog succeeded in reaching land, only to fall dead immediately on leaving the water. The Governor and all of his companions were much grieved at the loss of this particular greyhound, for it was a rare hunter and very necessary for the conquest. Within the short span of its life, it had made skillful and admirable attacks on the Indians both by day and by night.

—*Garcilaso de la Vega*

Gainesville, Florida
Sunday, November 11, 1984

Today we began our work on the De Soto trail. Not really *our* work. Charlie's work. It is only mine in that I am here with him while he is doing it, keeping him company and conversing with him about it. I draw on my old college degree in anthropology. I draw on the research that has gone into my past published work, three novels for young people that were set in the time and culture of the Cherokees of the old Southeast. For years I have accompanied Charlie to professional meetings and have sat through many scholarly papers about Indian life. I am, therefore, a knowledgeable layman, but no more than that. Charlie is the professional here, the anthropology professor whose research on the southeastern Indians is widely respected. This is his project. I have come along as wife, companion, and reporter.

Our intent is to drive the entire De Soto trail from beginning to end, although we are not really starting at the beginning. We covered the beginning a year and a half ago when we drove down to Tampa Bay and looked at possible landing sites for the expedition. From Tampa Bay we drove along what Charlie thought was the trail the army followed inland and north up the peninsula. We got as far as this general area of central Florida when we ran out of time and had to go home. So this time we are starting at Gainesville, and we have six weeks to spend on the road. We must be home by Christmas so that Charlie can get ready to resume his teaching at the University of Georgia in early January.

When we drove that first segment of the route more than a year ago, we did not try to cover De Soto's very footsteps. That would have been impossible in an automobile, or even on foot, since the actual route, the very soil upon which it lay, cannot be known with certainty. We drove as close to where Charlie thinks the route must have been as the present road system will permit. We stopped and looked at rivers and swamps and general features of the land to see if they matched the descriptions given in the Spanish chronicles. That is what we will be doing again, as well as talking to archaeologists along the way. Everything depends on where the Indian towns were located in 1540, and the archaeologists are the ones who know that. We have already begun the archaeological dialogue here in Gainesville with Jerald Milanich. In fact, we are staying in Jerry's home tonight. He is curator of archaeology at the Florida Museum of Natural History, and he is interested in De Soto.

We went to the museum today and spent four or five hours going over the large-scale maps which Jerry had spread on the floor in one of the labs. He is fun to work with. There is a playfulness about him, a youthful exuberance, even though he is actually getting on into middle age and is a solid and established scholar. He and his students have been hard at work on the De Soto route for the past year. They have done a wonderful job of digging out old maps and identifying the oldest roads, which usually followed Indian trails that had been there for centuries. De Soto was not cutting his way through trackless wilderness. He had native guides who led him along well established trails. Jerry has also made use of current vegetation maps. Vegetation indicates soil type, and this is particularly useful information here in Florida, where so little soil is suitable for agriculture. The hardwood zones are the fertile areas, and that is where you would expect to find the sites of Indian towns. When we were last here, we were struck by how little anyone seemed to know about where the protohistoric archaeological sites in Florida were located. But Jerry is getting a good handle on that now. I thought he and Charlie worked well together today, good give and take. After lunch Jerry took us for a drive to a place at the edge of Gainesville where there is a little stretch of a very old road which he thinks could have been an actual part of De Soto's trail. It was an unpaved, sandy alley in a residential area and it looked authentic enough to fire our imaginations, even though there is no way actually to be sure about it. We returned to the museum and worked with maps for the rest of the afternoon.

This evening we had a nice dinner with Jerry and his wife, Maxine, and their daughter, Nara, here at their home. Now we have retired to our guest quarters. Very comfortable. Tomorrow we start out on the trail.

Charlie has fallen into a peculiar mood. He saw me writing just now and asked me what it was about.

"Jerry Milanich and the De Soto route," I said.

He shook his head in amazement, as if he had not really believed that I was going to keep a journal of this trip. "You may be the only one who gets a book out of this," he said. "I may never finish one."

I was puzzled and looked more closely at him, trying to see what he meant.

"Why aren't I taking notes?" he asked. Then he added in a heavy tone, "I really got tired today."

Some sort of defeatedness has overtaken him, as if he feels himself running out of steam, irreversibly. I trust it is no more than a reluctance to take the plunge into the work. Surely his energy and enthusiasm will pick up as we go forward.

It is true that he has not made any notes tonight. He is reading a detective novel.

Madison, Florida
Monday, November 12

Tonight Charlie is working on De Soto. No more motivation problems. We are in a motel room trying to settle into our new routine. I am not used to writing while someone else is in the room, but there is not much choice here. It is not so bad while Charlie himself is at work, but we may run into trouble when he wants to watch television: I know I cannot write in the same room with a television. We will have to work out some compromises. There is a pleasant silence while we both work. No type-writers, since we compose in longhand. I am writing in a spiral-bound notebook, which is handy for taking anywhere. Perhaps if I need to I can retreat to the bathroom and do some of my work while taking a bath. I have always enjoyed long baths, so much so that as a child I used to do my homework in the tub—so I have had practice at aquatic writing. Of even greater concern than finding a place to write is finding the stamina to keep a full record of our days. I want to try to capture our entire experience of search and discovery, and I can already see how important it will be to keep up with it each day. There is so much happening. If I fall very far behind, it will be impossible to catch up.

This morning, back in Gainesville, we rose around eight o'clock. I had gotten a good night's rest, Charlie not so good. He said he was awake for hours, mired down in that swampy mood he was in. But some time during the night he found his way out of it, and this morning he was ready to go.

We left Jerry's house around nine-thirty and met Marvin Smith down-town for coffee. Marvin is one of the two graduate students who first began work on the De Soto trail with Charlie five years ago. With Chester DePratter, the other collaborator, they brainstormed the entire route in a few month's time. If Charlie had known then how many years of work were going to be required to carry it forward from brainstorm to solid scholarship, he might never have started the project. But now it is too late to turn back. Marvin and Chester have moved on to more specialized interests, leaving the main part of the route work to Charlie. They do, however, still keep a hand in and help out where they can.

Marvin is in Gainesville finishing his doctoral degree at the University of Florida. We had a pleasant visit with him, enjoying the relaxed familiarity of an old friend. We talked about the high interest that was shown in De Soto at the annual conference of southeastern archaeologists last week. And we talked about Marvin's prospects for employment when he finishes his work here, which will be soon. He suggested names of some archaeologists who might be able to help us as we travel along the route. We lingered, had more coffee, then said goodbye to him and started on our way.

We headed out northwest on U.S. 441. I did the driving so that Charlie could study maps and look things up in the four chronicles of the expedition. The Spaniards, at this point at which we were joining them, had been in La Florida for three months. La Florida was the name they gave to all of eastern North America. They only had the vaguest idea of what kind of land La Florida was and no idea at all of how large it was. They had done some sailing around the edges of it and had prodded at it with a few failed attempts to gain a foothold on its coasts, but in the fifty years since the New World had been discovered, most of the attention of Spain's conquistadors had been focused on Central and South America. Hernando de Soto had played a large role in those more southern adventures, especially in Peru where he was third in command under Francisco Pizarro in the conquest of the Incas. This had made him an extremely wealthy man, and he should have been content to settle down with his Inca gold. But he wanted a land of his own, where he would be governor, first in command. So he went back to Spain and invested most of his fortune in a new expedition, which was very large and well outfitted. There were over six hundred soldiers, several hundred servants and slaves, three hundred horses, and a herd of pigs, which were brought along for famine food.

This great expedition landed at Tampa Bay in May 1539. They spent the next two months exploring the area around the bay. They found the native people there too primitive to support a Spanish colony—there was no agriculture to speak of, no granaries of stored food to feed the army. And there was no gold. When they inquired of the Indians where they might go to find a people as civilized and wealthy as the Aztecs or

Incas, they were directed north. So in August they set out, going inland a little way from Tampa Bay and then turning northward. They came up past present-day Ocala and then past Gainesville, perhaps walking along that same sandy road we saw with Jerry yesterday. And now we were joining them as we drove toward Alachua, a modern-day town with a Native American name.

Charlie thinks that it was in the vicinity of Alachua that the Spaniards came to the Indian town they called Malapaz. Usually they used the local peoples' names for the towns they passed through, but this one they called by a Spanish name—"Bad Peace"—because its chief had tricked them with his supposedly peaceful overtures. The Spaniards, following what was becoming their standard procedure, captured thirty men and women from the chief's town, the men to serve as burden bearers, the women as servants and concubines. The chief sent word that if the Spaniards would let the captives go, he himself would take their place and see that the army was supplied with food and with a guide to lead them north. The Spaniards accepted this proposal, but the chief deceived them by sending an imposter in his place. The Spaniards released the thirty captives and then found that the one captive they now held was not the chief and had no power to make good the chief's promises. That captive himself tried to make his escape the next day, bolting away to rejoin a group of his people hidden in the woods. But the Spaniards sent one of their great war dogs after him. It knew the man's scent and rushed into the crowd of Indians, singled out the fleeing captive, and pulled him down. The rest of the people escaped, but this man was recaptured and presumably spent the rest of his days—which would have been few—laboring in Spanish chains.

From Alachua we took Florida 241 north to the Santa Fe River. The Spaniards mention crossing a river at about this point. In order to cross it, they had to make a bridge, which they did by felling pine trees. We stopped to see if the Santa Fe seemed suitable for that crossing. It was a small, serene river with water like dark tea. We walked down beside it, enjoying the beauty of it. The river cut through a bed of wet sand in which low, twisting trees stood among little shallow pools of brown, cypress-stained water. As I went back among the trees, I realized I should be looking out for snakes and maybe even for alligators. It was this stop at the Santa Fe that brought back to me how much fun it is to follow De Soto's trail: these frequent stops, this getting out of the car and walking around to look at the terrain. This is a way to really see the country. You do not have to be out walking around in odd places very long before you lose the feeling of being a stranger, or at least of being perceived as a stranger. You feel that people must think you live nearby, or why would you be out there studying with interest a field or a river bank?

We drove on across the Santa Fe into what Charlie thinks was the territory of Aguacalequen, between the forks of the Santa Fe River and Olustee Creek. A mile or two north of the Santa Fe, we turned left and headed for Olustee Creek, only about a mile to the west. At this point the Spaniards crossed another river that required a bridge, and we needed Olustee Creek to be that river. Charlie was very pleased to see that it was a substantial stream of water, one that would have required a bridge had the water been up at all, and maybe even if it was only as we saw it today. Again we got out of the car and walked down to the river's edge. This, too, was a black-water river. Its banks were about ten feet high. Just before the water reaches the present bridge, it divides to go around an island and the current rushes a little there. Charlie needs high banks for Olustee Creek—about twenty-five feet of height—to fit a dramatic event in the narratives in which Indians stood on the opposite bank of the river and shot at the Spaniards and killed one of the war dogs, which had broken loose and was trying to swim across to get at them. Olustee might be wide enough. What we need now is to find a place where it cuts through a ridge—limestone would be nice— so that high banks flank the river. We have no idea if that would be a likely possibility or not. Charlie will have to talk to some Florida people about it.

From the Olustee we drove on west a few miles and picked up U.S. 441 again, turning north to Lake City, which is in the Indian province of Uriutina. We stopped at Alligator Lake on the southern edge of the town—the large lake that undoubtedly gives Lake City its name. Charlie feels that the principal town of the Indian province must have also been here beside the lake. We stopped at a boat ramp, a quiet place with a long dock that ran out into the water. The afternoon was beginning to wane. The sky was clear and the air cool, almost cold. There were loons on the lake. They would swim along like ducks, then suddenly dive beneath the water, completely disappearing, and come up far away. Out on a little island a large white heron stood like a sentry.

Around the shore were grand old cypress trees, huge at their bases. Two large kingfishers flew out of the tops of the trees, making a racket that sounded almost like pileated woodpeckers. One seemed to be chasing the other. We lingered as long as we could and then got back in the car and left Lake City on U.S. 90, heading west toward Live Oak.

We were looking now for the vicinity of the Village of Many Waters. De Soto's men called it this because it rained so hard for two days that the Spaniards could not move. And when they did start out again, they got mired down in a terrible swamp. Charlie expected the Village of Many Waters to be around Wellborn. And sure enough, for about five miles beyond Wellborn we passed through three different places that could have been the swamp—perhaps that whole stretch was what bogged them down. The land here was noticeably lower than that before or after it, full of willows and cypress. The roadbed through it was on an embankment.

As we neared Live Oak the land rose and became fair and open again. Charlie thinks Live Oak is the approximate location of Napituca, a town where the local inhabitants and the Spaniards engaged in a battle. The Indians fared badly, no match for horsemen with lances. To save themselves, the defeated warriors jumped into two ponds that were there in the field of battle and swam to the middle, beyond range of the Spaniards' crossbows and arquebuses. They stayed there, treading water, waiting for dark so they could crawl out and slip away. Though the ponds were large, the Spaniards had enough men to surround one of them effectively, and none of the warriors in that one got away, though all escaped from the other one.

Well, not far from Live Oak we came to a field with several sinkhole ponds scattered through it. We were thrilled. We stopped and took pictures. The sun was getting lower and was bright and sparkling on the water. Beside the largest of the ponds was a beautiful old willow tree with a large, twisted trunk. We were amazed to have found multiple ponds just where we needed them. We did not pass any other place like that all day—only right there at Napituca. Which is not to say that was the very site of the village and the battle, but we could see that the land around Live Oak was exactly right for it.

Leaving Live Oak, we took Florida 51 to the southwest, following a new interpretation of the route that Charlie had worked out with Jerry on Sunday. This new proposal was an effort to bring the army into an area with ravines several days beyond this point, a requirement that Charlie's earlier version of the route seemed not to be meeting satisfactorily.

It is this sort of fit into a chain of events that makes or breaks any theory about a particular segment of the route. What happens in one place has to lead to what happens in the next place and that has to lead to what happens after that. A river wide enough to be crossed by a bridge, for example, might have to be followed by a suitable archaeological site for an Indian town within so many miles, which must be followed in a certain distance by another river, which must be followed by a ravine or a lake or whatever it is the chroniclers say they encountered next. This is one of the real differences between Charlie's effort to reconstruct the route and the attempt that was made by the U.S. De Soto Commission fifty years ago. The man in charge of that route was John R. Swanton, who was an anthropologist at the Smithsonian Institution. Swanton was a pioneer in the study of the Native Americans of the Southeast, the first to produce a comprehensive scholarly account of this distinctive aboriginal culture area. His talent was more for collecting a lot of diverse and often unrelated details than for putting together a cohesive big picture. His De Soto route reflected this. He was successful in producing a general outline of the route, but almost nowhere did he make accurate connections between the specific places De Soto visited and the actual details of archaeology and geography. Indeed, it would have been almost impossible for him to have done so as far as the archaeology was concerned. The archaeological knowledge of his time was very limited compared to the present. The field was in its infancy and its pictures could be painted only with broad strokes. So Swanton's route was a good start, but it was by no means the last word. He himself was well aware of this and said so. And yet it has become the "official" route and has assumed an almost sacred inviolability in the minds of many people, particularly those through whose communities the "official" route passes. But Charlie's chain of evidence, if he can sustain it, will eventually prove strong enough to bring the needed revisions to the old route.

We were trying, then, to find a route west from Live Oak that would fit the chain of events that lay ahead. Charlie thought that perhaps from Live Oak they followed a course that would have hooked them up with the trail that later became known as the Old Mission Road, after the Spanish friars who established a presence there in the seventeenth century. This would put De Soto's crossing of the Suwannee at Dowling Park, he thought, though in fact we did not have a map of the Old Mission Road before us and I do not think we had it quite right. Anyhow, we went from Live Oak to Dowling Park through truly lousy terrain—scrubby pineland, obviously unsuitable for farming, only sparsely populated. At Dowling Park we crossed the Suwannee and stopped to look at the river. This is what we needed for Olustee Creek—high banks, wide river. But there is almost no doubt that the Suwannee was not the one where the dog was shot—the Suwannee, rather, was the one they called the River of the Deer, a larger river than the others they had crossed, and on the other side was the province of Usachile.

What we needed now, starting about two leagues (five or six miles) from the river, were four leagues of good agricultural land that could have supported continuous scattered hamlets. This was an Apalachee-like settlement pattern, the kind found archaeologically around Tallahassee, and it implied good agricultural land. Well, the first ten miles from the Suwannee crossing up toward Madison was the poorest country we have seen yet. The road skirts along the edge of San Pedro Bay, a huge area of low swampy land that is nothing but pine scrubs. "This can't be it," we said as we drove through it. Then near Madison the land began to rise and suddenly we were in good farm country. That high land extends eastward from Madison toward the Suwannee, so we could see that Charlie's earlier reconstruction of the route that put the crossing further north at Ellaville was better, even though that still left the problem of the ravine that would come later.

We drove back east along U.S. 90 to the Suwannee, about twelve miles. There are still today scattered farmsteads continuously along that road up to within four or five miles of the river, and then the land descends gradually into pineland. We stopped beside the Suwannee, at a little park on the western side. The river was beautiful here, cutting through high limestone banks. On the opposite bank was a place of bubbling water that must have been a spring coming out of the limestone. It churned and frothed and sounded like water going over shoals. I had never seen anything like it.

We drove back west for a few miles and then cut up north to intersect Florida 6. Turning east on that, we went back to the river, though this time it was to the Withlacoochee, which runs into the Suwannee just before the crossing at Ellaville, where we had just been. We stopped at the Withlacoochee, again at a little park on the west bank, and got out to look at the river. We saw that there was a large stream of crystal clear water flowing into the brown water of the river. When we walked back along the clear stream to see where it was coming from, we found a beautiful little spring in a deep pit in the limestone. The water was bright coppery blue in the deepest part. We could see to the absolute bottom of it, all the fish that were in it, the exposed tree roots that had grown into it, and all the little hollows of the limestone. There was no sand or dirt around the edge of it, just this white, water-smoothed, knobby stone. We could see the place down deep in the pool where the water was coming in, a place in the rock wall where there was a little disturbance. It was beautiful. We were the only ones there. The afternoon was very late, and it was getting cold. A kingfisher flew by along the river. We stayed around for a while, reluctant to leave, then finally returned to the car and headed west to Madison to find a motel for the night.

We ate dinner in Madison at the Stone Fox Restaurant, a quirky little establishment that seemed to be *the* place to eat in that town. When people bring their children in, cartoons are shown on the wall for them, and the man who appeared to be the owner entertains them with unusual toys. I found myself watching the faces of the people there; they all looked familiar, like the people I grew up with in Tifton, Georgia, which is only eighty miles or so to the north. It is remarkable that people's faces are so much the same in particular geographical areas. The voices, too, sounded familiar to me—a southern Georgia–northern Florida variant of southern dialect. I could not begin to say what the components are, except that these people—my people—are mumblers. Like Jimmy Carter.

Wakulla Springs, Florida
Tuesday, November 13

Charlie woke up this morning worrying about Olustee Creek. It does not seem to him to be wide enough for the incident with the dog. A dog could have been across there in a flash, he says. Of course, we do not really know how it would be if it were in flood or if the water level was simply higher in 1539. Jerry told us that the water level in northern Florida is lower than it used to be because of phosphate mining, but we do not know if that applies to Olustee Creek. Maybe it was the New River rather than Olustee Creek that De Soto crossed as he was leaving Aguacalequen. But it would have taken too much time for us to have gone back to check out the New River. Charlie will have to deal with this problem later.

We left Madison this morning and went west on U.S. 90 toward the Aucilla River. What we needed here was a "great woods," as the Spaniards called it—a climax hardwood forest—followed by a pine wood (*piñar*), in which the Spaniards spent the night. The next day after the pine wood they came to the village of Agile on the east bank of the Aucilla River. So we needed something like one and a half days of travel before Agile, with a *piñar* at the end of the first day. The great woods implies a buffer zone between Indian polities, since hardwoods grow on good agricultural soil which would otherwise have been settled and farmed. The buffer zone was between the Timucuans and the Apalachees, who were hostile to each other.

The route west from Madison looked all right for hardwood forest—it was fertile farmland. We expected to come to pine woods by the time we got to Greenville, but we did not really find enough pines there to suit us. It is piney, but there are still hardwoods, too. We did not feel it looked right, so we turned south to drop down below a large swampy area, and then we cut back east toward Madison on a lower road, exploring an alternate route. In the mission days of the seventeenth century there were two ways to go from Madison to the Aucilla crossing—a high road and a low road—and in between were the villages of the Timucuans, an area that became known as the San Pedro Old Fields. We drove back along the low road, looking again, in reverse order, for a *piñar* and then a great woods area. It was a lovely morning. The sky was clear with only a few high, thin clouds. The air was cool, in the low fifties. The countryside, as soon as we got a little way from Greenville, was rolling agricultural land, very peaceful. We were driving now on county roads and seldom saw another car. We could make U-turns when we needed to go back and look at something, and we often did. We were gratified to come upon a historical marker for the mission of San Pedro, pleased that we were in the right place even though we had not had a map of the Old Mission Road to go by. The country right around the old mission site was pastoral and serene. Most of the land was in pasture with cattle grazing on it. Great live oaks stood solitary in the fields, draped in Spanish moss. We stopped to take pictures. I turned off the engine and got out, even though it was Charlie who was manning the camera. I just wanted to be out there with all that beauty.

The San Pedro Old Fields would do fine for the great woods if the archaeology shows that the Timucuans moved into that area only after the friars arrived in the seventeenth century. If there was no occupation before that, in the sixteenth century, then it probably was in fact a great woods when De Soto came through. And the lower road is longer than the U.S. 90 route and might work better for travel time, assuming Usachile was around Madison. The reason for taking the lower road would have to be explained—perhaps it was drier. Certainly the mission-period Spaniards made use of it. But we still needed a *piñar*, so we headed back toward Greenville again, trying to make mixed forest into pinewood but unable to convince ourselves. This time, however, we could see that the land around Greenville is definitely pinier than what came before, and as we went on west of Greenville, it became even more so as the elevation dropped toward the river. So we decided the army must have slept in a pinewood somewhere in the vicinity of Greenville.

We ate lunch sitting on an old concrete bridge abutment beside the Aucilla River. It was a pleasant little swampy river—the water hardly seemed to be moving at all. It was brown and clear and not very wide or deep. The Spaniards describe a swamp with much more water, but there is no doubt in anyone's mind that the Aucilla is the eastern boundary of the province of Apalachee. The fact is that all these Florida rivers seem to have been carrying much more water in the sixteenth century. De Soto, coming through here late in the summer, had difficult crossings at most of the rivers. Today only the Suwannee would be hard to cross, unless all the others were in flood.

After lunch we drove down a dirt road that ran south beside the river. We wanted to go down to the railroad tracks which run east and west, parallel to U.S. 90, about a mile to the south. Railroads usually follow the oldest roads, and the oldest roads usually follow the aboriginal trails, and so we thought the railroad would be more likely than U.S. 90 to be on De Soto's exact path. Charlie was looking for something like the dense woods the Spaniards had to fight their way through after crossing the Aucilla. There was only a narrow path for them to follow through those woods, and the Apalachees hid among the trees and harassed them every step of the way. We intended to drive down to the tracks, take a look, and drive back.

We went along through terrain that would do fine for dense swampy woods, found the railroad tracks, and then saw that our dirt road curved to the right and followed the tracks west into the town of Aucilla, only about another mile away. So we went on instead of turning back. The land got better very quickly, and before we knew it, we were seeing farms. We felt this was indeed a very old road. It went into Aucilla through the town's back door. Just as we reached the edge of town, the road and tracks cut through a hill and there were red banks on either side of us—the red hills of Apalachee. Those red hills are what made Apalachee such a fertile land.

Aucilla is a tiny town and a very old one. We wondered if the Apalachee town of Ivitachuco might have been located there. It was the first town the Spaniards came to after crossing the swamp. As we left, driving west, the land became low and scrubby again for several miles. We were on county road 158, which seems to have been close to the old main road—it followed the railroad tracks most closely. We were going west from Aucilla to Drifton, parallel to U.S. 90 but about five miles south of it. A few miles before Drifton the land rose up into the red hills proper. Now the terrain was definitely hilly, and it was fertile, with handsome farms. We took a side trip north of Drifton to Monticello to get some coffee and found Monticello to be a much more prosperous town than any we had seen since Lake City. This was just how Apalachee struck the Spaniards after they had come through the Timucuan country.

From Monticello we got back on county road 158 and headed west to Lloyd. What we were looking for now was a "deep ravine" where the Apalachees harassed the Spaniards as they went across. It was this ravine that we were worrying about yesterday when we were trying to find a different crossing of the Suwannee, hoping to make the distance to the ravine come out right. Even though this was hilly country we were going through, I was skeptical that we would find anything that could be described as a ravine. I told Charlie so. "You're not going to find one," I said. I was getting tired and did not want to keep on looking so hard for things.

As we drove along, it seemed that I was right: rolling hills but nothing rugged. Then just before we reached Lloyd we crossed a short bridge. Charlie was studying his map, but I looked over the bridge and saw what looked amazingly like a ravine, though it went by so fast I was not sure.

"That was a ravine!" I exclaimed.

"Where?"

"Back there!"

We made a U-turn. There was a little dirt road that went down beside the bridge to a creek, and we drove down it and got out and looked—steep banks, ten or twelve feet high, a substantial stream of clear brown water. Nothing huge and dramatic, but it could definitely be called a ravine. It was the only thing we saw in all our driving today that could be, and it came in exactly the right place. Charlie took a picture and we went on.

We wanted next to go west from Lloyd to Capitola, but there was no road shown on our map, only the railroad track. We thought we were going to have to turn south in Lloyd and go down and pick up U.S. 27, go west on that, and then cut back north to Capitola. But in Lloyd, county road 158 seemed not to end as our map indicated but to cross the main road and go on toward the west, following the tracks. We stopped at the intersection. This was the center of Lloyd, this crossroads, and about all there was of it. There was an old man sitting on the porch of a weathered store building on the corner. Charlie rolled down his window and asked him if 158 went to Capitola.

"Eh?" he said, cupping his hand to his ear. He was holding a fly-swatter in his other hand.

Charlie asked again in a louder voice, pointing across the road. "Is this the way to Capitola?"

"That's right," the old man said, nodding encouragingly. "Four mile down the road." He reached out and swatted a fly.

So off we went, past a couple of truly ancient wooden buildings, large commercial ones, abandoned, unpainted, and darkly weathered. We knew this was an old road. Great live oaks grew close beside it. We had hardly gotten out of town when the pavement ended, changing to washboarded, sandy dirt. If we had not asked the old man about it, we would have turned back. But instead we went on with a certain amount of confidence, trusting that Capitola was indeed only "four mile" ahead. After a couple of miles I started noticing an old ditch-looking feature near the road, and it occurred to me that it might be the original roadbed, older even than the one we were on. We stopped for a moment and got out and looked at it. We were not sure, but it was possible. We saw more of it all the way to Capitola.

Capitola was very small. I hardly remember anything about it, except that we got back on paved road there, which was a relief. Chaires was only a mile or two away; the road to it followed near the tracks. All of these little towns—Aucilla, Drifton, Lloyd, Capitola, and Chaires—are on an old road that in historic times was the main road from Tallahassee to St. Augustine. But now there are two other roads that carry all the traffic, U.S. 90 to the north and U.S. 27 to the south. These towns have been left in the middle of nowhere. Only the railroad comes through, and I doubt that any train ever stops.

From Chaires we went a mile south to U.S. 27. Before heading west to Tallahassee, we turned east to take a look at the St. Marks River, about a mile away. Immediately after we turned left onto Highway 27, we passed a dirt road going off to the right that was marked with a street sign saying "St. Augustine Road."

"What?" we said, wondering if this could be an actual remembered segment of the old road itself. It certainly seemed to be in the right place.

We checked out the St. Marks, which was only a swampy area, no visible water, and then came back and turned down St. Augustine Road. We wanted to see if it would take us into Tallahassee. It was going south when we turned onto it, which was not promising, but very soon it bent around to the west. The live oaks beside it were big and old and made a canopy overhead. The roadbed was deep. There was no mistaking that it was some kind of historic road, whether it was the very one that went back to Spanish times or not. Tallahassee was about ten miles away. We still were not sure this would take us there, but we were finished with our trail work for the day and had nothing more to do but go find a room for the night. So we stayed on the road. There was actually quite a bit of traffic on it for an unpaved road, and it had a number of homes along it. We stopped beside a pasture of goats to take pictures of a place where the trees made a heavy canopy and the roadbed was especially deep.

After four or five miles we crossed a paved road, and beyond that the old St. Augustine Road was paved. There was a historic marker confirming that it was indeed the old Spanish road. Now we were in outlying Tallahassee, and there were residences all along the road and still the canopy of live oaks overhead. Finally we came to the perimeter highway that runs around Tallahassee. The old road crossed it and ran on into town, but we turned south and headed down to Wakulla Springs to spend the night in a fine old resort hotel.

Reading Garcilaso tonight, I figured out why we have been having so much trouble with the dog-in-the-river incident. We have been assuming that Garcilaso knew exactly where that story fit into the itinerary of the expedition. But Garcilaso, who was not there and who wrote his story second-hand, often got things mixed up, and this seems to have been one of those times. He had the dog being shot while the army was in Aguacalequen. There were two river crossings there and Charlie assumed he was talking about the second one. But the high banks in the incident and the width of the river clearly indicate that it did not happen in Aguacalequen at all but later when the army was crossing the Suwannee. That is the only river in this part of Florida that fits the story. We should have been skeptical from the beginning. We knew Garcilaso could garble things. He patched his narrative together from so many different stories. So Olustee Creek will do fine for the second crossing in Aguacalequen, if the archaeology confirms it. We do not need high banks or a wide crossing there.

From now on Garcilaso is out for nailing down the route. He only adds confusion. He is good for the stories he tells, but not for anything hard and factual.

Albany, Georgia
Wednesday, November 14

We got up this morning and had a lovely breakfast by a window in the dining room of the Wakulla Springs Lodge. Then we went out and took a ride in a glass-bottom boat. It was fun—a bit hyped, but fun. It certainly was a thrill to look down and see schools of catfish and bass and alligator gar—one especially monstrous gar. But even though Wakulla claims to be the largest spring in the world, it was not nearly so enchanting to us as that little spring near Madison that we found on our own a few days ago. The three or four fish we saw swimming in that little spring were worth all the schools of fish in Wakulla with its chainlink fence and its four-dollar boat ride.

We went straight from the boat to the car and drove up to Tallahassee to talk to John Scarry and Calvin Jones at the Florida Department of Archives and History. They are the ones who know best the archaeology of northern Florida, especially the Apalachee area in Leon and Jefferson counties. Calvin, who is an older man and has been around a long time, has done more work than anyone on the Spanish missions and has probably done more survey work in the whole state of Florida than anyone else has done. Which is not to say that most of Florida has been surveyed. The gaps in archaeological knowledge always amaze me, though if you consider how painstaking the gathering of archaeological data is, it should not be surprising that so much is still unknown.

The question we pursued with Calvin and John was, Where did De Soto cross the Aucilla River? Which is the same thing as asking, Where, in 1539, were the towns of Agile and Ivitachuco, which were on either side of the crossing? Calvin had excavated the seventeenth-century mission site of Ivitachuco southwest of Lamont, and he was convinced that this is where Ivitachuco was in 1539. He felt that the area around the mission had been continuously occupied all the way back to the Archaic period, more than three thousand years ago. This would mean that the crossing of the Aucilla was south of the place where we were yesterday. Charlie was not sure that Calvin was right about that. We looked at evidence for both crossings, but in the end we could not decide.

We did, however, find out some important information about water levels in northern Florida. We asked Calvin and John about it, and they told us that there are great fluctuations. The rainy season there is July and August, normally, though it can also stretch into September. They get heavy rains, several inches at a time—three, four, or five inches is not uncommon—and it can come almost every day. The rivers swell very greatly while carrying off this water, though they carry it off quickly and then subside. Also there is fluctuation on a larger cycle as sinkholes open up and close. Lake Jackson, just north of Tallahassee, periodically goes from being a huge lake to being almost dry—recently from sixty-five hundred acres down to a thousand and then back up again.

So De Soto came through northern Florida in the rainy season, which helps explain why the rivers were so much higher for him than they have been for us. That is one question answered, at least.

CHAPTER TWO

Georgia Pecans

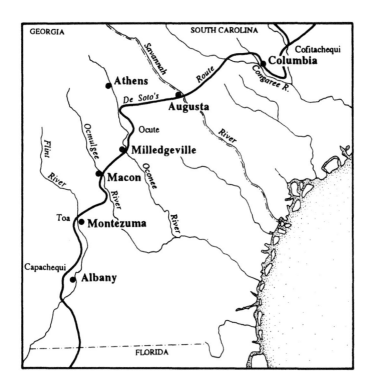

On Wednesday, the third of March, in the year 1540, the Governor
left Anhaica Apalachee. . . . He had ordered his men to go provided
with maize for a march through sixty leagues of desert. The cavalry
carried their grain on the horses, and the infantry theirs on the back;
because the Indians they brought with them for service, being naked
and in chains, had perished in great part during the winter. . . .

They arrived at a town by the name of Capachiqui, and on Friday, the eleventh, the inhabitants were found to have gone off. . . .

The Governor left Capachiqui, passing through a desert; and on
Wednesday, the twenty-first of the month, came to Toalli {or Toa}.

The houses of this town were different from those behind, which
were covered with dry grass; thenceforward they were roofed with
cane, after the fashion of tile. They are kept very clean: some have
their sides so made of clay as to look like tapia. Throughout the cold
country every Indian has a winter house, plastered inside and out,
with a very small door, which is closed at dark, and a fire being
made within, it remains heated like an oven, so that clothing is not
needed during the night-time. He has likewise a house for summer,
and near it a kitchen, where fire is made and bread baked. Maize is
kept in a barbacoa, which is a house with wooden sides, like a room,
raised aloft on four posts, and has a floor of cane. The difference
between the houses of the masters, or principal men, and those of
the common people is, besides being larger than the others, they have
deep balconies on the front side with cane seats, like benches; and
about are many large barbacoas, in which they bring together the
tribute their people give them of maize, skins of deer, and blankets
of the country. These are like shawls, some of them made from the
inner bark of trees, and others of a grass resembling nettle, which,
by treading out becomes like flax. The women use them for covering,
wearing one about the body from the waist downward, and another
over the shoulder, with the right arm left free, after the manner of the
Gypsies: the men wear but one, which they carry over the shoulder in
the same way, the loins being covered with a bragueiro of deer-skin,

after the fashion of the woolen breech-cloth that was once the custom of Spain. The skins are well dressed, the colour being given to them that is wished, and in such perfection, that, when of vermilion, they look like very fine red broadcloth; and when black, the sort in use for shoes, they are of the purest. The same hues are given to blankets.

—*A Gentleman of Elvas*

Albany, Georgia
Thursday morning, November 15

We left Tallahassee about one o'clock yesterday and drove north-north-west to Albany. We made only two brief stops—at the Ocklochnee River, in Florida, and at the Flint River, in Georgia. The Flint was impressive—wide and swift, a large river carrying a lot of water. It has high banks, and the trees along it are draped with Spanish moss. This part of the country is just beginning its autumn leaf season, sweet gum being the most striking with its red leaves. Because so many trees in southern Georgia are evergreens, autumn here does not put on much of a show.

After crossing the Flint near Newton, we drove on into Albany. I felt waves of nostalgia as we came close to the heart of my home territory: pine trees; pecan groves; large farms; crisp, neat towns that look, architecturally, like the 1950s and 1960s. This part of the South did not come alive economically until after World War II. That was the time when I grew up here, playing in pine woods and pecan orchards. Even today there is nothing more beautiful to me than farm buildings nestled in the shade of neat rows of pecan trees. As we drove along yesterday, the weeds beside the road looked so familiar that I wanted to get out and lie down in them. I knew just how they would smell. It is remarkable how much time you spend in close contact with things of the earth when you are a child. It is never like that again.

We got to Albany around four-thirty, checked into a motel, and called Eugene Black, Jr., a local lawyer who is interested in archaeology. Charlie has communicated with him in the past about De Soto in southwest Georgia, and Gene has been very helpful in supplying information about local sites. He knew we were coming through on this trip and had offered to take us out to see the territory of the Indian province of Capachequi. This was the first society De Soto encountered after Apalachee.

Gene invited us to his home for dinner, which was very kind, considering the fact that he had not known we would be arriving yesterday. We had not met him before this, but we took to him right away and to his wife Edith. They are around my age, mid-thirties, both of them impressively intelligent. Edith teaches Latin in a public high school. Gene is a lawyer who is willing to handle civil rights cases, and he takes a strong interest in local politics. Edith is also active in public life, especially in the political realm. She seems strong as steel. In a town in which more than half the population is black and most of the white population is conservative, they struggle to uphold liberal values of social justice. They characterize themselves as two of the last white Democrats in Dougherty County. (It has only been two weeks since Reagan creamed Mondale in the presidential election.) Gene Black is a fan of W. E. B. Du Bois, who came to Dougherty County around the turn of the century and used what he learned there as the basis of his book *The Souls of Black Folks*. Gene brought out a copy of this during the evening, using it to make a point in our conversation. He wants to write a new history of Albany for its coming sesquicentennial. His would be black history as well as white history. W. E. B. Du Bois would have a prominent place in it.

Gene Black's other passion is archaeology. He grew up in Albany, and as a boy he liked to walk the fields and pick up artifacts. (This is only one of the ways he makes me think of Jimmy Carter—they are the same kind of people, a particular product, it seems, of this part of the country.) Gene studied archaeology on his own in his younger days, and while he was at the University of Georgia working on his law degree, he spent much time in the anthropology department talking to graduate students and professors, although he and Charlie never met there. Edith claims that Gene's dream is to quit law and become an archaeology professor, but he seems to me to be too well anchored in the real world for that. It was striking to talk to him about De Soto after spending these last few days with archaeologists. Lawyers are intrinsically different from archaeologists. They deal with everyday reality, not with theories. Their thinking is more concrete. They are sharper at weighing evidence. As I watched Charlie and him working together over the maps, I realized that Charlie was more like Gene than he is like other anthropologists. Had Charlie not come from a farm in Kentucky, had he had any training in middle-class social skills when he was growing up, he probably would have become a doctor or a lawyer instead of a scholar. He has that kind of sharpness of mind. I think it is one of the reasons he has been such a misfit in academia. He is not swayed by the current fashion of ideas. He thinks for himself and makes his own path and tries to stay in contact with hard reality.

We had a lovely evening with Gene and Edith. At about ten-thirty we said goodnight and came back to the motel to get some sleep.

It is early in the morning now, and Charlie is still sleeping. I made myself get up to write. We are meeting Gene at a restaurant for breakfast at seven-thirty. Then he is going to take us out to the Chickasaw-hatchee Swamp.

Athens, Georgia
Thursday night, November 15

We met Gene this morning at the appointed hour, had a bite to eat, and then rode with him to the Chickasawhatchee Swamp, which is several miles west of Albany. As we were driving through the countryside, he told us about the desperate economic condition of this section of southern Georgia. The counties surrounding Dougherty County are among the very poorest in the state. The farm economy has gone bust, and no economic alternative has arisen. The counties have little tax base left. Indigent people crowd into Albany like landless peasants into Mexico City. Infant mortality has reached Third World proportions, he says. There is not much public money for health care or schools.

Just before the Civil War, Dougherty County was one of the wealthiest counties in the South. The land had only recently been opened and the soil was still fertile. Then came the Civil War with its economic ruin. The South in general and southwest Georgia in particular did not get back on its feet again until after World War II. They enjoyed two or three decades of prosperity. But then in the 1970s came the energy crunch, soaring interest rates, and a government farm policy that threw farm prices to the mercy of the international market. Crops depending on human labor could no longer compete, but the huge farm machinery required to replace labor was incredibly expensive. Nor could farmers compete any longer without irrigation equipment, which was again terribly expensive. To justify such an investment in machinery, farmers had to buy more land. All of this purchasing of land and equipment was done on credit, at high interest rates. The resulting debt payments have been more than most farmers can handle. Foreclosures have become rampant in the last few years. What land is being bought, is being bought by multinational corporations for hunting preserves or for row crops—peanuts, soybeans, cotton—crops that can be grown with machines, which only large corporations can afford to buy. Much of the land is not being bought. Gene has a client who has been trying for two years to sell a two-thousand-acre farm. Farm communities are dying, small businesses folding. People are beginning to be frightened, he said.

A large corporation—a paper company—owns most of Chickasawhatchee Swamp. Not only do you have to have the company's permission to go back there, you have to have keys to the various gates. Gene took care of all of that for us. He has spent a lot of time in years past driving the logging roads of the swamp and walking around looking for sites. He has encountered ten-foot rattlesnakes and wild pigs—little long-legged pigs with shaggy black hair and fearsome tusks. Part of the swamp is a wildlife refuge. There are alligators, wild turkeys, deer, and possibly cougars, and there have been reports of bears. We hoped to see some wildlife, but we wanted to see bears, cougars, and wild pigs only at a distance, and ten-foot rattlers not at all. We were lucky in that the weather was very cool, in the forties—cold enough to keep the snakes at home. We were also fortunate that this has been an unusually dry autumn, only two hard rains since Labor Day. The swamp was drier than Gene had ever seen it. That meant we were not seeing it as it typically was when it was home to the people of Capachequi, but it also meant that we could drive around on roads that were impassable in wetter seasons. Of course, there were dry spells when the Indians were living there, too.

It was not dry when De Soto came through. It was exceedingly wet. He had spent the winter in Apalachee, somewhere around Tallahassee, and had left there in March heading north. Sixteenth-century armies did not carry food with them on their marches, either in Europe or in the New World. They lived by foraging, which is to say by seizing food from the people through whose land they were marching. It is unlikely that De Soto would have made the difficult crossing of the Flint

River had he not been looking for food. His ultimate destination at this stage of the expedition was Cofitachequi, in South Carolina, which he had been told was a rich province—he was hoping for another land like that of the Aztecs or Incas. He had no reason to go west of the Flint except that his army might otherwise have run short of food. They had brought with them from Apalachee enough corn to sustain them through sixty leagues (twelve travel days) of unpopulated land. If they could find any food at Capachequi, this would be additional insurance against starvation.

The Flint was too wide to bridge. They built a barge, then found the current so strong they had to use a chain to pull the barge across. To make a long enough chain for the job they had to take the chains off the Indian slaves they had captured in Florida. The strength of the current broke the chain twice, but they added some ropes to the effort and finally got everybody across.

The Chickasawhatchee Swamp is about ten miles west of the Flint River. The people of Capachequi lived on high pieces of ground in the very heart of the swamp. It seems an unlikely place for people to live, but in fact the creek bottoms in the swamp provide some of the only naturally fertile soil in this whole southwest Georgia region. The swamp itself is actually quite beautiful. When the Indians were there, the forests on the higher land would have been mostly hardwoods, not the pines the paper company has growing there today. Cypress grows in the low places, a beautiful tree with its wide-flaring base. Old ones are tall and majestic and their bases huge.

According to the chronicles, De Soto and his men came to the first town of Capachequi, then on the same day left that town, crossed a bad swampy place with water up to the horses' girths, and came to the main village. Our purpose in poking around the swamp was to see if we could narrow in on exactly which village sites these were. That Chickasawhatchee Swamp was the land of Capachequi was not in doubt. Charlie had already worked that out and felt confident about it.

Gene knew of four village sites in the swamp. Two of them were close together, separated by a narrow strip of swamp, and may have been two sections of a single village. Garcilaso seems to be describing Capachequi when he tells about a province in which some of the towns were connected by wooden bridges going out over stretches of swamp. You could certainly imagine that at this particular site. Gene and Charlie both felt this was the first village De Soto encountered. They differed, though, on which one was the second. We drove to each of the candidates. The swamp crossings for both were over the main channel of Chickasawhatchee Creek, and the water even in this dry season was five feet deep—deeper than a horse's girth, which throws doubt on both sites. But Charlie's swamp crossing was wider, at least, which matched the chronicler's description of a huge sheet of water. And his site had a mound, a flat-topped earthen pyramid ten or twelve feet high. You could imagine the chief's house on top of it and the village and cornfields below. Gene's site was large, but it did not have a mound, and Charlie feels sure that if the mound site was occupied when De Soto came through, it would have been the main town. De Soto always went to the main town. I think Gene was at least partly persuaded. But as he pointed out, we do not even know where all the village sites are in the swamp. The ones that have been found are in areas that have been cleared of timber by the paper company and plowed, which turns up potsherds where there were villages. More will likely be discovered in the future. Before we can ever know exactly where De Soto went in Chickasawhatchee Swamp, much more archaeology will have to be done. But meanwhile we do know that De Soto visited this swamp and found here a Native American society called Capachequi. What happened to these people after De Soto's visit we do not know. Many would have died of European diseases. The survivors probably joined the Creeks or the Apalachees. A few of their descendants may have later been Seminoles.

We got back to Albany about noon, said goodbye to the Blacks, and headed north up the west side of the Flint. Our next stop was the De Soto Nut House in the tiny town of De Soto in Sumter County, Jimmy Carter's home county. The De Soto Nut House sells peanuts, pecans, and nut-laden candy. We appreciated the humor of the name. I took Charlie's picture in front of the sign, of course. I also took a picture of him standing beside the De Soto city limits sign. In the grass directly across the highway from that sign we found evidence of a Hispanic presence—two empty tequila bottles and two lime halves, well squeezed. Charlie said this was proof we were on the right trail.

The town of Leslie is no bigger than the town of De Soto and is directly adjacent to it, no countryside between. There is surely a story of why there are two towns instead of one, but we neglected to ask anyone about it. We stopped in Leslie to buy pecans at an establishment called Deriso Farms. "We buy and sell pecans," the sign said, meaning it was a wholesaler, a good place for us to buy a large quantity—thirty pounds—to give to friends. We went into this place—it was more like an office than a store—and were greeted by an amiable gentleman, about sixty years old. He had a light stubble of beard on his face, wore a neat suit of work clothes and a cap that said Deriso Farms. He was extraordinarily friendly, seemed pleased that we wanted thirty pounds, and said he would have to go over to the warehouse and make up a box for us. Then he picked up the phone and called the warehouse and told them to send somebody over to pick him up. You could tell by the way he did it that he was the boss of the place, though his manner was by no means self-important. He explained to us that his own truck was tied up with a load of pecans or else he would drive himself over. He had a gentle, earthy face and was pleasantly talkative. He sounded like Jimmy Carter. His name was Mr. Deriso, with the accent on the first syllable. His ancestors came from Italy in the old days, he said.

The man arrived to pick him up, and we followed in our own car to the warehouse. It was a big place, occupying several large buildings in a railroad yard in the heart of downtown Leslie. He took us in through the back door of what must have been the main warehouse. There were huge sacks of pecans stacked all around. The sacks were coffee sacks with "Café do Brasil" printed on them. Mr. Deriso began showing us his pecans. He had them for seventy-five cents, seventy cents, sixty-five cents, and sixty cents a pound. The seventy-five cent ones were paper-shells. He gave us some to try, breaking open the shell with a tool I had never seen before—an inspector's tool, he told me. It cut the shell more than crushed it. He would first cut off the two ends and then cut away about half of the rest of the shell. It was easy to lift the meat away from what was left.

"We'll take thirty pounds of these," I told him.

But he wanted to show us more. He seemed to be genuinely enjoying himself, and it was not because of the prospect of making a sale. Thirty pounds of pecans was nothing in a place like this. It seemed, rather, that he simply liked his business and enjoyed telling people about it. He cracked some Stuarts for us. This is the standard pecan, he told us. Most people who have pecan trees in their yards have Stuarts. They are better for roasting than papershells. They have less oil. Some people prefer their flavor, too. None of the pecans were quite what they should be this year, he said. There is an aphid that has made its appearance in the orchards and is immune to every insecticide they have tried to use against it. The aphid attacks the foliage of the tree, which takes nourishment away from the nuts.

All the while he is telling us this, he is cracking open pecans and giving them to us faster than we can eat them. He showed us another variety, developed by university researchers. It has a dense, heavy meat, but it has not been a success. No one is planting this variety anymore.

We stuck to our decision for papershells. He poured thirty pounds of them into a flat, traylike apparatus with a funnel-shaped opening on one side, and he and one of his men began picking through the nuts, taking out the ones with parts of their shells cracked off. The machines that pick them up break a lot of them, he told us.

We did not know they had a machine for picking up pecans. He described it for us. It has rotating paddles that sweep up the pecans— along with leaves, twigs, and trash—from raked windrows in the orchard. It is the paddles that break so many of the shells. A stream of air in the machine picks up what the paddles sweep in and blows it back to a conveyor belt that empties it out into a trailer hooked onto the back. Hydraulic lifts empty the contents of the trailer into farm wagons, and the nuts and debris are taken to another machine, a cleaner, that separates the nuts from the leaves, twigs, and soft-drink cans. At this point there are people who are supposed to pick out the damaged nuts, though they obviously do less than a thorough job of it. Mr. Deriso and his man spent a good five minutes picking through our thirty pounds.

After the nuts have gone through the cleaner, they are brought to the warehouse, where they are put through another machine that sorts them into sizes. This is done for the later benefit of the shelling machines, which can handle only nuts of uniform size. The sized nuts are sacked in the big coffee bags and shipped out.

There are two primary markets for pecans. The first is people like us who buy small quantities from packing houses or from roadside stands. This market begins in early November and ends at Thanksgiving. After Thanksgiving the shellers take over, and they are by far the larger market. They set their prices ahead of time based on an official estimate of the size of the crop. Mr. Deriso complained that the estimate was far too high this year—something like a 135 million pounds, when the actual crop was going to be only around 95 or 100 million. This artificially lowered the price.

Mr. Deriso poured our thirty pounds into a sack about the size of a large bag of dog food. We stuffed it into our already full Karmann Ghia, knowing we were coming home tonight and would not have to travel that way for long. Saying goodbye to Mr. Deriso, we headed north toward the Indian province of Toa.

We think Toa was along the Flint River, in the vicinity of Macon County or a little north of there. Very little archaeological surveying has been done in this area, so we had no hope of locating Toa with any precision on this trip. De Soto and his men crossed the Flint River in Toa, and so we spent our time looking for likely crossing places. We first checked out the river at Montezuma. De Soto had a hard time with this crossing. The first bridge they tried to put across the river was swept away by the swift current. The second one held. The current at Montezuma was indeed quite swift. It made whitewater where it broke over a log that was lodged in the shallows near the shore. But the river at that particular point looked a little wide to bridge.

We decided to look farther north for a narrower crossing. Gene Black had told us about a ferry we could take across the river near Marshallville—the only ferry still operating in the state of Georgia, he said. We headed for that. We went north about ten miles and then turned east toward the river on Georgia 127. About two miles from the river we turned onto a dirt road, still 127, and saw at once that it was very old, with trees touching overhead and its roadbed worn down between the banks. A sign said the ferry operated from six o'clock in the morning until ten at night—generous hours, I thought. It also said there was no charge.

Driving down to the ferry on the old unpaved road gave us a feeling of going back in time. At the river there was a concrete ramp leading down to the water's edge and a sign that told us to blow our horn for the ferry. We could see the ferryman's house across the river and the ferry tied up over there. The river was not wide—no more than a stone's throw. We did not have to blow our horn. The ferryman was out in his yard talking to someone, and as soon as he saw us, he headed down to the boat and in just a minute or two he was across.

The ferry was large enough for only one car at a time. It was a flat boat with a deck of wooden planks, a steel railing along either side, and steel ramps on both ends that are never raised. The ferryman noses the ramps onto the concrete approaches on the shore and you drive on one end and off the other. The ferryman was a black man named William English. He wore a Georgia Department of Transportation uniform. Through the car window he handed me a clipboard that held a passenger list. I had to write down the date, the time (it had been fifteen minutes since the last passenger had come across), my name, our tag number, our home state, and the make of our car. By the time I had done that, we were on the other side. Charlie had been out of the car taking pictures of the river. Even though the ferry had stopped, I got out, too. Mr. English told us to take our time, take all the pictures we wanted. We talked to him a little about the river. He said the water was high right now. We pointed to the middle of the channel where we had just crossed and asked him how deep it was. Seven feet, he told us. Deep enough for De Soto to have had to have bridged it, we thought, thinking Georgia 127 might be on the old main trail and this might have been De Soto's crossing.

"Is it ever shallow enough to ford," asked Charlie. "Can you ever wade across it?"

"Oh, yes," said Mr. English. "Wade across it and walk across it."

"So it gets pretty shallow sometimes."

"Oh, yes. It's not a deep river."

"But you said it was seven feet," I said.

"Only right here where they've dug the channel for the ferry," said Mr. English. It was true—that was the spot we had asked him about.

"Up there, then," I said, pointing upstream. "How deep is it there?"

"About three feet."

"And this is high water?"

"That's right. We just had rain."

So it seems that De Soto did not cross at the Marshallville ferry. It must have been somewhere downstream, probably in the vicinity of Montezuma.

We left Mr. English and drove west through Marshallville to Perry, where we wanted to take a look at Big Indian Creek. De Soto's men were losing heart by the time they got to Toa. La Florida was not looking very attractive to them. To spur their interest De Soto set out suddenly with a party of cavalry and dashed forward, as if he knew something about what lay ahead that the men behind did not know. The horsemen rode all day and after nightfall came to a deep stream of water that caused them some difficulty in fording. Big Indian Creek in Perry is a decent-sized creek, but it does not look as if it would have given them much trouble, even at night. So either it has silted in and is no longer as deep as it once was, or else De Soto crossed it somewhere downstream where it was larger.

We did not check it out any further. The afternoon was getting late and we wanted to see the Ocmulgee River before nightfall. We can work on this part of the route at our leisure at some future time, since it is only two or three hours from home.

We drove northeast and stopped beside the Ocmulgee at a bridge just south of Warner Robins. The Ocmulgee in this stretch has a huge swamp with it, a wide meander zone that makes it suitable for an incident that was supposed to have happened around here. The cavalry waded to an island, either in the river or in the swamp, where an Indian village was located. They raided the village for food and then left it and went on up toward the Indian province of Ichisi around Macon.

It was late when we stopped at the river, almost dark. There was heavy traffic on the highway, many trucks. Big cargo planes were coming in low to land at Robins Air Force Base. I was tired and did not get out of the car. Charlie had to walk a very long way to reach the middle of the bridge to take a picture. That was our last De Soto effort for the day.

We left the route and drove home to Athens, a two-hour trip. We will spend a couple of days here catching up on things—sleep, laundry, mail. It is good to be in our own house for a change.

Columbia, South Carolina
Sunday, November 18

We left home about four-thirty yesterday afternoon and drove back down to Macon to pick up the route where we had left off. We spent the night in a sleazy motel south of Macon on U.S. 41, which used to be the north–south corridor before Interstate 75 was built. The motel had a satellite dish that was controlled from the office, and at about ten-thirty, while we were watching the fourth quarter of the Georgia-Auburn football game, there was a blink on the screen and suddenly we were watching the Playboy channel. That was certainly an eye-opener for us. We did not know that hard-core pornography had come to television. All through the night as we tried to sleep we heard sounds of coming and going outside. Our lodgings seem to have been more a brothel than a tourist motel.

We stumbled out on the De Soto trail this morning bleary-eyed and slow-witted. We checked out a couple of creeks that were close by, which is why we had chosen that particular motel. Both creeks filled the bill for what we needed. Echeconnee Creek is large enough to drown a man, which fits a situation that was said to have happened there. The other one, Tobosofkee Creek, is smaller and has swamp on each side, indicating it sometimes carries a lot of water—the map shows it draining a large watershed. The chronicles say this creek rose up suddenly while the army was crossing it after a rain, and the men were endangered, though this time none were drowned. We then drove into downtown Macon to take another look at the Ocmulgee River. Parking the car, we got out and walked onto the bridge. The Ocmulgee is a large river, wide but not terribly deep, especially not in such a dry autumn as this one has been. We could see from the grassline along the bank that the water level was about a foot lower than it had been earlier in the year. I was surprised at how clear the water was—we could see the bottom in all but the deepest parts. That, too, may be because of dry weather. Surely after a rain it is as murky with red mud as are the rest of Georgia's rivers.

We ate a rather luxurious breakfast at the Hilton Hotel, which restored us somewhat from the sleaziness of that red-light motel last night. Then we left Macon behind. The Ocmulgee Valley above and below Macon was the province of Ichisi. Somehow I could not focus on the Ichisi Indians very well. The continuous urban sprawl of Macon and Warner Robins overwhelmed the distant past. All the river and creek banks in the area were so littered with trash that any natural beauty was obliterated.

So we were leaving Ichisi without having gotten much of a feeling for it. In the eighteenth century the Ocmulgee was called Ocheeseehatchee, which is Muskogean for "Ocheesee River" or "Ocheesee Creek." Ocheesee is the same word as Ichisi. There was a trading post there in the very early eighteenth century and a number of Muskogean-speaking people lived along the river and its tributaries. They were called at first the Ocheesee Creek Indians, or Ocheesee Creeks, which soon was shortened to Creeks. The name stayed with them as further events forced them to move west to the Chattahoochee and beyond into Alabama, where they joined other Muskogean speakers. Eventually that entire confederation was called Creeks, though a distinction was made between Upper Creeks, whose origins were in Tennessee, northern Georgia, and northern Alabama, and Lower Creeks, whose origins were farther south. If there were any Ichisi descendants still living in the eighteenth century, they would have been Lower Creeks.

So Macon was an important place for Native Americans of both prehistoric and early historic times. It is located on the fall line between the piedmont and the coastal plain. For Europeans the fall line meant the head of navigation. For the native peoples it provided two different ecosystems to exploit for food, and good fishing in the shoals of the fall line itself.

Elvas says in his chronicle that the Indian houses changed when they came to Toa. Behind them houses were covered with grass. From Toa on, they were roofed with cane in the manner of tiles, and the walls were plastered with clay. There is definitely a difference in the archaeological material from the Tallahassee area, on the one hand, and the Macon area on the other. Archaeologists think of it mainly in terms of pottery styles, the distinctive ways in which different groups of people shaped and decorated their pottery. The late Mississippian archaeological component from the Tallahassee area is known as Fort Walton phase. That would have been the material culture of the Apalachees. The Ichisi people, around Macon, were part of Lamar phase, which has a wide distribution from central Georgia into South Carolina, northern Georgia, and a little way over into Alabama. Not much is known yet of the archaeology of the Capachequi and Toa areas, but from what Elvas says, we would expect that Capachequi, down near Albany, was more closely related to Apalachee, or Fort Walton phase, than to the Lamar-phase cultures of the Macon area and northward. David Hally, an archaeologist who works with Charlie at the University of Georgia, thinks we will find the ceramics in Chickasawhatchee Swamp to be primarily Fort Walton phase with a Lamar influence. It makes me excited just to write that. This De Soto route is shedding so much light on the aboriginal Southeast. If they do find Fort Walton pottery in Chickasawhatchee Swamp and then go up to the Flint around Montezuma and find a good-sized chiefdom—Toa—with full-blown Lamar pottery, then we will know we have the route right. And if we have the route right, then we can say with a high degree of certainty that in 1540 there was an Indian society called Capachequi living around Albany, the remnants of which probably later joined the Apalachees. And we will know that the people of Toa lived on the Flint around Montezuma. Their remnants were probably later living among the Ichisi Creeks near Macon and later still among the Lower Creeks on the Chattahoochee. We have never before had names for these prehistoric Native Americans. We could only call them by their pottery styles—Fort Walton people, or Lamar.

From Macon we went northeast toward Milledgeville, looking for the neighborhood of the Indian town of Altamaha. We were in the piedmont now. One of the chroniclers describes the change in terrain. No more pinewoods, he said. And no more swamps—the rivers have firm banks. We stopped in Milledgeville and walked along the banks of the Oconee River. The morning sun was glittering so brightly on the water we could hardly look at it. The current was swift. Upstream a little we could see a line of shoals.

We were coming now into the political territory of Ocute. Altamaha was the first town, farthest downstream, and was in a tributary relationship to Ocute, though it seemed to maintain a certain independence of identity. The chief of Altamaha, perhaps seeing an opportunity to get free of Ocute, asked De Soto whether he should stop paying tribute to Ocute and pay it to the Spaniards instead. But De Soto, knowing he was just passing through but still wanting to seem to be lord of the land, said that Ocute was his brother and the chief of Altamaha should keep on paying tribute as he had been. Altamaha is the name that was later given to the river that is formed in the coastal plain by the joining of the Ocmulgee and Oconee rivers. That may imply that Altamaha finally did get free of Ocute and moved farther downriver. Sometime after De Soto—perhaps partly as a result of the De Soto expedition— the tributary system of all the chiefdoms of the Southeast broke down, and the chiefdoms crumbled apart into more egalitarian societies. Along with the end of tribute came the end of the building of mounds. The days of a hereditary chiefly elite endowed with great power had passed.

From Milledgeville we drove northeast to the present-day town of Sparta. Just north of Sparta was the home territory of Ocute, which was said to be the most powerful chiefdom in this part of Georgia— more powerful than Ichisi is the implication. We were driving through the heart of the piedmont now, a rich cotton country in the years before the Civil War—a region that considered itself vibrantly alive, not stultified like the coastal aristocrats, but more settled and cultured than the rough, newly opened regions to the west. Some of the more admirable of the southern political leaders came from the piedmont—admirable mainly for their moderation and their efforts to preserve the Union before the war broke out.

Today the piedmont is only lightly farmed. Some of the land is in pasture for cattle, a little of it is cultivated, but most of it is planted in pines for paper and lumber. Most of the towns we drove through—Sparta, Siloam, Greensboro, Crawfordville—are not much beyond where the Civil War left them. The post–World War II boom that hit the towns of southern Georgia seems not to have reached these piedmont towns. The coastal plain is well suited for large-scale agriculture. The piedmont evidently is not.

We drove on north to Greensboro, which is near the Indian town of Cofaqui, the last town subject to Ocute. Then we headed east with De Soto into the great wilderness of Ocute. This was an unpopulated buffer zone that stretched on for more than two hundred miles. De Soto and his men got lost in it.

We stopped at Crawfordville at the Alexander Stephens State Park and ate our lunch sitting on the back steps of the home of the vice-president of the Confederacy. At this point we were only about forty miles from our own home, but we went right on as if we were tourists from three states away. It was the first time we had ever been to the Alexander Stephens home. It seems we only do that kind of thing as tourists. The woman who was the hostess at the park was nervous because we would not come inside. But we preferred to poke around the backyard with its outbuildings (the privy had four holes). We felt we would lose the feeling of being back in time if we went in and submitted to the official tour.

From Crawfordville we followed U.S. 278 to Augusta. This is the old main road and also the route of the railroad. In the not so distant past there would have been cotton fields all along the way. Today it looks more like the wilderness it was when De Soto came through: mostly woods, some pastures, every now and then a field of soybeans, just now being harvested.

In Augusta we stopped to look at the Savannah River—not that there was any doubt about where it came in the route, but Charlie wanted a picture of it. It was overwhelmed by city: highway and railroad bridges, electric wires. We took an unsatisfactory picture and went on. The chroniclers describe the Savannah as wide, with a strong current and many flat rocks, which is exactly how it looks today. They lost a number of pigs to the current as they crossed and had to hold onto each other in a human chain to keep from being swept away themselves. It was, however, shallow enough to ford.

We passed through the community of Silver Bluff and saw a county road named De Soto Road. This was where the Swanton Commission put the Indian province of Cofitachequi in the 1939 version of the route. Charlie thinks Cofitachequi was much farther east, in the center of South Carolina.

Just south of Augusta we made a brief stop àt Redcliff State Park (we were now in South Carolina), which is the home of the Hammonds of Redcliff from antebellum times. I had read a volume of the family's letters in the past year, and I wanted to take a look at the place. We sat at a picnic table and ate some cheese and crackers and rested a few minutes, and then we went on.

We were still following U.S. 278. Our next stop was the South Fork of the Edisto River near Springfield, a stop Charlie was dreading because he needed a large river here and it did not seem from the topographical maps that the South Fork Edisto was going to be very big. This had been a major problem in reconstructing the route from Ocute to Cofitachequi. The solution Charlie had finally come to, the one we were checking out, was that after crossing the Savannah, the expedition followed a strong trail that led southeast to the coast (at least later there was a strong trail here), and thus diverged from the course they should have been following along the fall line to the east and northeast, which would have given them a much easier crossing of the South Fork, higher up. All the chroniclers say that their guides did not know where they were going. The people of Ocute were at war with Cofitachequi, but that war was waged only by small parties that encountered one another while hunting in the wilderness. The people of Ocute never went to Cofitachequi—either for raiding or for any other purpose. Therefore they did not really know how to get there. Six days out of Ocute the trail by which the Indian guides were leading the Spaniards petered out, and after that they got completely lost. It was while they were lost that they crossed the South Fork down in the coastal plain—near Springfield, Charlie thought. That solution seemed to work best for the distance they had to cover before the crossing and after it. But he dreaded seeing how small the South Fork would be in actuality. The chroniclers said it was a difficult crossing.

Well, it was the high point of our day when we got there and saw it. It had a wide swamp on either side and the channel itself looked fairly deep and wide even now in this dry autumn. De Soto was there in April. The water would have been out of its banks—you could see it would take very little to spill it over into the swamp. The water in the river was black from cypress trees.

So the South Fork Edisto would work. We had to go next to look at the North Fork, taking South Carolina 3 toward Swansea. We needed the North Fork Edisto to be small and so easy to cross that the chroniclers would not have mentioned it. The road to it ran almost due north, and we had driven out of the coastal plain into low hills by the time we reached it. It was a welcome sight: firm banks (no swamp), narrow channel, and a ripple of shoals. They could have easily walked across it, even with higher water. We were very happy. This was one part of the route we had not been sure about at all.

Now we headed on into Columbia, following U.S. 321 north. De Soto covered this stretch in bewilderment and dire distress. The army was making seven or eight leagues a day—as much as twenty miles—so desperate were they to find people and corn. What they found next, though, was a river as large as the Savannah had been. This is the Congaree, which is formed by the Saluda and Broad rivers coming together in Columbia, which like Macon and Augusta is at the fall line.

We wanted to look at the Congaree and found a fine old bridge across it in the middle of downtown Columbia. The afternoon was very late, the sun just above the trees on the horizon. The bridge was the old-fashioned kind with concrete balustrades. It had a sidewalk on it, and we walked out to the middle. The river was beautiful. It is huge—amazingly wide—but also very shallow here and full of rocks. There was an island in the middle. Each branch that went around it was as wide as any river we have seen yet on the route. People were fishing along the banks in the gathering twilight, and there was no urban ugliness here. Maybe the Congaree is too majestic to lose its beauty to a city. On the east side of the river a diverted channel came flowing out through the vaulted brick arches of an old hydroelectric plant. There were eight arches and the current was strong as it rushed out to rejoin the river. Behind this was a huge old textile mill, many stories high, with all its many windows bricked up. The story of the southern piedmont after the Civil War, and particularly after 1900, is textile mills: uprooted country people, mill towns, a cash economy, low wages, union struggles. The Carolinas are the heart of it.

We stopped here in Columbia for the night. Tomorrow we head up toward Tennessee.

CHAPTER THREE

Tennessee Zinc

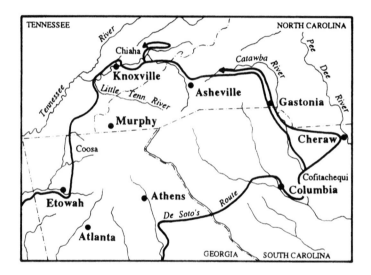

During all the days of their march from Tali the chief of Tali had corn and mazamorras {hominy mush} and cooked beans and everything that could be brought {to them} from his villages bordering the way. Thursday they passed another small village, and then other villages, and Friday the Governor entered Coosa.

This chief is a powerful one and a ruler of a wide territory, one of the best and most abundant that they found in Florida. And the chief came out to receive the Governor in a litter covered with the white mantles of the country, and the litter was borne on the shoulders of sixty or seventy of his principal subjects, with no plebeian or common Indian among them; and those that bore him took turns by relays with great ceremonies after their manner.

There were in Coosa many plums like the early ones of Seville, very good; both they and the trees were like those of Spain. There were also some wild apples like those called canavales in Extremadura, small in size. They remained there in Coosa some days, in which the Indians went off and left their chief in the power of the Christians with some principal men, and the Spaniards went out to round them up, and they took many, and they put them in iron collars and chains. . . .

On Friday, August 20, the Governor and his people left Coosa, and there stayed behind a Christian named Feryada, a Levantine; and they slept the next night beyond Talimachusy, and the next day in a heavy rain they went to Itaba, a large village along a fine river, and there they bought some Indian women, which were given them in exchange for looking-glasses and knives.

—*Rodrigo Ranjel*

Mascot, Tennessee
Monday, November 19

We are staying with a Tennessee archaeologist, Richard Polhemus, who lives with his parents in the old company town of a defunct zinc-mining operation near Knoxville. We drove five hundred miles today. Most of the day we were in the South Carolina piedmont, the land of textile mills.

We left Columbia about seven-thirty this morning and headed northeast to Cheraw. This was not on De Soto's main trail, though Cheraw was a place where a part of his army visited. Cofitachequi, in the heart of South Carolina, had been a disappointment to De Soto. He had been led to believe that he would find gold and silver there, but he found only a few pieces of copper, some slabs of mica, and a rather large store of low-quality freshwater pearls. Furthermore, the native population seems to have been decimated by a recent epidemic, possibly one that had spread inland from contact with Spanish sailors along the coast. Consequently there was little corn in the granaries. The Indians themselves were suffering food shortages. To help feed his army De Soto sent part of it up to Ilasi, a tributary town with a store of corn, which Charlie thinks was located near the present-day town of Cheraw. They later rejoined the main army as it headed north on a trail farther west.

If we had followed De Soto's trail from Columbia, we would have gone southeast to the Indian town of Aymae in the forks of the Wateree and Congaree, where those two rivers come together to make the Santee. Then north up the Wateree to Camden, the heartland of Cofitachequi. All of this portion of the route we have already traveled while working on the expedition of Juan Pardo, the Spaniard who came through this part of the country thirty years after De Soto, following much the same trail. Likewise, we have driven the route taken by both De Soto and Pardo north from Camden and then northwest to the Indian town of Chiaha over here in Tennessee. We had not driven the side trip to Ilasi, a digression taken by both Pardo and that detachment of De Soto's army. What Charlie specifically wanted to check out was Thompson Creek just west of Cheraw. When Pardo and his men left Ilasi after several days of heavy rains, they had to wade through water a mile wide (half a league) with ice on the surface. Thompson Creek empties into the Pee Dee River at Cheraw, and Charlie reasoned that backwater from the Pee Dee in flood would create that kind of situation at approximately the place where U.S. 1 crosses Thompson Creek today, about three miles west of Cheraw.

On the way there we drove through miles and miles of sand hills—

ancient beaches covered with pines and a kind of scrubby oak that was a beautiful red in this peak of the leaf season. The sand hills were largely unpopulated. Paper companies owned part of them, and another large area was state forest. There was some farming, evidently more than we could see from the highway, since for a time we passed more soybean combines than cars—three combines, to be exact. The car total eventually surpassed the combine count.

Outside Cheraw we found Thompson Creek, with a flood plain that was very wide, though not an entire mile across. We stopped at a country store that had a lunch counter and poolroom in it and asked whether Thompson Creek got backwater from the Pee Dee and whether it ever backed up to anything like a mile across. There were four people in the store, three men and a woman—the woman and one of the men seemed to be the proprietors. Yes, indeed, they told us. It turns into a terrible swamp and goes as far upstream as Chesterfield, seven or eight miles up the road. So bad a swamp, one of them said, he once lost a car in it. The Pee Dee can almost dry up at times, they said, and the swamp gets dry as well, "but come a heavy rain and you never seen so much water." The biggest flood one of them had ever seen was back in 1945. It had been feared that the train trestle over the Pee Dee would wash away. A train was driven out onto it and parked there to hold it. And it held.

It was only after we had driven away and were several miles down the road that we realized that we had no idea *how* the man had managed to lose a car in the swamp. There was a story there. I am sure he would have been happy to tell it.

Cheraw is a textile-mill town—J. P. Stevens on the east side of town, Burlington Mills on the west. If there were other mills, we did not see them. We left and headed west on South Carolina 9, an old road. The sun was coming out after a heavy sky and scattered drizzles. I had thought we would have to drive through rain most of the day, but instead the sky cleared to a fresh, washed-clean blue with fluffy white clouds and a temperature of about sixty-five degrees. The leaves were at their absolute peak of beauty—the loveliest foliage we have seen yet. There was hardly any traffic on the highway. We passed through ancient farming communities, nothing left of them but a few old unpainted buildings. In front of an abandoned store that stood alone beneath some pecan trees in what must have been, even in its heyday, a tiny community, there was an old gas pump and an antique Gulf Oil sign of the kind you never see anymore except in the movies. It made us feel back in time.

As we got a little higher in the piedmont, we began passing through more and more textile towns until by the time we got to Lancaster, near Rock Hill, the region had become decidedly prosperous. While we were eating lunch in Lancaster, we heard an announcement over the radio that congressional hearings were being held in the city of Rock Hill concerning pending legislation aimed at limiting foreign textile imports. The public was urged to attend.

When we reached the town of Chester, we turned north on U.S. 321, another old road, and headed toward Gastonia. We were back on the main trail of De Soto now. The country from Chester through York was some of the most inviting we have traveled through so far. Partly it was the sparkling weather and bright autumn leaves, but I also remember noticing the attractiveness of this land on our earlier Pardo travels, which took place in other seasons. The piedmont gets higher here, the hills more abrupt. As we neared Gastonia the number of textile mills multiplied until just south of Gastonia there seemed to be one every mile—and here we even began to see manufacturing plants that produced textile-mill equipment. Gastonia is a large and prosperous town. We were in North Carolina now.

U.S. 321 from Gastonia to Hickory is a ghastly road. By the time we reached the end of those twenty-five miles, we were swearing never to drive that stretch of highway again. There is continuous occupation along it—town, residences, town, residences, without cease. The highway is heavily congested—we were never free of exhausting traffic. There is manufacturing all along the way—textiles, primarily, but also a heavy presence of furniture manufacturing. But despite this obvious economic base and despite the heavy population, U.S. 321 is unimproved from Gastonia to Hickory. To drive it is like going back to the 1950s—hardly any stretches of four-lane, not even any passing lanes. When we finally reached Interstate 40 in Hickory it was like coming out of a time warp. By then we were so exhausted that we decided to take I-40 all the way to Knoxville, since we still had the Blue Ridge Mountains to cross. Even at that we were past seven o'clock getting here.

The part of the route that we were missing by taking the interstate was the stretch from the Indian town of Guaquili (present-day Hickory) to that of Chiaha (Dandridge, Tennessee). We drove this several years ago. In fact, the stretch of I-40 along the Pigeon River through the mountains was the first De Soto traveling we ever did. This was back at the beginning when Charlie and Chester and Marvin were working so closely together. Charlie thought De Soto had gone down the Pigeon River to get through the Blue Ridge, coming out at Newport. Marvin thought he had gone down the Little Tennessee River, coming out south of Knoxville. Chester did not have a strong opinion on this section of the route, though as I recall he was leaning toward the Pigeon. Richard Polhemus had tried to tell us that the Pigeon was too rugged for there to have been a strong trail there, but it was only when we drove it, trying to take De Soto along it, that we realized he could not have gone that way. So we spent that night in a motel in Newport, got up the next morning, and drove up the French Broad River, taking the route backward, and it fit beautifully. That was when we learned that it takes traveling the route to confirm the work that has been done with maps and archaeology.

We were exhausted by the time we got here to the Polhemuses' house, but the moment we met Richard's parents, new life flowed into us. They are delightful. The story of zinc mining in Tennessee is fascinating and so much alive here in this company house. The evening was a hundred times better than the day. But it kept us up late and I shall have to wait until tomorrow to write about it.

Maryville, Tennessee
Tuesday, November 20

We slept well last night in comfortable guest quarters in the Polhemuses' house. Jim and Bea Polhemus made us feel like treasured guests. We arrived at their home last night worn to a frazzle from that long drive, the last of it through high mountains in the rain. Richard met us just off the interstate. He is a young man, thirtyish, dark-haired, and tall, or perhaps he only seems tall because he stands with a bit of a stoop. Reserved and mannerly, he smiles quietly and says little until the subject turns to archaeology. Then he comes alive. Archaeology is the heartbeat of Richard's life. He has been engaged in archaeological projects in Tennessee since he was a boy, and though he does not yet have a doctoral degree or a full-time professional job, he is nonetheless a fully legitimate archaeologist in the eyes of the other professionals. Charlie and I have gotten to know him in recent years through Charlie's work on the Pardo and De Soto routes, and we always enjoy his openness and sincerity and his genuine enthusiasm for Tennessee archaeology.

We knew Richard lived with his parents, but that was all we knew about his home life, except that his father had something to do with mining. We thought they lived at the edge of Knoxville. As it turned out, Richard led us to a little town about fifteen miles from the city. I saw as we were winding up the street to his home that all the houses looked alike, they all had the same porches, most of which had been enclosed to make sunrooms. I knew from that sameness that this was a company town.

The weather had turned very cold since we crossed the mountains. It was in the thirties and we shivered getting out of the car and going to the house. Jim Polhemus came out to greet us—a handsome, friendly man who looked to be about my father's age, mid-sixties. He seemed genuinely pleased to have us there. Inside the door I met Bea, a happy-faced woman who laughs a lot. Their house was unpretentious, but lovely and tasteful. I immediately felt at home. There was a fire in the fireplace and we stood in front of it and warmed ourselves. Jim brought us drinks— he said he had anything, so I asked for sherry, which I seldom request, but it seemed just the thing to go with sitting by the fire.

We sat down in comfortable chairs and nibbled Goldfish crackers, and I asked where we were. This is Mascot, they told us. A company town for a now-defunct zinc mine. The mine closed down because the zinc ran out. Most of the people still living in the town are retirees. The young people have all moved away. There are no children to hire to mow the grass.

The company does not own the houses anymore. Several years ago they let the residents buy them. But the company still owns all the rest of the land around there and what is left of the mining facilities, which are gradually being dismantled and carted away. For most of its life the mine was owned by the American Zinc, Lead, and Smelting Company. In the early 1960s that company sold out to a British mining company; so for a while, said Jim and Bea, they were "under the British."

Why would a British company want a zinc mine in Tennessee, I asked?

The British are aggressive miners, said Jim. They own mines all over the world—gold mines in South Africa, for instance. But sometimes they make a mistake. The zinc mine went broke while they owned it.

Which was too bad, said Bea. They met some very nice people while they were under the British.

A multinational mining company owns them now and still uses some of the aboveground facilities in connection with other mines they have in the area. But they are not doing well. This last quarter was the first time they failed to pay dividends to their stockholders. Primary industries are in trouble in America today, said Jim. He did not know why.

Jim Polhemus came to Mascot from Connecticut in 1938 after dropping out of college. His father had been in mining—had, in fact, designed some of the facilities at Mascot—and his grandfather had been in mining, too. Jim worked at first with a pick and shovel and lived in the dormitories where the single men lived and ate in the mess hall. It did not take much hard labor to make him see that he should have stayed in college, so he went back and earned a degree in mining engineering and then returned to Mascot to a better job. Bea, also from Connecticut, came down and joined him. They brought up three children. By the time Jim retired he was General Manager of Surface Operations Above Ground. Their house, the one we were staying in, was in the management section of the camp. It had once been the doctor's house.

Jim is an intellectual. He has always been interested in archaeology, and in the 1940s he became friends with Madeleine Kneberg and Tom Lewis, who were, in effect, the anthropology department at the University of Tennessee. He is interested in the history of mining in general, but especially of the mine at Mascot. When he heard one day that all the old records were going to be dumped down a hole, he went and salvaged what he could, picking out the most important things he could find. He was only given six or seven hours to do it. He showed us some pictures he had salvaged that were taken during the boom era right before World War I. There were once a thousand men underground, he said. A lot of zinc was needed in World War I to make brass.

The shaft underground was huge, said Bea. Like a cathedral. She went down into it only once. If a woman went down there, all the men would come out. Jim told us that zinc does not occur in beds like coal, so the underground mines look different from coal mines. Zinc does not occur in a regular pattern. It is where it is. You follow it until you have dug it all out. There at Mascot they dug up close to the surface of the ground and that created unending sinkhole problems, since they were mining in limestone. Water getting into the mine was the worst problem they had. Sometimes a sinkhole would open up and a whole creek would come flowing in. Jim spent much of his time plugging up holes.

He talked about unions—you could tell that labor relations had been a large and disturbing part of his life with the mining company. He was management, in opposition to unions. And yet many of the men in the unions were men he had once worked with. He knew them as individuals. He talked a lot about the kind of company it was— a "gentle" company, he said. A one-man company, despite the public shareholders. He felt the company genuinely cared for its employees. When layoffs came, they would lay off the single men first and let the men with families keep working. And they would give the single men one day's work a week so they could hang on. He gave many examples of the decency of the company. There was never any bloodshed, he said, referring to union activity. There were no head-knockings.

During dinner the conversation shifted to archaeology. We talked a lot about Tom Lewis and Madeleine Kneberg, who were friends of the Polhemuses. There were so few archaeologists in the South up until the 1960s. The ones who were here were the pioneers, and the names of almost all of them have become legend. Certainly Lewis and Kneberg are a legend. Tom Lewis came to Tennessee during the Depression, when the Works Progress Administration (the WPA) was assigning great numbers of workers to archaeological projects. The government would say to an archaeologist: Here are two hundred men—put them to work. Ordinarily archaeological crews are small, five to twenty people. There has never been anything like those WPA excavations. They took archaeology in the South a giant step forward, even though their methods in those days were crude compared to the present. Tom Lewis worked at Norris Dam first and then at other sites.

Madeleine came a little later than Tom, and the two of them eventually married. Her degree was in physical anthropology, which meant she was not specifically trained for archaeology. But then, Tom's degree was not in archaeology either. In those days, especially in the South, many archaeologists lacked formal training. Madeleine was considered to be the smarter of the pair. She was also a talented artist and would draw scenes of Native American life based on their excavations.

Despite the valuable contribution they made to the archaeology of the region, Tom and Madeleine left the University of Tennessee on their retirement with a certain degree of bitterness—hurt feelings, anyway. The new, more rigorous and "scientific" style of archaeology was sweeping the country, and even the South was affected. More money was available in the national economy, and anthropology departments in the South began to grow from the underfunded, understaffed holding actions they had always been. Kneberg's and Lewis's style of popularizing archaeology was frowned upon now. We archaeologists are scientists, the young scholars said. We should be talking primarily to ourselves—ours is a scientific dialog that the lay person cannot understand. Archaeologists like Kneberg and Lewis, with their strong commitment to educating the public, were considered less than true scholars.

There was unpleasantness in the university. Kneberg and Lewis were instrumental in founding an anthropology museum on campus, but the anthropology department, which was separate, turned its back on them. There was a great mess of a controversy, and Kneberg and Lewis retired from the university as soon as they possibly could and left without ever looking back. Madeleine, in her eighties, is living today in Florida. Tom has died.

We slept well last night, and this morning we got up to the smell of coffee and bacon. Jim, of whom I had grown very fond, was sitting at the table, which was all set with glasses of orange juice and cups of steaming coffee. I allowed myself the luxury of sitting down without offering to help Bea. She seemed to have everything under control. Richard and Charlie joined us, and we drank our coffee while Bea scrambled the eggs.

I told Jim I would like to start the day with a tour of the mining town. He seemed pleased. But he said he would have to let Richard be the one to conduct the tour. It was too cold outside for him to function well. Jim has emphysema—real problems with his breathing. He told us he and Bea had been to a retirement party last week for one of the fellows in the company who used to work here in Mascot and more recently has worked in one of the nearby operations.

"He was in terrible shape," said Jim. "All the old guys are broken down. They've all got breathing problems. I don't know what we did to them. But we did *something* wrong. That lime dust wasn't supposed to hurt you. But we've all got breathing problems."

He said it quietly, looking down at his hands as he toyed with his coffee cup. It was that same disturbed tone that had underlain all his talk about the company. He knew that much had happened here in Mascot that was not exactly right. And yet in large measure he was the company—he had given it all of his intellect, all of his talent. He had developed new methods of extracting zinc from the ore. In the end he was one of three top men in the company there at Mascot. He is a gentle and humane man. He was proud of what the company had accomplished there, proud of what he had helped them do. And yet there was this underlying ambivalence.

Bea objected when Jim said he would let us take the tour without him. It was he who knew all the history and stories of the camp, she said.

"Dick grew up here," said Jim, still in that quiet, thoughtful mood. "He can show them the place from a different perspective. I see things differently. I'm the one who had to push people around to get them to work."

Jim Polhemus is a good man. I felt great tenderness toward him. He is a woodcarver and makes small, graceful pieces. When we left him, he could not come with us to the door. He was standing by the kitchen table, leaning on it, coughing and trying to catch his breath.

Murphy, North Carolina
Thanksgiving Day, November 22

We have left De Soto's trail and come to my parents' home for Thanksgiving. Since leaving Mascot we have spent two days on the route, driving from the Indian town of Tanasqui to that of Coosa—all of it within the province of the great chiefdom of Coosa. All, that is, except Tanasqui itself, which was just east of Coosa's frontier.

We went with Richard Polhemus to look at the supposed site of Tanasqui on the point of land where the Pigeon and French Broad rivers come together, just outside present-day Newport. Actually, De Soto did not visit Tanasqui. He went by it without mentioning it. It was Pardo who went there, but only on his way *to* Chiaha, not on his way back, which meant that it was a little way off the main trail. Charlie, Chester, and Marvin are the ones who suggested that Tanasqui was in this particular location. It is one of the most testable hypotheses of their Pardo route. The Pardo documents say that the town was located between two rivers, with the rivers forming defensive barriers on all but one side, and across that open neck of land was a palisade with three towers. This was the first time Pardo and his men had seen a palisaded town. They asked the people of Tanasqui what the palisade was for, and the people said, To protect us against our enemies.

On the basis of Charlie's route, Richard Polhemus has gotten some funds from the National Geographic Society to survey the site and try to find the village of Tanasqui, with its palisade with three bastions. A very large farm covers the tip of the peninsula. Richard has been walking the land, taking core samples and looking for sites. Of the several sites he has found, all but one are of the wrong time period. That one, however, might turn out to be right. He took us there Tuesday morning to show it to us.

It was not exactly as we had imagined it. We had imagined the village on the farthest tip of land with a palisade closing it in on the land side. Actually that is not a very reasonable arrangement. Swollen waters would flood the village if it were down that close to the confluence, and if it were back from the confluence any distance at all, the neck of land would become too wide for a palisade of any reasonable size. The site that Richard has found is not down in the bottomlands at the confluence but up on a ridge on one side of the point of land, back about a quarter of a mile. On the western side of the ridge is a steep bluff dropping down to the Pigeon River, which runs right beside the site. The sides of the ridge that face the confluence to the north and the French Broad River to the east drop steeply to the bottomlands below. If the trees were cleared you could see the French Broad several hundred yards away. The south side of the ridge, facing up the peninsula, does not drop off steeply from the village site. It is across *this* neck of land that one would expect to find the palisade with three towers. And in fact, there is an intriguing fencerow just about where you might expect the palisade to be. It has been there a long time and has some very old cedar trees growing in it. It may have nothing to do with the old palisade, but it makes it easy to imagine one being there.

There have been many good ideas in archaeology that have not held up when the excavation was done, and this could well turn out that way. But the site looked good for Tanasqui. It was not the way we had first imagined it, but the location on the ridge does in fact fit the description quite well. The rivers *are* on either side, and when you consider the fact that the bottomlands would have been the town's cornfields, then you can accept this description with no trouble at all. And the village is in a location that would have needed a defensive palisade on only one side—the steepness of approach would have protected the other sides.

There is still a possibility that the site will turn out to have been occupied at too early a date. Or that there will be no palisade to be found. That would certainly make problems for this leg of the route. But evidence for other parts of the route leading up to Newport and away from it is growing stronger and stronger, and it seems increasingly likely that Tanasqui will eventually be found at that site or one close by. If it is found, it will clinch the route—at least a major segment of it. If it is not, we shall have to be content with less certainty.

Richard Polhemus was the first of the archaeologists Charlie and Chester and Marvin talked to early in their work who saw that they were on to something important. In large part this was because it shed new light on his own work and confirmed some of the ideas he had been developing over the past several years. About these I will write tomorrow. Right now I have to stop and make scalloped oysters for Thanksgiving dinner.

Athens, Georgia
Friday, November 23

We got home about dark last night, full of turkey and pumpkin pie and feeling happy to be back on our own again, free of the chaos of family gatherings. The house was cold as a tomb, but we built a fire in the woodstove and enjoyed standing around it, having a drink and listening to a "History of the Beatles" on the radio.

Today while we were eating lunch in a restaurant near the campus, we talked about Tanasqui and what an important site it could be. If Richard finds that palisade—and especially if he also finds some sixteenth-century European artifacts—it will confirm the route and in so doing will take the archaeology of that area a giant step forward. This is a Pisgah-phase site, which is early Cherokee. Until now archaeologists have maintained that Pisgah had ended by 1500, with Qualla phase replacing it—that is, Qualla grew out of Pisgah and had done so by 1500. The main difference between the two phases, besides ceramic styles, is that Pisgah sites are compact and fortified, whereas Qualla sites have dispersed settlement and no palisades. This implies that Pisgah was locked into some kind of conflict with its neighbors that Qualla no longer had to contend with.

When Charlie and Chester and Marvin first started asking about possible De Soto sites in this area, the knowledgeable archaeologists told them that the only sites known were Pisgah sites and those were too early—pre-1500. Charlie started saying, "Then maybe you have the end of Pisgah dated wrong. Maybe Pisgah ends with De Soto and Pardo, most likely as a consequence of them."

Roy Dickens at the University of North Carolina at Chapel Hill is the most respected authority on Pisgah-Qualla. When Roy saw Charlie's route, he liked it. He liked the sense it made of archaeology. He liked Dallas phase in the Tennessee Valley belonging to the ancestors of the Creeks instead of the Cherokees, even though he and others had argued it the other way since the 1960s. Before that, Lewis and Kneberg had maintained that Dallas was Creek, but as their old-fashioned, supposedly unrigorous style of archaeology fell into disrepute, so did their theories. Yet according to Charlie's route, Lewis and Kneberg were right.

Roy himself has been quite willing to change his theories in the face of new evidence. He is also willing to entertain the possibility that Pisgah extended through De Soto and Pardo instead of ending just before. This is something we have found over and over while tracing the route: the archaeological picture reveals major shifts in Indian culture during this general time period, but archaeologists have almost always dated the shifts at 1500, shying away from De Soto's entrada, as if there were something unscientific about using De Soto to explain anything—when, in fact, early European contact was one of the most disastrous things that ever happened to Native American societies. Disease, a shaken worldview, the collapse of the chiefdom political structure: surely this would show up in the archaeology. So if Richard's site does turn out to be Tanasqui, we will have Pisgah phase lasting through Pardo—1568.

De Soto did not visit Tanasqui, or if he did, he did not mention it. He was headed for Chiaha, which was only a few miles downriver near present-day Dandridge. We did not spend any time on this leg of De Soto's route, since we had covered it when we drove the Pardo route earlier. What we did need to do this time was check out a revision Charlie had made in the Pardo route.

After Pardo first visited Chiaha in 1567, he went from there to a town called Chalahume and then to a nearby town called Satapo. The Pardo chronicler says that in going to Chalahume they went west from Chiaha and traveled over difficult country with hard climbing and passed by mountains more rugged than any they had seen before. When they were leaving Satapo, they were told of a better route back to Chiaha, and they took it.

Well, west of Chiaha is the low hilly country that lies east of Knoxville. When we traveled the Pardo route earlier, we had been well pleased with the way Charlie's reconstruction of the route matched the terrain all the way to Chiaha. But the route west from Chiaha made us very uneasy. How could they say, after coming down the French Broad River through the high mountains, that this land east of Knoxville was more rugged than any they had passed through before? Maybe it was that until now they had followed river courses through mountains without having to do any climbing, we reasoned lamely. Maybe these hills wore them out just because they had to go up and over them instead of following stream courses through them. But we felt something was not right. After all, they had come through Swannanoa Gap—the eastern continental divide. That was a big up-and-over.

But Charlie felt that he had the Pardo route essentially right, at least to Chiaha. He and Chester and Marvin published it, and when they came to this last leg from Chiaha to Chalehume, they said they were unsure of it, but gave an interpretation, putting Satapo and Chalahume somewhere near Knoxville.

Later Charlie got in touch with Dwayne King, a scholar whose specialty is Cherokees, about the names of the towns from which some chiefs came to meet with Pardo while he was in the mountains. Charlie wanted to know how many of them were Cherokee towns. Dwayne put the ones he could identify as such into three categories: those that were definitely known Cherokee towns, some of which still exist today in new locations; those that were probably Cherokee because the words had meaning in Cherokee; and those that were possibly Cherokee because the words, while untranslatable, could have been Cherokee words.

But Dwayne was also interested in the definitely Creek towns of Satapo and Chalahume. The name of the Cherokee town of Citico had always been puzzling. Citico is not a Cherokee word. It has no meaning in the Cherokee language. But if a Cherokee were to try to say the word Satapo, he would pronounce it Sataquo. The reason for that is that Cherokee does not have bilabial sounds. In much the same way that English speakers have difficulty with uvular sounds, like the French *r*, Cherokee speakers had trouble making sounds that required putting their lips together: *m, p, b*. Sataquo, anglicized, would become Sataco—or Citico.

Charlie started looking at the maps again. The eighteenth-century town of Citico was on the Little Tennessee River. What if that had once been the Creek town of Satapo? Suppose the Creeks had abandoned the area and the Cherokees had moved in, still remembering some of the old place names that the Creeks had used. He started trying to take Pardo from Chiaha to the site of Citico and then back to Chiaha by an alternate route, as the documents indicate. The travel time worked when he took him down the east side of Chilhowee Mountain, and it worked again when he took him back up the west side. That route involved some travel over rugged terrain. Much of it was through valleys, but there were a few ridges that would have to be crossed—one especially had some height to it. And as the Spaniards were going along that route to the east of Chilhowee, they would have had a view of the spectacular Great Smoky Mountains, which rise to the east of the valley they were following. More rugged mountains than any they had seen before—more rugged than any others in eastern North America.

The town Pardo visited right before Satapo (or Citico) was Chalahume. It was not far from Satapo—a mile or two upstream. In the eighteenth century there was a similarly located Cherokee town named Chilhowee—another name with no meaning in Cherokee. Cherokees trying to pronounce the name of the Creek town of Chalahume would change the *m* to a *w:* Chalahuwa. Chilhowee. It was beginning to look as if the Cherokees had in fact come in after the time of the Spaniards and taken over abandoned Creek towns. That was an exciting discovery.

We left Richard at Tanasqui—he wanted to collect some core samples before he went home—and we set out to trace Pardo's trail alongside Chilhowee Mountain to the Little Tennessee River. We went to Sevierville and took U.S. 441 south toward Gatlinburg. We were looking for a little road we could see on the map that turned off to the right just before Pigeon Forge. But before we knew it, we were in Pigeon Forge itself, without having recognized our turn-off. We stopped at the Pigeon Forge Information Center—tourism is the major industry here, spilling over from Gatlinburg and the Great Smoky Mountains National Park. The lady at the desk told us to proceed down the road and turn right at the second light. This did not seem right to me, since the map clearly showed our road turning off *before* Pigeon Forge. There was a three-dimensional relief map in the Information Center and we studied that to try to find the route we wanted to follow. If we could find this road near Pigeon Forge, we could follow it to Walland, about halfway to the Little Tennessee. That road, according to the map, was unpaved part of the way, but we were confident it would carry us through. Beyond Walland, though, it did not look as if we would be able to drive exactly where Pardo went. We could walk it. A trail was indicated for part of the way, connecting two segments of the road we wanted to follow. But we had no time for a hike. So we decided that if we could get to Walland, we would take the Foothills Parkway along the crest of Chilhowee Mountain, which was clearly not an old road—nobody would ever go that way without an automobile and a modern highway.

We got in the car and drove down to the second traffic light and turned as we had been directed to do. This road was too broad and well traveled to be the one we were looking for. We came to a little road that went off to the right with a sign pointing to Laurel Grove Baptist Church. Laurel Grove was a town on the road we were looking for, so we left the big, smooth road and headed down this narrow one with rough, lumpy pavement. This took us closer to the base of Chilhowee Mountain, so we felt it was the right way.

When we came to Laurel Grove, which was only a tiny community, the pavement ran out. We checked the map. That was what our road was supposed to do. We were in the right place. So on we went. It was not a bad road. It was narrow, but it was graveled—much like the road our house is on in Georgia. We were in a pretty little valley with a creek in it.

"Walnut Creek," said Charlie. "The rugged ridge they crossed was at the head of Walnut Creek."

We soon left the valley, and the road began to climb a little.

"Going up the ridge," Charlie said optimistically. But this was supposed to be a climb that made the soldiers complain. We came to the top and the road leveled out. I could have walked up that hill in fifteen minutes without a word of grumbling. I told Charlie so.

"This has to be it," Charlie said testily. "Stop and let me take a picture of the rise in the land." He had that frustrated tone he gets before he admits he is wrong.

"There's no rise worth taking a picture of," I said. "This is not what you think it is." I was referring to this whole route alongside Chilhowee Mountain.

"It has to be," he said sharply. He was not giving up on it. I stopped the car, and while he got out to take a picture of nothing that would illustrate anything, I sat there wondering what we were going to do now. If this part was not right, it brought the whole Pardo route into doubt again. There had somewhere to be some terrain that fit that leg of the journey from Chiaha to Chalahuma. We could not go back to believing that it was east of Knoxville.

Charlie got back in the car. "Let's go on," he said.

"Maybe that wasn't the ridge you saw on the topo map," I said. "Maybe we haven't come to it yet."

He nodded, a little more subdued. "Let's just go on and see what we find," he said.

So on we went. It was pretty country, the little mountain road winding past scattered houses—some seemed to have been there for generations; others looked like the homes of former city people who had come looking for some mountains to live in. After a while the houses were few and far between, and then they faded out altogether. We were in forest. The road began to climb. The creek was close beside the road now. That first little climb had not taken us to the top after all.

The road got steeper and began to wind. The hillside came sharply and steeply to the stream bed with a narrow shoulder cut into it for the road. The trail that was here before the road was cut must have gone along the very edge of the water—it was quite a narrow pass, steep and high. We came to a place where we could look down at the valley dropping away below us.

"How's this?" I asked Charlie happily.

"Terrific," he said and got out and took a picture.

It was not as high and long a climb as Swannanoa Gap, but it was more pinched in by mountains on either side. It would have been a much less traveled trail, an Indian backroad, and it may have had some difficult stretches in it—places that were precarious for Spanish soldiers loaded down with heavy backpacks. Unlike the first little ridge we went up, this one could be said to fit the chronicler's description.

When we got to the top, we stopped and got out for a while just to enjoy the mountain forest. Then we headed down the other side. There was another mountain stream beside the road. As we followed it down, we watched it get larger, flowing along beneath the laurels.

We came out of the forest into another open valley, and now we could see the nearest mountains of the Great Smokies to the east. When we arrived at the little town of Walland, we found it to be not so isolated a place as we had expected, given our unusual entry route. Walland is on the Foothills Parkway, and it looked as if there were always a few tourists wandering around there. The countryside was full of summer homes.

We got on the Foothills Parkway to go the rest of the way to Chalahuma. We considered this a poor second choice for driving Pardo's route, since we would be going along the top of this long mountain ridge, while he would have been going along the valley at the foot. But once we got up there, we were thrilled with how much we could see. There were spectacular vistas on both sides of the road.

Chilhowee Mountain is very narrow. It does not properly belong to the Blue Ridge Mountain chain but to the Ridge and Valley geographical province that lies to the west of the Blue Ridge. The rock of the two mountain chains is different. The Blue Ridge is mostly granite. The Ridge and Valley is limestone and sandstone. The mountains of the Ridge and Valley are long and narrow and run in straight lines, northeast to southwest. I did not realize how narrow they could be until we got up there to the top of Chilhowee.

We could look off to the left and see down below us the valley that Pardo would have been walking through. And beyond that valley rose the Smokies in all their majesty. I have never had such a magnificent view of the Smokies in all the years I have traveled through this region. We could see tiers of mountains, lower ones in the foreground and high, massive ones rising up behind with snow on their peaks. These are old mountains. The peaks have been worn down and gentled. Trees grow to the very top and break up the stark whiteness of the winter snows.

There were places on the Foothills Parkway where we could look to the east and see this scene of the valley below and the Smokies beyond and then look to the west and see the first wide valley of the Ridge and Valley region, with the next ridge rising far in the distance against the horizon. We could see the city of Maryville down in the valley. The Great Warriors Path ran along this valley, and that is the trail Charlie believes Pardo and his men followed on their return to Chiaha. The documents say they went back by a different trail from the one they had followed in. So from our vantage point on top of Chilhowee Mountain we could look down on both routes.

The day was getting late by the time we descended the mountain. Chalahume (or Chilhowee) was right there, where Happy Valley, which runs along the southeast side of Chilhowee Mountain, joins the valley of the Little Tennessee River. The site of Chilhowee is now under water, as are Citico and all the other Native American towns that once lay along the Little Tennessee. The area has only recently been flooded by Tellico Dam—one of the newest dams built by the Tennessee Valley Authority. This was done over the adamant objection of the Cherokees, whose ancestors lived in the valley in the eighteenth century. It was a thickly populated area back then. There were nearly a dozen towns, all of them well documented in the historical record. Much frontier history transpired here. This was the home of Sequoyah, who invented the Cherokee syllabary.

Besides being rich in history, it used to be a beautiful little valley for its own sake. We visited it several times while archaeological excavations were going on in the years before flooding. Archaeologists would have preferred the valley to have been preserved for unhurried excavations far into the future, but as it was, a great deal of salvage archaeology was done and a great deal of information collected. Richard Polhemus worked here, as did many others.

A relatively large number of sixteenth-century European artifacts have been found in sites along the Little Tennessee River. It was for this reason that Marvin had argued strenuously in the beginning for De Soto and Pardo to have followed the Little Tennessee River through the Blue Ridge instead of the French Broad River or the Pigeon. It was only after the evidence for the French Broad began to mount up that he reluctantly abandoned the route down the Little Tennessee. But it was hard to explain why there were so many Spanish artifacts there if none of the Spanish explorers visited the towns. De Soto visited Bussell Island at the mouth of the Little Tennessee, but he did not come upriver.

So no one has been happier than Marvin about the prospect of bringing Pardo onto the upper Little Tennessee. His interest in De Soto had been kindled in the first place by his interest in sixteenth-century European artifacts—especially in rare glass beads, which are highly diagnostic as time markers. (Particular styles were manufactured only in particular decades.) Why not use the distribution of sixteenth-century European artifacts to roughly plot out where De Soto went, he asked? Because such artifacts could have been moved all over the land by the Indians, some people answered. But Marvin went on to show that these artifacts ended up very quickly in burials. They were not being handed down through generations. They were going with their owners into graves that could be dated to the sixteenth century. This does not mean that they did not move around at all, but that they did not move around for long. It is reasonable to assume, he argues, that they usually stayed in the same general area, or at least in the same polity, in which they had been acquired from the Spaniards.

The burials on the Little Tennessee that have yielded these early Spanish artifacts are burials belonging to the Dallas archaeological phase. This is a cultural phase that precedes (lies under) the archaeological remains of the Overhill Cherokees of the eighteenth century, and there are major differences between the two. The question has always been, Were the Dallas-phase people ancestors of the Cherokees?

When the modern Cherokees were arguing with the TVA about Tellico Dam, they claimed that the Little Tennessee Valley was their ancient homeland—by which they meant truly ancient, a thousand years at least. Madeleine Kneberg and Tom Lewis had concluded in the 1940s and 1950s that the Dallas people were ancestral to *Creeks*, not to Cherokees. But then Roy Dickens and Joffre Coe, at the University of North Carolina, and most of the people at the University of Tennessee came along in the 1960s saying that the people of the Dallas phase were early *Cherokees*, not Creeks. The concept of cultures evolving in place had come into vogue. The idea was that sharp changes in the archaeological record can be explained by internal change in society rather than by replacement of one people by another.

When Pardo and De Soto crossed the mountains into the Tennessee Valley, they visited towns that were definitely Creek: Chiaha and Coste (Koasati) were still Creek towns in later centuries, though they had moved considerably southward. And according to Charlie's route, the Spaniards came to the first of these towns, Chiaha, far up in the Tennessee Valley, north of Knoxville. This, as it turns out, coincides with the northernmost limit of Dallas-phase sites. It was for this reason that Richard Polhemus, who has been working on Dallas for years, liked Charlie's route when he first heard about it. It made sense of his archaeological data. It told him more clearly than Kneberg and Lewis or anyone else had ever been able to tell him before that the people whose archaeological record he had been studying for so long were Muskogean speakers, the ancestors of some of the Creeks who later lived farther south in Georgia and Alabama. His territory suddenly filled up with names: Chiaha, Coste, Satapo, Chalahume, Tali. And all these towns were politically subject to Coosa, a chiefdom that, according to Charlie's route, was located in northern Georgia. We know they were subject to Coosa because both De Soto and Pardo said they were. When the Spaniards crossed the mountains from North Carolina, it was to reach a town called Chiaha, which was subject to the great chief of Coosa. And as they traveled beyond Chiaha down the Tennessee Valley, they passed through towns which they were told were all subject to Coosa.

So the Cherokees were relative newcomers to the Little Tennessee Valley. The modern Cherokees are correct in saying that the valley was the home of their ancestors, only not their *ancient* ancestors. The richness of eighteenth-century Native American history in that valley should have been enough in itself to have stopped the TVA from flooding it. But if you add to that the ancient history of the Creeks and the footsteps of the early Spanish explorers, it becomes even more regrettable to have lost this land.

As for myself, I could not forget the beauty of that little valley as it once was with the river's morning mist lifting above the archaeologists' camp where we had stayed one night. The lake that has taken its place is narrow and ugly. It stretches from mountain base to mountain base, obliterating the valley completely with all its rich centuries of history and prehistory. It was impossible to look at it and imagine the land that was once here or the Indian towns nestled in it or the Spanish explorers walking over it or the English and French traders packing their goods in. In a way, I regretted having come back to see it at all.

We spent Tuesday night in Maryville. Wednesday morning we left Pardo behind and headed for Lenoir City to hook up with De Soto at the Indian town of Coste. That left the De Soto trail from Chiaha to Coste untraveled, but since the chroniclers say they followed along the river (the Tennessee), we have no major problems with that leg of the route.

We tried to take back roads from Maryville to Lenoir City and got lost a time or two. We saw a lot of pretty Tennessee hill farms, but we also wasted a lot of time. Finally we made it to Lenoir City, and after bumbling around some more, we found Bussell Island, a large island right in the mouth of the Little Tennessee River. The terrain is complicated by the presence of Tellico Dam just upstream from Bussell Island, so close it almost touches it.

Charlie thinks the Indian town of Coste was located on that island. Here some of De Soto's men robbed a granary and the inhabitants bristled more dangerously than any had done since back in Apalachee, in northern Florida. To appease the chief, De Soto had to pretend to punish his soldiers, when in fact stealing corn was what the expedition was all about by that time. They were not finding gold or large native societies who could be peasants for Spanish lords. They were still hoping they would eventually find such riches, but in the meantime the quest that drove them from day to day was food for their bellies—Indian corn stored in granaries, to be precise. The largest granaries were in the large societies with high-ranking chiefs to whom tribute was being paid. The wider the chief's influence, the bigger the granaries. Once De Soto had gained the upper hand in Coste, he was able to get the people's corn away from them. But even larger stores of corn lay ahead. Coste was itself subject to Coosa, and Coosa was where De Soto headed next.

We followed his trail down the Ridge and Valley country without trying to pinpoint his steps exactly. The details in the narratives are somewhat sketchy for this leg of the route, but we did not worry about it too much. We knew where we were going. Charlie and Chester had located Coosa by using material from the Tristán de Luna expedition— yet another Spanish venture, this one coming up into Alabama and Georgia from the Gulf Coast twenty years after De Soto. Coosa is under Carters Lake near Chatsworth, Georgia, and there are only so many ways to get there from Lenoir City—the ridges and valleys dictate where the roads go. The route Charlie thinks De Soto took follows the railroad tracks, which, of course, usually follow the oldest roads, which usually follow the Indian trails.

We drove south on U.S. 11 to Athens, Tennessee, passing through some of the richest farmland we have seen yet in our travels. These were not large farms, but they were serious ones, with livestock in the fields and good barns with silos. The supporting economy—the feed stores, the farm equipment dealers, the stockyards—seemed healthy. The rural towns appeared to have life in them. Perhaps if we had stopped and asked a few people, we would have found that farming was in trouble here, too, but from the look of things it was not in as much trouble as it is in most of the other areas we have driven through.

At Athens we took Tennessee 30 to pick up another major corridor a little further to the east. This was U.S. 411, which took us south beside another railroad track. The land was hillier and poorer here, no longer many farms. De Soto encountered only a few small towns along this stretch. His chroniclers did not bother to name them. Just below the Tennessee town of Etowah we crossed the lovely Hiwassee River just downstream from a place where it comes into the valley through a spectacular notch in the mountains. There was a De Soto marker there, our path crossing Swanton's once again. We lingered a little while to enjoy the river and then headed on down 411 toward Georgia.

The northwest corner of Georgia is carpet country. By the time we reached Chatsworth we were passing one carpet mill after another, some of them shoulder to shoulder. But despite this strong manufacturing presence, this did not appear to be a prosperous land. Many of the homes we saw were quite poor.

All the way down from Tennessee we had been following mountains that ran north and south, and this was still true as we drove through Chatsworth. Had we not already been confident of our location for Coosa, we would have been worried at this point, since Coosa was said to lie just to the south of an east–west range of mountains. But we knew we were coming to the southern end of this north–south range. By the time we got to Carters Lake and turned east to drive along the shore of Coosa, the mountains were to the north of us. They looked to us as if they were running east and west, and they had looked that way to the chroniclers, too.

We had been to Coosa before, back in 1969, to visit David Hally's archaeological excavation—another salvage project conducted in a race against time while a dam was being built. The site Dave was digging was the Little Egypt site. He had no idea it was the capital town of the grand chiefdom of Coosa. There was no way he could have known it from the archaeology alone. The Coosa people, like other Native Americans of this early time, had no written language. They could not leave their name behind. All Dave knew was that he was digging a mound center whose people belonged to the Barnett archaeological phase, diagnosed primarily by the style of pottery found there, a local variant of

Lamar-style pottery with a strong minority presence of the Dallas style. This was back when it was still believed that Dallas was Cherokee. Everyone was pretty sure that Lamar, which has its center of distribution around Macon in central Georgia, was Creek. So this mixture of Dallas and Lamar in Barnett-phase sites was puzzling. Archaeologists did not know how to interpret it. Pottery was made by women, so if there was Cherokee pottery there, it must mean that Creeks were taking Cherokee wives. Or whole families of Cherokees were moving in. But that was difficult to believe, since Creeks and Cherokees spoke vastly different languages and were seldom on friendly terms. Dave also knew that sixteenth-century Spaniards had been in the area. Excavation had yielded not only some diagnostic long blue beads, but also a steel dirk.

It was not until Charlie and Chester nailed down Coosa that the Little Egypt site suddenly made sense. This was early in their reconstruction of the route, when it was only beginning to dawn on them that Dallas was Creek instead of Cherokee. In their initial effort to bring De Soto south from Chiaha, Charlie and Chester and Marvin had kept him on the Tennessee River for the entire distance to Coosa and had placed Coosa at a large mound site near Chattanooga, on the Tennessee. De Soto did not say that he stayed on the river. They just assumed that he did.

But then came the night when Charlie was awake in the wee hours, as he often is, unable to sleep. He went into the spare bedroom, so his light would not bother me, and read for an hour or two—as he often does. This night he was reading the papers of the Tristán de Luna expedition. In 1560 a party of Luna's men, including some who had been with De Soto, revisited Coosa from the floundering Spanish colony in lower Alabama. The Coosas were having trouble with one of their tributaries, the Napochies, who had decided they would not pay tribute anymore. The chief of Coosa asked the Spaniards to join forces with him to go to war against the Napochies, to encourage them to mend their ways. The Spaniards agreed and went with the warriors of Coosa to the town of the Napochies, which was a three-day journey from Coosa and was situated on the banks of a very wide river, two crossbow shots across. This could only have been the Tennessee River, and this meant that Coosa itself was not on or near the Tennessee. So Coosa could not have been at Chattanooga. In fact, it looked as if it might have been the Napochies who were at Chattanooga.

So Charlie got out a map and started trying to figure out where to put Coosa. It had to be three days from the Napochies, who were on the Tennessee, and a particular number of days from Coste—distances from two points that both had to fit. He tried placing Coosa on the Coosawatee—somewhat upriver from Little Egypt, since at that moment he had forgotten about the Little Egypt site itself. Then he plotted De Soto's route southward from this new general location of Coosa, using the travel time given in the chronicles. This made the Indian town of Itaba land on the great Etowah archaeological site. That was when he realized that Itaba was the same word as Etowah. Spaniards do not have a true *w*. They have a bilabial spirant, made by putting their lips not quite together, and they write it with a *b* or a *v*. No one ever realized before that Itaba was Etowah. It is so obvious now that we know it, but until that night, no one did. No one had ever seen the two words fall together like that on a map. It was a stunning confirmation for this section of the route. Charlie said he just closed the Luna book, put the map aside, turned out the light, and went back to sleep.

The next day he went to Chester DePratter with the new Coosa. He still did not have it pinned down to a site. They started going over Luna's description: two streams coming together in the town.

"My God," said Chester. "That's Talking Rock Creek and the Coosawatee. That's the Little Egypt site."

The rest of Luna's description fit as well. Mountains to the north running east and west: anyone can stand there and see them. Continuous population for several miles up and down the valley: there were Barnett-phase farmsteads all up and down the river. Beyond Coosa all is forest: Little Egypt is at one of the entryways to the Blue Ridge Mountains, which would have been uninhabited forest except for isolated valleys where Cherokees were living (making Pisgah and Qualla pottery, not Dallas).

It was a very good fit. It made sense of the pottery: Coosa held political sway over Dallas towns to the north; thus the mixture of Dallas pottery with Coosa's Lamar pottery. Even the meaning of the word *Coosawatee* added support. It was the Coosawatee River that was dammed up to make Carters Lake. The Little Egypt site was on its banks. Coosawatee is a Cherokee word. Cherokees lived there in the late eighteenth and early nineteenth centuries, until they were forced west to Oklahoma in the 1830s. Coosawatee is the Cherokee word for "old Coosa place."

We reached Coosa late in the afternoon of the evening before Thanksgiving and spent some time driving around the shores of Carters Lake, trying to find a good place to take a picture of the east–west mountains to the north. There was no one else around. We were driving slowly down a little road that led toward a boat ramp when a gray fox came trotting out of the woods into the road in front of us. We stopped, and it stopped. It stood still for a moment or two, looking at us. Then it trotted on across the road into the woods again.

CHAPTER FOUR

Alabama Rain

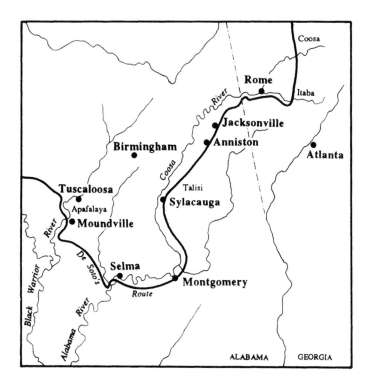

After the end of the battle {at Mabila} . . . they rested there until the 14th of November, caring for their wounds and their horses, and they burned over much of the country. And up to the time when they left there, the total deaths from the time the Governor and his forces entered the land of Florida, were one hundred and two Christians. . . .

Sunday, November 14, . . . the Governor left Mabila, and the Wednesday following came to a fine river. Thursday, the {18th}, their way lay over bad places and through swamps, and they found a village with corn which was named Talicpacana. The Christians had discovered on the other side of the river a village which appeared to them from a distance to be finely situated.

On Sunday, the 21st of November, Vasco Gonçalez found a village half a league distant from this named Moçulixa, from which they had transported all the corn to the other side of the river and had piled it in heaps covered with mats; and the Indians were across the river, and were making threats. A barge was constructed which was finished the 29th of the month, and they made a large truck to carry it to Moçulixa; and when it was launched in the water sixty soldiers embarked in it. The Indians shot countless darts, or rather arrows. But when this great canoe reached the shore they took flight, and not more than three or four Christians were wounded. The country was easily secured, and they found an abundance of corn.

The next day, Wednesday, the whole force came to a village which was called Zabusta, and there they crossed the river in the boat and with some canoes that they had found in that place; and they tarried for the night in another village on the other side, because up above they found a fine one, and took the chief, whose name was Apafalaya, and carried him along as guide and interpreter; and this stream was called the river Apafalaya.

—Rodrigo Ranjel

Selma, Alabama
Sunday, November 25

We left home early this morning and drove to Cartersville to pick up the trail again at Itaba. The Etowah Mounds are a real treasure—high, grass-covered, flat-topped, pyramidal mounds. This is a rich site that has yielded some of the finest artifacts of any archaeological site in North America. It is now a state park with a fine museum attached to it. We could not get onto the grounds today—the park is closed on Sunday mornings—but we had been there a number of times before, so it did not matter much. We drove a little way down the road and stopped and got out to look at the mounds from what would have been the town's agricultural fields. This is still good farmland. The ground had recently been plowed. These are the bottomlands of the Etowah River. When De Soto was here, it rained so much that they had to wait six days for the water to go down before they could cross the river.

In De Soto's day Etowah, or Itaba, was not the great political center it once had been. Had he come a few hundred years earlier, it would have been Coosa paying tribute to Itaba rather than the other way around. The exquisite artifacts that have been excavated and the huge mounds are associated with that earlier time. By the time De Soto got there, its time as the center had passed, and Coosa was on the rise. There seems to have been an inherent instability in chiefdoms. They rose and fell. Chester DePratter examined this at length in his doctoral dissertation.

We left Itaba and went southwest on Georgia 113, looking for a town between Cartersville and Rome called Euharlee. Charlie felt De Soto went through Euharlee on his way to the Indian town of Ulibahali at Rome. Euharlee is probably the way the first white west-Georgians pronounced Ulibahali. Euharlee takes its name from Euharlee Creek. The people of Ulibahali must have once lived along its banks.

We could see from our map that to reach Euharlee we were to turn off 113 onto an unnumbered road and go through a little town called Stilesboro. There is a huge power plant that dominates the Etowah Valley. You see its two tall smokestacks from miles away, from the Etowah Mound site, from anywhere in the valley, and there is a haze that hangs in the air—like city air in the open countryside. This monstrous plant, it turns out, is at Stilesboro. We got a little lost and ended up driving most of the way around the plant's perimeter. Besides the two tall stacks that go up into the clouds, there are four short fat towers. A lot of steamy stuff was pouring out of two of the short towers. A thinner vapor—probably worse—was coming from the tall stacks. It made a strange scene, juxtaposed as it was against the little community of Stilesboro.

We finally got around it and found our way to Euharlee—a tiny town, old, consisting mostly of small white churches. We did not linger but headed on northwest toward Rome. We bypassed Rome without trying to see the archaeological site that Charlie thinks might have been Ulibahali. It is under some tennis courts at the country club. Marvin Smith is from Rome and has been to the site. We know it is of the right time period—Barnett phase. That is enough for now.

Barnett is the archaeological phase that goes with the chiefdom of Coosa, so we were still in the territory of Coosa proper. De Soto had taken the chief of Coosa hostage in order to get cooperation along the way from the people who were subject to him. For the chief, who was used to being carried around on a litter and treated with great deference, it must have been humiliating to be dragged along by this invading army. His sister was a prisoner, too. The inhabitants of Ulibahali did not take kindly to the situation and began to make some hostile moves toward the Spaniards. But the situation was defused, evidently by the chief himself, and the army went on. Several members of the expedition stayed behind in Coosa—Feryado, a "Levantine"; Robles, a black man who was ill; another slave, who evidently ran away; and a Spanish gentleman who either got lost or was killed. The only thing the chroniclers knew about this last one was that he disappeared while they were in Coosa and they never saw him again.

Coosa was the most appealing land the army had been through up to that time. It was populous and there was plenty of food. Later, when Tristán de Luna's colony was starving at Pensacola Bay, some of the De Soto veterans among them led an expedition north to find Coosa again. They were disappointed in what they found. It was no longer the fine place it once had been. The population had probably been decimated by disease. And the Coosa chief was losing his widespread power, as is evident by the fact that the Napochies, who lived over on the Tennessee near present-day Chattanooga, were refusing to make tribute payments. His powerlessness at the hands of De Soto probably had a lot to do with that. De Soto took many slaves in Coosa—captured them by force. It was not a good time for the grand chief, who was supposed to have the power of the Sun on his side.

De Soto visited two more towns of Coosa as he went west from present-day Rome. We think these were the King site and the Johnstone Farm site. Dave Hally excavated the King site several years ago. It was occupied for only about fifty years, right around the time of De Soto. In Dave's excavation Spanish artifacts were found. And in the part of the village that was not excavated, a relic hunter coming in later found a sixteenth-century double-edged sword. The skeletal material that Dave's crew recovered from the site included a large number of individuals (at least fifty) with evidence of wounds inflicted by steel weapons. These were all women or older men—no warriors and no children. There is nothing in the chronicles about any kind of violent episode in the vicinity of the King site. Robert Blakely at Georgia State University, who has studied these skeletal remains, has speculated that these were slaves taken by De Soto and killed or wounded later in Alabama at the battle of Mabila and then carried back home by their relatives. Either that or there was a lot more carnage on the whole expedition than the chroniclers were recording.

Nobody has excavated the Johnstone Farm site, but Dave and Marvin surveyed it recently—walked the plowed fields—and found Barnett-phase pottery. So we know it is of the right time period.

We did not try to go look at either of these sites. We headed south to Cedartown and then west into Alabama. De Soto spent the night in the open near the Georgia-Alabama state line. Then the next day he came to Tuasi, near present-day Piedmont. We passed through some fairly poor land to get there—hilly land abandoned by farmers, grown up in pines and scrub, like so much of the southern piedmont. To me it looks ugly. I like to see land in farms, with pastures and cultivated fields. Where there is forest, I want to see mature forest, more hardwoods than pines, trees that have some size and dignity and a certain amount of space around them. But because of the pulpwood industry there is not much mature forest in the South, just these pine forests that are harvested once they reach a certain size.

We were still going through ridge-and-valley country. Tuasi was near Piedmont, in a wide valley. The land was more attractive here. It was being farmed. One of the chroniclers said Tuasi was the first town of Talisi. But because it was such a long way to the next town, Charlie thinks Tuasi will turn out to be not the first town of Talisi, but the last town of Coosa.

But still De Soto kept the chief of Coosa with him. Evidently the chief held some sway over Talisi, though it seems not to have been as firm as his hold on the Dallas-phase people to the north. Talisi had the great chiefdom of Tascaluza on the other side of it, so it was in a position to play the balance-of-power game. It seems, though, to have been more closely allied with Coosa than with Tascaluza.

It took De Soto four days after Tuasi to reach what Charlie thinks was the first town of Talisi. As we drove on through the ridge-and-valley piedmont, I was more and more amazed at the extent of Coosa's territory. The most northerly town subject to him was Chiaha, way back up in the Tennessee Valley near Newport, Tennessee—almost to Virginia. And here we were going deep into Alabama, still in Coosa's territory. I had somehow had the idea before this that Talisi was closer to the Georgia line.

We went through Jacksonville, an antebellum cotton town in a wide valley. There was a square in the middle of town with a Confederate soldier high on his pedestal, facing north; a Confederate cannon, also pointing north; and four bronze plaques commemorating various Confederate worthies—generals and such—contributed by Jacksonville to the Cause.

I have lived in the South almost all my life, and these north-facing Confederate soldiers on their high stone pedestals are everywhere. It is easy to laugh at them now, but to laugh is to forget how hard it is to lose, and no section of America ever lost more than the white South lost in the Civil War. They lost the war itself. They lost horrendous numbers of their sons and brothers and husbands. They lost all the money and resources that were squandered on the war, and they lost the very underpinning of their economy—the labor system upon which it had been based. And on top of all that, they lost their moral ground. Separate from the North they could assert their own moral code: slavery is not evil, they could say, or at least it is a necessary evil, the white man's burden. But united with the North, under the ruling power of the North, their very way of life was defined as evil. It is not easy to accept even small reversals in one's life. To be a white Southerner after the Civil War was a little like being an American after Vietnam—only the Civil War was closer to home, and the white South's defeat was total.

As we were leaving Jacksonville, we passed a gang of motorcyclists heading into town: a huge gang, maybe two hundred. They were a club of some kind, a mixed group, some ordinary-looking people, some wild ones—a new kind of Alabama rebel, long hair streaming out behind, weird paraphernalia. One fellow had on a shaggy, Viking-style helmet—it looked as if it was covered with buffalo skin and had two long horns on it. Sitting behind another biker, a girl clutched a giant teddy bear. It would have been interesting to have been in that staid Confederate square in Jacksonville when they rode by. As we went past them a police car was in the middle of them—siren and blue lights— pulling over one of the many riders who were not wearing helmets.

We went on through Anniston, a long strip of a city that is to be commended for its synchronized traffic lights. From Anniston we drove to Taledega. And south of Taledega we turned west to Childersburg on the Coosa River. This finally was Talisi. Here De Soto released the chief of Coosa, who went away weeping because his sister was not released, and because he had been taken so far from the heart of his territory, his sacred land.

From Childersburg De Soto followed the river south to Tascaluza's province, which began around Montgomery. From the map we could see that we could not go along the river that way—there were no roads whatsoever, and the reason was not at all apparent. The road we had to take paralleled the river but at a considerable distance from it—fifteen or twenty miles.

Actually we could go to one Indian town below Talisi—Casiste, which Charlie thinks was near the little remnant plantation community of Talladega Springs. We found Talledega Springs to be a very isolated place. The population balance has not changed since plantation days— mostly blacks living there and a few whites. There was a huge brick plantation house that might have been antebellum but probably was not. It was old, though. Just to the south of Talledega Springs were some very high, steep-sided, rocky hills—small mountains, actually. They showed up on our map only as a single contour line, giving us no indication of their ruggedness. This was the reason no roads went south of here. The land was uninhabitable, except possibly right along the river in the old days. Today the river valley is flooded by a continuous series of dams.

So we went back to the east to Sylacauga and headed south from there toward Montgomery. We drove through miles of these rugged hills, wilderness except for the bottomlands along the occasional creeks that intersected it. As we went on and on through the hills it began to dawn on me that they were a geographic boundary between Coosa's ridge-and-valley province to the north and Tascaluza's upper coastal plain to the south. Talisi was at the southern end of the ridge and valley, a separate polity, but geographically more connected to Coosa than to Tascaluza. Again I was amazed at how Charlie's route is fitting the land. De Soto went through only a few small towns along this hilly stretch of the Coosa River. The chroniclers say little about them but characterize one as a "wretched village." That is what you would expect in a place like this.

We finally came down out of the hills into rolling farmland. We drove into Wetumpka at sunset and decided to push on to Selma before stopping. This was Tascaluza's territory, stretching out along the great Alabama River. A year or so earlier we had driven this part of the route from Montgomery to Selma to Cahaba, which is just south of Selma and is where the Battle of Mabila may have taken place. De Soto's route from Montgomery to Selma was south of the river, but we felt no need to retrace that stretch again, so we cut across from Wetumpka on the north side of the river and drove west through the gathering darkness. Before us was a thin crescent moon with two bright stars above it. The sky was perfectly clear, a pure deep blue coming down into the pink of the sunset. By the time we reached Selma—only six o'clock—the sky was blacker than black, with the crescent moon and the two stars shining brightly white. We could see the rest of the moon's sphere in shadow.

Tomorrow we are going to Moundville to talk to Jim Knight about the archaeology of the country we have been driving through today.

Tuscaloosa, Alabama
Monday, November 26

After we had moved ourselves into this motel in Tuscaloosa tonight, I went looking for my journal and could not find it. My journal! A hundred pages of the De Soto trail! I nearly died. I knew I could not reproduce those pages. I knew, too, that I could not have lost them. The entire first third of the trip could not be lost. And yet it is so difficult to believe what you know in your heart of hearts. I was so agitated that Charlie made the call for me to the Selma motel where we stayed last night. I stood by him and waited while the man on the other end of the line went to look. Waited and waited. Gave up hope. And then I heard Charlie say, "Then you've got it?" I had left it—my spiral-bound notebook in a small leather briefcase—in our motel room.

Dear God. It was like going off and leaving your child in a strange place and not realizing for hours that you had done it. So tomorrow we will have to begin by driving back to Selma. Only sixty miles away—it could have been worse. In the meantime I carry on with loose paper . . .

This morning we headed out from Selma for Moundville, a trip that would normally take an hour but took us three, in our usual De Soto trail fashion. From Selma we went southwest to Hazen to pick up the trail just north of the Indian town of Mabila, which we think was at or near Cahaba. At Hazen we took a county road north to Marion Junction. It was a pleasant day, cloudy but not raining, cool but not cold. There was almost no traffic on the road—an occasional pickup truck. The farms here were huge—enormous fields of gently rolling land. You could seldom see more than one farmhouse at a time. It was only when we passed the Black Belt Agricultural Experiment Station that I realized we were in the Black Belt—a particular geographic zone that runs through Alabama and Mississippi. I have seen parts of the Black Belt in Mississippi, and it has this same apparent fertility (the soil *is* black, or at least gray) and the same big fields.

We went through Marion Junction and on north toward Marion, evidently a sister community of some sort, though almost twenty miles away. Before we reached Marion, the land became abruptly hillier, the soil turned red, and we could see four or five farmhouses at a time instead of just one. These were poorer houses, although generally well cared for. We were back in the piedmont again. It was satisfying to see a section of southern piedmont that is still being farmed intensively. But I would guess that if we were to come back in ten years, we would find most of those little farms grown up in pines. Even today we passed a farm every now and then that had already been abandoned.

From Marion we went northwest to Greensboro and from Greensboro to the Black Warrior River. On this entire leg of the journey, from Cahaba to the Black Warrior, the Spaniards marched through empty country. They were following a trail that took the high ground between two river systems, with only one or two small creeks to cross. They carried with them two days' worth of food, but it took them four days to cover the distance.

They came to the Black Warrior River near the present-day town of Eutaw. "We came to a fine river," they said. There is a huge swamp bordering the Black Warrior at Eutaw, so it is hard to know exactly how the trail came in there. We know they turned north and started up the river at this point, but it would seem strange if they went into the swamp to do that, though they might have. There are trails through swamps—ridges of high ground. And we know they had to go through swamp to cross Big Brush Creek and Five Mile Creek, which empty into the Black Warrior just upstream from where the expedition first came to the river. They say in the narratives that they had to go through swamp at these points.

Charlie and I crossed the Black Warrior and went to Eutaw just to see it. De Soto did not cross the river here. We found it to be a nice old town. It looks as if it has plenty of life in it, though it certainly is in the middle of nowhere. The population must be at least 70 percent black, judging from the sample of people we saw on the streets. As someone who grew up in a small town in southern Georgia in the days of segregation, it does my heart good to visit these small southern towns and see black people living in them as full citizens. The steak house where we ate in Selma last night was the most thoroughly integrated restaurant I have ever been in. The clientele was truly half white and half black. And so were the employees.

Coming back across the river, we turned down a little side road and found a state park on the bank of the river with a boat ramp and picnic tables in a peaceful grove of trees. There were three or four pickup trucks with empty boat trailers parked there, but no other people. We found a shady table beside the water and ate our lunch. The air smelled good under the trees. The sky had cleared partly and the sun was sparkling on the water. It was a welcome rest.

After lunch we drove on up to Moundville, fifteen miles north, stopping at Big Brush Creek and Five Mile Creek to take pictures of their swampiness. Once again Charlie gets just the terrain he needs. After these two creeks the land gets higher, and Elliotts Creek, which flows past Moundville, has well-defined banks, no swamps.

Moundville was a staggering sight, even though we have seen it before. There are so many mounds there, all of them large—some huge. The state of Alabama has done well to preserve the site. It is the second largest mound site in all of North America, the largest being Cahokia, just east of St. Louis.

We found Jim Knight in the archaeology research lab. He was expecting us and we were glad to see him. He has become a friend in recent years. A young archaeologist and a very strong one scholastically, he will probably become one of the grand old men of southeastern archaeology before his career has ended. He already has the manner of a grand old man. There is no boyishness in Jim. He has a serious demeanor and speaks with measured words, often pausing to think things through before he answers a question. He is in charge of the lab at Moundville. I was surprised to see how many people work there—upward of a dozen, many of them students at the University of Alabama at Tuscaloosa, which is not far away.

We spread out our map of Alabama on a table in the library and started looking at the route with Jim. He knows the Talisi area, back around Childersburg. He has done a great deal of surveying there and has excavated some eighteenth-century Kymulga-phase towns. Kymulga, like Barnett, is a variant of Lamar (the dominant pottery type in central Georgia), and it is more closely related to Barnett than to any other phase. That fits the route very well. The De Soto narratives imply some kind of connection between Coosa and Talisi, but Talisi does not seem to have been firmly in Coosa's sphere. De Soto released the chief of Coosa when he reached Talisi rather than after he had traveled through it, which implies that the chief would not have done him much good there in getting food and burden bearers and women from the Talisi people.

Jim said he thought Ulibahali and Tuasi were separate chiefdoms also, because De Soto treated for what he needed with the chiefs of those places rather than with Coosa. However, the people of Ulibahali did make an attempt to free Coosa, and Coosa stopped them, which Charlie thinks implies that Ulibahali was in Coosa's sphere. Because of its location, he thinks Tuasi probably was, too. What is really at issue here is the nature of the power of the grand chief over his tributaries.

Jim has basically liked Charlie's route through Alabama, again because it makes sense of the archaeology. His Kymulga-phase sites fall precisely in De Soto's province of Talisi. The only problem is that he has been working primarily on sites that are clustered up Tallasseehatchee Creek, several miles from the Coosa River. The De Soto chronicles specifically say that Talisi was on a large river, with towns and fields on both sides of the river. But there may not be any contradiction. Jim's Kymulga sites are later, mostly eighteenth-century—that later period has been his primary research interest, and he looks for those sites to excavate.

When Charlie first started asking him about sites in this area several years ago, Jim said that all the sites were away from the river. My tendency would have been to say, "All right. We have it wrong. Talisi must be up Tallasseehatchee Creek and De Soto was wrong about the big river." But Charlie said: "There have to be sites along the river. Has anybody looked?"

Well, it turns out that over the years some surveying has been done, and there *have* been a few sites reported along the river. And these *do* tend to be early Kymulga-phase sites, which puts them in the De Soto time period. There was also a "Lamar" site, probably Kymulga, reported lower down Tallasseehatchee Creek by Lewis Larson, an archaeologist from Georgia, but this was an oral report, never written up, and Jim had never been able to learn where it was. As we were leaning over the maps yesterday trying to figure out where the main town of Talisi might have been, Jim kept referring to Larson's "lost Kymulga site." He had a feeling that site might be it. Charlie said he thought the main town of Talisi would be at Childersburg, where Tallasseehatchee Creek comes into the Coosa River. Jim, however, said that area had been well surveyed and the site we needed was not there.

I kept losing faith, having flashes of dread that none of it was going to work out. But Charlie stood firm. "Maybe I'm off a town or two," he said, "but I have the province right. And the main town *has* to be on the river."

Jim looked through a book that summarized the sites in the area, checking once more to make sure there was not a site he had overlooked that might have some early Kymulga in it. He ran his finger down the brief descriptions, skimming the lists of the styles of potsherds that had been picked up from the surface of the ground at the different sites.

"What's this?" he said suddenly, indicating with his amazement that he had found an early-Kymulga site. "Why didn't I know about this?"

He looked to see where it was located. It was exactly where Charlie had wanted it, at the confluence of Tallasseehatchee Creek and the Coosa River. Right there at Childersburg. Jim rushed to the site files to get a fuller report. "It's big," he said. "Two hundred by four hundred meters. The biggest one on the river."

Now we had the capital of Talisi. New juice flowed into us. We moved on down the route, talking about the archaeology of the Montgomery area. This we had already worked on with Craig Shelton, Ned Jenkins, and David Chase at Montgomery on a previous trip. Charlie is fairly satisfied with that leg of the route, though there could still be some shifting from site to site. The archaeology of the protohistoric period is interesting and it is amazing how well it fits the route. It is beginning to seem likely that Moundville III–phase pottery coincides with the territory of Tascaluza. There is an eastern boundary for this pottery that occurs right around Montgomery, which is where De Soto found the first of Tascaluza's towns. The pottery style east of there is a variant of Lamar, with connections back to Georgia. Tascaluza's Moundville III–phase pottery is completely different from that. Its connections run west toward Mississippi. In culture and language Tascaluza appears to have been western Muskogean rather than eastern Muskogean. That means he was more a Choctaw than a Creek.

Tuscaloosa
Tuesday, November 27

I got back my journal. Thank God. We went to bed at eight-thirty last night and got up at five this morning. I wrote for an hour or so, adding to yesterday's account, and then we drove down to Selma to retrieve my journal. From there we drove back to Moundville, arriving about ten-thirty.

But I still have not finished writing about yesterday. Charlie had arranged to meet with Bruce Kuerten at Moundville—or rather, Bruce had arranged to meet with Charlie. Bruce is a filmmaker who works for the public television station at Auburn University. Charlie has been one of the consultants for a film they are making about the Native Americans of the South during the historic period, beginning, of course, with De Soto. They now have the first act written, which is the De Soto section, and they wanted Charlie's reaction to it. He told Kuerten he would be in Moundville this week, so Kuerten said he would come here to meet with him. And he did. He showed up at Moundville in the early afternoon. There were two other young men with him, Anderson Luster and John DeJulio. They had the storyboards for the first act, and we sat down at a table in the library to look at them.

I had never seen storyboards for a film before. They are little watercolors of the scenes as they will appear on camera. Everything that is going to happen on camera is illustrated, showing the exact camera angle for each shot. This is assembled in a loose-leaf notebook with two pictures to a page and directions for shooting the scene beneath each picture. In another notebook they had the text of the narration.

The first act will only last twenty minutes on film, but it took us nearly two hours to go over it. It is about De Soto and Chief Tascaluza and the Battle of Mabila. It was exciting for us to see visually depicted the very events we had just been working on in our travels. The film team had thoroughly researched the material world of the conquistadors and were paying great attention to the smallest details. There in vivid color were De Soto and his men, looking much as they must have looked. And there was Tascaluza presiding over his people from atop a mound. Kuerten was trying to get every detail of the village right. He was going to try to use some of the techniques that were used in *Star Wars*, blending live action with paintings of settings so that outdoor scenes will look real in places where they need sets that would be too elaborate to construct realistically and too expensive for the brief shot or two they would need of them.

We had a fine time with these guys. They are talented and full of energy. Anderson Luster is the artist. It was amazing how beautiful each of those little watercolors were. We talked about everything as we went along, and Charlie and I both made suggestions. Kuerten scribbled notes. It will be a very good film, at least this part we have seen. It all looked authentic to us, given what we know about the subject matter.

The De Soto portion of the film ends with a portrayal of the epidemics that followed in the wake of the expedition. A sick Spaniard drops a handkerchief along the trail, and a little girl comes along and picks it up. She comes down with smallpox, and soon everyone is ill, everyone dying. The full horror of this is depicted so that people will realize what an enormous catastrophe these European diseases were for the indigenous peoples. It was far worse than the bubonic plague in Europe. It was more comparable to nuclear war. One-half to three-quarters of the population died. The chiefdoms collapsed and the surviving people reorganized themselves along simpler lines, coalescing into smaller territories. No more mounds were built after De Soto's time. By the time the British reached the interior of the Southeast in the late seventeenth century, there were no Indian societies to compare with what De Soto saw. There were only a very few remnants of the old social order—little groups like the Natchez on the lower Mississippi, who called their chief the Great Sun and carried him around on a litter.

By the time the film people left, it was after four o'clock. We made arrangements with Jim Knight to return to the Moundville lab the next morning to work further on the route, especially on the chiefdom of Apafalaya, which we think was in the Moundville area. He promised to take us around and show us some sites.

We drove into Tuscaloosa and found a motel. That was when I discovered my journal was missing. I was exhausted from having slept only three or four hours the night before, which was why we went to bed at eight-thirty. These are strange hours we are keeping on this trip. Time itself is strange. It moves so slowly. We can hardly believe that it has been only two weeks since we started out in Florida. It seems like two months.

Tuscaloosa
Wednesday, November 28

We had another good day at Moundville yesterday. When we arrived there, at midmorning, the sky was heavy with clouds, a cold front moving in. There would soon be rain, but we could not go out to look at sites until we had studied the maps and made some determination of which sites might have been the towns De Soto visited. Jim Knight was ready for us in the library, and we went right to work.

De Soto had marched north to this area from Mabila, a four-day trek for which they had brought only a two-day supply of corn, so they arrived hungry. Before they reached any towns, they came to a fine river. We had wondered about this, because of the large swamp around the Black Warrior River at the place where they first came near it. It would have been wasted effort for them to have waded through the Eutaw Swamp just to get a look at the river, when their trail lay parallel to the river a mile or two away, along the edge of the Pleistocene terrace— that is, on the high ground. Our question was: Is the Eutaw Swamp completely natural or is it the result of damming on the Black Warrior? Jim had the man who could answer questions like that.

"Let me go get Lawrence," he said.

He disappeared for a moment and came back with Lawrence Alexander, a tall, dark-haired, unassuming man in his thirties. Lawrence held himself back a bit as we gathered with him around the table to look at an old 1909 soil map of Hale County. He was there, tracing with his finger the swamp soils on the map, and yet he did not move into the center of things and at first spoke only in answer to our questions.

The Eutaw Swamp was indeed the result of damming, he said. He showed us on the old map the low places that would become swamp but that were not yet swamp when the map was made. He pointed out the high places with the good soil, and the alluvial fans along the streams, and the terrace that the trail followed—where the railroad track lies today. He spoke of the land with what seemed a total grasp of all its many variables. He understood it in scientific terms, the different soil types and how they were formed. He understood the land through time, through human history, how it was used, where the roads and trails were, why things are as they are. This is the knowledge of books and formal learning, and yet he carried it like the knowledge of those occasional wise persons you run into in out-of-the-way places who are not formally educated but who have accumulated a wealth of knowledge from paying close attention to the world around them. I was not sure what sort of person Lawrence Alexander was, whether he was a formally trained professional archaeologist or one of these other people who so often link up with archaeologists and learn to speak their language. It was not the sort of question I could ask at that point without running the risk of insulting him—although I have more respect for local wise men, in general, than I do for trained scholars. As we talked he gradually became less reticent and more central in the discussion. No doubt he had been sizing us up as well.

So the problem of the Eutaw Swamp was solved. We had De Soto coming unimpeded to the banks of the Black Warrior. Then the army started up the trail along the terrace. It was November, cold and rainy, and the chroniclers complain of bad swampy places. This would have been where the trail crossed Big Brush and Five Mile creeks. Lawrence assured us there would have been swamp along those creeks then as now—wet swamp if it had been raining.

Then the army reached Talipacana, the first town of the chiefdom of

Apafalaya. There was corn there, but they needed more—it took a lot of corn to feed an expedition of as many as a thousand people with one to two hundred horses. A contingent of soldiers was sent out to find more, which they did at the next town, Moçulixa (pronounced "Mosulisha"), which was on the river. The only problem was that the people of Moçulixa had fled the town and taken all their corn to the opposite bank and had it heaped there under mats. They made threats to the Spaniards, saying they would kill them if they tried to cross the river.

Hearing of this, De Soto devised a plan. He had a barge built secretly within the camp where the Indians could not see what was going on. Then the Spaniards made a large sled and dragged the barge half a league to the river, still trying to keep the element of surprise. When the barge was launched, sixty men and three horses boarded it and crossed to the other side. The three horsemen set about securing a landing for the rest of the army, and the foot soldiers fought their way to the corn. The Indians tried to resist, but when they saw this was impossible, they melted away into the canebrake. The corn having been secured, the rest of the army crossed the river, passed through the town of Zabusta, and came to another town, where they camped for the night. The next day they entered yet another town, which seems to have been the main town.

This was more or less the scenario as Charlie understood it from the narratives. He felt that Moçulixa may have been at the Moundville site itself; it was not the main town but was nonetheless some sort of center, since corn was stored there. The Moundville site, like Etowah, had passed its glory, the occupation at this time being smaller than it had been in an earlier era when all the many mounds were in use. Most of the mounds were probably overgrown with trees in De Soto's day. But it may still have been the central town for this southern end of the chiefdom—a regional center within a larger polity. The Moundville site was a candidate for Moçulixa because it was on the river.

If Moundville was Moçulixa, and Charlie was not insistent about this but thought it a good place to start, then Talipacana, according to the way he understood the narratives, would have to be back along the trail to the south at a distance of about half a league (a mile and a half), the distance they dragged the barge. There was a site back on Elliotts Creek that was squarely on the trail. It was a large enough site to have had a good supply of corn for the hungry army. Lawrence and Jim felt it was the best candidate.

But it was too far from Moçulixa and the river, more than a whole league. "That won't do," said Charlie. He was insistent that they dragged the barge only a half a league. Two chroniclers, Ranjel and Elvas, said so. Both are reliable. There were other sites in the neighborhood, but they were too small and too far from the main trail. We could not make anything fit for Talipacana.

So we skipped over it for a while and tried to take the army on from Moçulixa, still assuming it to have been at Moundville. This worked well. There is a large site across the river, upstream a little way, that could have been Zabusta, the town they came to first on the other side. And a day's journey above that, another large site that could have been the main town of Apafalaya. So if we could find Talipacana, we might have a fit.

We went back to the map of sites in the area below Moundville and tried again. Still that site on Elliotts Creek looked like the best one. It was the first town they would have come to. It had large, fertile fields for corn. It fit in every way except for the half league they dragged the barge. We could not have them dragging it an entire league—three miles. But if this town was *not* Talipacana, why was it bypassed when the army was so hungry? We tried to find another site for Moçulixa. Nothing worked. We stood around in silence for a while, staring down at the maps. We had run out of alternatives. There was nothing more to try. It was not going to fit.

"Let me look at the narratives," I said to Charlie. "Let me read about that barge."

He gave me the books. "Biedma doesn't say anything about it," he said. "It's in Ranjel and Elvas. And in Garcilaso, though he scrambles it, as usual."

Everybody stood around, still staring at the maps. I read Ranjel and then Elvas. Having seen everything I had seen that morning, pouring over the maps, looking at all the sites, at the roads, at the lay of the land, I found when reading Elvas that his account seemed to fit what we had. He says that the town they came to after Talipacana was on a great river. The clear implication is that Talipacana was not. That would fit the Elliotts Creek site. The town on the river he calls Zabusta. What happened to Moçulixa? He does not mention it. Nor does he mention the corn on the other side, though he says there were hostile Indians there. And he says the barge was built within the town of Zabusta. Did he mean Moçulixa? Had his memory condensed these two towns into one? He says they dragged the barge half a league upstream to launch it. If they had built it at Moundville—Moundville being Moçulixa—they would have *had* to drag it that far because Moundville is on a high bluff and to get down to water level to launch a boat, you would have to go half a league up or down the river.

We started going over it all again. Everybody came alive. We wrangled around until we had come up with a new interpretation of what the chroniclers were describing. The army came through a day of bad swamps and arrived at Talipacana, on Elliotts Creek. From there they sent out cavalry to reconnoiter. Moundville sits on a high bluff on the outside of a sharp U-bend in the river. Directly across the river the land is low and boggy. Upstream from that, still on the other side, up the right-hand stem of the U from Moundville, is the large Wiggins site, the site of Zabusta. The cavalry could have seen it clearly from their side of the river. They also found Moçulixa, which was not so fine a town, a half a league away from Zabusta, but on the opposite side of the river. It was the Moundville site itself. The Indians had carried their corn across to the low caney land on the inside of the bend. No one lived over there; the land was too low. There were no houses in which to put the corn, so they left it in the open and covered it with mats.

De Soto moved his army to Moçulixa. He built the barge there and dragged it half a league upstream to launch it and put some men on the other side. Some of the men went down and got the corn, the Indians melting back into the canes. Others went upstream to Zabusta and secured a landing for the entire army. The land on the Moundville side of the river was high and much better for the journey upstream than the low land inside the bend. The army went up and crossed at Zabusta and then went further upstream to the Tu 46/47 site, which is a large site also on the river (and which does not yet have an informal name in addition to its scientific one). Between the Wiggins site and Tu 46/47 are plenty of bottomlands on which there would have been other towns, any of which could have been the one in which they spent the night before reaching the main town.

We stood around looking at the maps, talking about things. Why did the Spaniards not mention the mounds? There are a *lot* of mounds at Moundville. But after the first town in Florida the Spaniards rarely mention mounds, except when mounds are involved in the action. They say they put a cross on a mound at Ichisi, back in Georgia. And they say Tascaluza was seated on a mound when they arrived at his town, near Montgomery. But almost every town of any size had at least one mound, and they never mentioned them. In fact, they seldom gave a description at all of the towns except to say they were "fine" or "wretched" or "by a great river."

Most of the mounds at Moundville were in use in early Moundville III times, Jim told us. That was the peak for that site. De Soto came through in *late* Moundville III phase. Already a few burial urns were beginning to be used. Burial urns are the primary marker for the next phase—Alabama River. The change to Alabama River phase marks a major cultural change. Many characteristics are different then. It used to be believed that the shift was made around 1500 and that De Soto came through during Alabama River phase. But Caleb Curren, who has been working on sixteenth-century Spanish explorers in Alabama, showed that Moundville III was the correct association. Charlie does not agree with Curren's De Soto route through Alabama, which he believes puts everything too far south, but he does agree with his conclusion about the shift to Alabama River phase. It came after De Soto.

But as Jim was pointing out, the seeds of change were already planted before De Soto. The shift was underway. A few burial urns were being used, and the center of the Moundville polity had shifted north from the Moundville site to Apafalaya.

"Why was that?" Charlie asked. He was asking for their speculations, knowing no one had yet come up with a definite answer. The question has been around for a long time.

"Look at the soils," said Lawrence. "Look at where the fields are today." He pointed to the white places on the topographic map. "White means the land is cleared. See, almost all of it is north of Moundville. The good land gives out at Moundville. There's hardly any downriver from here."

I could see that that would mean something, but I was not sure what. If the center was going to shift, it would have to shift to the north. But why the shift?

"Was it that the thrust of population growth was to the north?" I asked.

"There was no growth," said Jim. "The population declined from early to late Moundville III."

So what had happened? We have seen the same thing over and over again throughout the Southeast. A decline of the big chiefdoms, the old centers falling and new ones within the same polities rising. A major change in the archaeological picture. The shift has been placed at around 1450–1500, but Charlie's De Soto work is moving it forward about a hundred years. Yet it was not De Soto alone who caused the change. His effect seems to have been to accelerate what was already happening. Back in North Carolina and Tennessee the shift was from Pisgah phase to Qualla phase—again, dated by archaeologists at 1450–1500. But at the Plum Grove site on the upper Nolichucky sixteenth-century artifacts have been found in an archaeological context that is a blend of Pisgah and Qualla, indicating that the shift was not yet completed when the Spaniards came through. The burial urns in Moundville III phase showed the same sort of thing.

What was it that happened in the late fifteenth and early sixteenth centuries to cause these changes?

"Climate," said Lawrence. "Something happened in the climate. The rivers changed."

"What do you mean?" asked Charlie.

Lawrence told us about the Moccasin Bend site near Chattanooga. He participated in excavations there. There was no Mississippian component, he said. There should have been but there was not. There was Archaic. And on top of that Woodland. But on top of that, where Mississippian should have been, there was a thick layer of sand. And on top of that Historic. The Mississippian layer had been scoured away by the river, and the sand deposited. The rivers had been running faster, carrying more water.

"You mean a little ice age?" said Charlie.

"Something like that," said Lawrence.

He was suggesting that the climate got colder for a while. I did not quite understand how the rivers showed that, and later I asked Charlie about it. If the weather is colder, he explained, it rains more, and the rivers carry more water.

Charlie liked the idea of a possible climatic change.

"Chester developed the idea of the cyclical nature of chiefdoms," said Charlie, "but no one has yet come up with a mechanism for it. Why did chiefdoms decline? Why did so many seem to go into decline in that pre–De Soto period? You know, it would not take many years of crop failure to bring down a corn-dependent chiefdom. I've always wondered if it could have been the climate. Could a climatic change like that be reconstructed?"

"It definitely could," said Lawrence.

It was a good discussion, all of us revved up, feeling that we were seeing the fog that shrouds the prehistoric past shift a little, thin just a bit. The small questions, when answered, shed light on the big picture. Did De Soto come to Moundville? Was this Apafalaya? If so, we suddenly know a lot more about these people in 1540. And if we know this much about what they were like in 1540, we can ask more directed questions about the change from 1400. And we can compare it with the enlarged picture of other places De Soto visited and piece together a little more of the big picture. That big picture is what everyone has been working on for years and years, wearing away at it, adding a piece here and a piece there. And occasionally there is insight that moves it all forward a giant step. This De Soto work seems to be doing that.

It was lunchtime by now. The four of us, Charlie, Jim, Lawrence, and I, headed to Miss Melissa's Café in downtown Moundville (there is a twentieth-century town alongside the prehistoric one). As we came out of the research lab, we all looked at the sky. The clouds were dark and low, but it still was not raining.

"Maybe it will miss us," I said hopefully.

"No, we'll get it full force," said Lawrence. "Can't you feel it?"

"Sort of," I said. "What is it I'm feeling?"

"The ions."

I did not know what he was talking about, but I could see that he did. There was no doubt in his mind that a storm was coming. He was feeling it in his body, and he understood exactly what it was he was feeling.

Miss Melissa's is a traditional southern downtown cafe of the best sort. We had a delicious lunch there. Then we went back to the lab and climbed into a four-wheel-drive pickup truck with a long cab: front seat and back seat like a car. It was coated inside and out with Alabama dirt. Charlie and I got into the back seat, stepping around a shovel on the floor. Jim and Lawrence got into the front, Lawrence driving. Now that we were finally going out to look at the sites, the rain began to fall. Perfect bad timing, you could say. But everything looked pretty in the rain; the swamps, the fields, the red dirt roads, the trees still holding their autumn color, and their leaves coming down with the rain. It was Lawrence who had the worst of it, manhandling the clumsy truck over all kinds of roads through that steady downpour.

We went first to see the supposed site of Talipacana. We drove south on a small paved road that followed the old trail along the edge of the Pleistocene terrace. Often there was swamp on the river side of the road. The site was on that same side on a patch of high land with good soil. To reach it we drove a very short distance down a dirt road through some woods. There was a sign nailed to one of the trees: No Coon Hunting.

"No *coon* hunting?" I said. "Specifically?"

Lawrence explained that the land was leased by a coon hunting club in Moundville. They wanted all the raccoons for themselves. I am not sure whether the real point of coon hunting is the raccoons, the coon hounds, or the male comaraderie. More the last two than the first, I think; but they would need the raccoons to put it all in motion.

The woods gave way to field when we reached the site. We sat in the truck and looked at it through the rain. You could see the mound, worn down by plowing. It was a large field, good for farming when the Indians lived here, still good today. If it had not been raining we would have gotten out and walked around, our eyes glued to the ground, looking for potsherds. But it was enough just to see the place. It makes Talipacana seem more real.

Lawrence wrestled the truck around and we went back out, drove past Moundville, and then, in order to cross the river, we had to drive all the way to Tuscaloosa, fifteen miles to the north. While we were driving along, Jim told us stories he had heard from Charles Fairbanks about how John Swanton traveled the route fifty years ago. Jim got his Ph.D. at the University of Florida under Fairbanks, who was one of the best of the old generation of southeastern archaeologists, the ones like Kneberg and Lewis who got their start in the WPA days. Fairbanks and David DeJarnette, Jim said, went with Swanton over the part of the route that was in their territory. Swanton could not drive, so he had to be driven everywhere. He would point to a spot on the map where he had decided there was a town De Soto had visited, and he would say, "Take me there." And he meant right to the spot, road or no road. When they got there, they would get out and walk over the ground. If they found anything at all—even an Archaic spearpoint from two thousand years ago—that was enough for Swanton. He would declare his town location valid, ignoring the objections of Fairbanks and DeJarnette.

At least we were doing a better job than that.

We drove across the river at Tuscaloosa and then turned south down the other side to look at the sites that we thought might be Zabusta and Apafalaya. We drove for a long distance on dirt roads. The sky had gotten very dark and the rain was pelting down. Lawrence did not let it slow him down much. He seemed at home on dirt roads. While we were driving along, Charlie asked him if he grew up in Alabama.

"California," he said.

For a moment that was hard to believe—he seemed to be of this place, as if he had been here all his life—but I did finally manage to assimilate it. Charlie asked him how he came to Alabama.

He said he came first to Tennessee. He liked it and stayed. That did not quite answer the question, but it seemed that it did. He said he had participated in the excavations in the Little Tennessee Valley. He knew Richard Polhemus and his parents.

A little more questioning and we learned he was from the southeastern part of California, near the Arizona border. He said he liked the desert. One could go out on the desert pavement and see all the trails that had ever been there. An amazing number of trails, major ones and minor ones. There was a trail to take you anywhere you wanted to go. The major ones were wide—he spread his hands to show us—about three feet. They showed so plainly on the desert floor that you could follow them from the air.

"Do you think it would have been that way in the Southeast?" I asked. "Trails going everywhere?"

"Yes," he said with definiteness.

"The major ones would have been that wide?" I asked. "Three feet or so?"

"Yes," he said.

Charlie told him that we had been wondering about the trails De Soto followed. What exactly had they looked like? There had to be headroom for the horses and riders. Horses like to have a lot of space above them.

In a virgin forest, said Lawrence, the limbs would be high. There would be plenty of room for horses.

He understood it so completely and made it sound so simple, I wondered why we had not known these things ourselves. And in a way we had. But we were not sure about it in the same way he was. His was not a false confidence, either. I am certain that he truly understood these things. He had a grasp of the physical world that I have rarely seen in anyone.

By the time we got to Zabusta (the Wiggins site), we had been driving for the better part of an hour, and yet we were only about three miles from Moundville as the crow flies. The intervening river made all the difference. The rain was letting up a little now. The site was on a farm, and one of the two mounds was in the yard beside the house. The river was close by, just beyond the house. These were much larger fields than at Talipacana. You could imagine the Spaniards on the other side of the river, seeing this town here and concocting that elaborate scheme to get across to it. But once they crossed they found there was an even larger town ahead.

Retracing the route we had followed in, we drove upriver to that one —Tu 46/47. We passed through alternating stretches of low wooded land, outright swamps, and fertile fields. I began to understand as I never have before what it means to say that the Native Americans farmed riverine soils. I thought of our trip through Chickasawhatchee Swamp in southwest Georgia, tracing the village sites from one high place in the swamp to another.

Tu 46/47 was also on a farm—which makes sense. The land that would keep its fertility without fertilizers when the Indians were here would still be good farmland today. The person who owned the land had built his barn on top of the mound, to keep the barn above floodwaters. It was better for the mound to have a barn on it than to have been plowed through the years and eroded away.

The rain had slacked off a good bit now and was not so bad as we drove back to Moundville. Jim expressed regret that the rain had come when it did, just as we went out to see the sites, but to me it felt just right. De Soto was in Apafalaya in this same season—late November— and it rained on him, too. Having seen Apafalaya in a cold rain with the yellow leaves falling down has brought a vividness that will be with me always.

That evening Jim and his wife, Judy, who is an editor at the University of Alabama Press, had us over for a tasty chili dinner. The three youngest of their children were there, a lively, happy little crew. At

some point in the conversation we found out that Jim was from Sylacauga, Alabama. I asked him about the marble quarry we had seen
Sunday as we were driving from Talledega Springs to Sylacauga. It was
a huge operation. We had driven past it for miles it seemed, though we
could not see much of it because of trees along the road that blocked
the view. When we were almost into Sylacauga, we crossed a railroad
track and saw along the track on both sides of the crossing giant blocks
of marble, stacked and tumbled like toy blocks. It was a strange sight.
We thought perhaps there had been a train derailment, and the blocks
of marble had been levered off the track and left there.

That was it exactly, Jim told us. It happened when he was a boy. A
train collided with an automobile and several people were killed. The
blocks have been there ever since. He said he had often wondered why
it was not worth anyone's trouble to load them up and carry them away.

"Is it high-quality marble?" asked Charlie.

"They boast in Sylacauga," said Jim, "that it's the second finest
marble in the world."

He said there was a famous Italian sculptor named Morelli who
actually came to live in Sylacauga for a time in order to have access
to this marble. All over that part of Alabama, he told us, there are
small Morelli sculptures in libraries and such places. People are proud
of them.

On the subject of De Soto, Jim said he had made a phone call to
the person who reported the Kymulga-phase pottery for the site at
Childersburg that we thought might be the capital of Talisi—the site at
the confluence of Tallasseehatchee Creek and the Coosa River. It seems
there is some mix-up. There is nothing definite for that site except a
lithic scatter—flint chips and so on. The pottery seems to have been
from a bag of sherds picked up at a nearby smaller site. So still no capital
of Talisi until more work is done.

Jim said they have a new mural in downtown Childersburg depicting
De Soto's arrival in the chiefdom of Coosa, with the chief being carried
on a litter. Swanton's route located Coosa at Childersburg. Unfortu-
nately, there is no report of the chief of Talisi being carried on a litter to
meet De Soto, so Charlie's revisions in the route will not be popular in
Childersburg.

CHAPTER FIVE

Mississippi
Back Roads

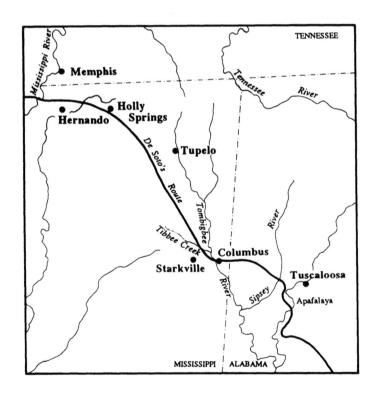

Having reached the province of Chicaza, . . . messengers from the Cacique arrived, saying that he and all his people desired to come and serve us. . . . The Cacique came, having with him a number of persons, who bore him upon their shoulders. He gave us some deer-skins and little dogs . . . and every day Indians came and went, bringing us many hares, and whatever else the country supplied.

In the night-time we captured some Indians, who, on a footing of peace, came to observe how we slept and guarded. . . .

As the enemy knew {thereby} whereabout our sentinels were set, they got amongst us into the town, without being observed, by twos and fours, more than three hundred men, with fire which they brought in little pots, not to be seen. When the sentinels discovered that more were coming in troop, they beat to arms; but this was not done until the others had already set fire to the town. The Indians did us very great injury, killing fifty-seven horses, more than three hundred hogs, and thirteen or fourteen men; and it was a great mysterious providence of God, that, though we were not resisting them, nor giving them any cause to do so, they turned and fled; had they followed us up, not a man of all our number could have escaped. Directly we moved to a cottage about a mile off.

We knew that the Indians had agreed to return upon us that night; but, God be praised, in consequence of a light rain, they did not come; for we were in so bad condition, that, although some horses still remained, we had no saddles, lances, nor targets {shields}, all having been consumed. . . .

We remained here perhaps two months, getting ready what were necessary of saddles, lances, and targets, and then left, taking the direction to the northwest, toward a province called Alibamo.

—*Luys Hernandez de Biedma*

Starkville, Mississippi
Friday, November 30

We left Tuscaloosa Wednesday afternoon and drove to Starkville—about ninety miles. It took De Soto six days to make the trip—through an uninhabited wilderness with many swamps. We think he followed a trail that ran about where U.S. 82 goes today. The sixty miles from Tuscaloosa to Columbus, Mississippi, is still more or less an uninhabited wilderness with many swamps. Between the swamps are rugged hills, grown up in pines. There were four creek systems that had to be crossed in that sixty miles, all with wide swamps. The first and largest was the Sipsey River. We stopped there to look at it. Charlie walked out on the bridge to take a picture, and I went down from the road into the woods. It was beautiful down there. The road was on a causeway, and the floor of the woods was low and flat and would have been entirely under water with a little more rain. It had rained fairly hard the day before, and there were pools of water all around. I could imagine James Adair, the English trader, making that difficult winter crossing of this river in the eighteenth century when the Indians nearly killed him and so did the swamp, which was very high and the winter very cold, and his toes froze. Over in the Chickasaw towns near present-day Tupelo the other English traders were taking bets on whether he would make it in.

I called Charlie down to join me, and we walked back a little farther and found the main channel of the river flowing through the woods. It was lovely and strange. There were almost no banks at all. The river was right there at ground level. Another few inches and it would spread over the whole swamp. We were only fifty yards from the highway, but the forest was all around us and James Adair seemed closer to us than the big trucks we could hear rumbling by.

We went back to the car and drove on. Before long we crossed the state border into Mississippi and came to Columbus on the east bank of the Tombigbee River. There were no Indians living on the east side of the river in De Soto's day, and the archaeology bears this out for the Tombigbee. We left U.S. 82 and drove a little to the north of town to take Mississippi 50 across the river toward West Point. Charlie felt this was the most likely crossing point for De Soto because it was above the mouth of Tibbee Creek, which empties a lot of water into the Tombigbee and would make a lower crossing more difficult. There was a wide swamp on either side of the channel of the river at the place where Highway 50 goes across. We stopped on the high, newly built bridge, and Charlie got out and snapped a picture. This was not the river as De Soto would have seen it. The Tombigbee has been altered—widened and straightened and deepened—for its entire course to make the Tenn-Tom Waterway, a highly controversial Army Corps of Engineers project that has been under construction for years and is now almost complete.

From the Tombigbee we drove on toward West Point. We were in a new country now—the Black Prairie—wide, level, gently rolling. Black earth. It was a welcome change after all those pine-covered hills. There were large farms here, huge fields in soybeans or pasture, big herds of cattle, horse farms. But few farmhouses. In places you could almost look from horizon to horizon and see nothing but fields. The houses we did see were modest—not at all the prosperity that the large farms implied. Either they belonged to tenants who worked for absentee landlords, or else the farm profits even on this fertile land were not very great once expenses and interest payments had been met.

We had reservations in Starkville at a better class of motel than usual—thanks to Mississippi State University, which is paying Charlie's expenses while he is here. In return he gave a lecture on campus last night—a presentation of his work on the entire route, with slides. There was much interest. The question-and-answer period went on and on, until finally it was adjourned to be continued at a reception at the home of John Peterson.

John is the director of the Cobb Institute of Archaeology, which houses all the archaeologists at Mississippi State—not a great number. The institute was established and liberally endowed by a Mr. and Mrs. Cobb, whose primary interest was the archaeology of the Holy Land. Southeastern Indian archaeology wormed its way in only gradually but now is fully accepted as a coequal research interest with the Middle East. It is a peculiar combination but evidently an effective one in this deepest region of the Deep South. Two things that traditional southerners have always been interested in are the Bible and the Indians.

Before the lecture yesterday evening we spent a very full day with the southeastern archaeologists from the institute, along with several outside people who know the archaeology of the area and had been invited to join us. The interest here in Mississippi has been greater than any we have encountered so far. At one point there were as many as eight or ten people standing around the maps with us in one of the archaeology labs.

When De Soto reached the Tombigbee after traveling through those six days of wilderness, he was met by a large force of unfriendly Indians lined up against him on the other side of the river. These were Chickasaws. The Spaniards built a barge in which to cross the river, and they used it to send across a captured Indian to talk to the Chickasaws and convince them not to oppose the Spaniards. The Chickasaws killed the messenger the moment he reached the other side.

The Spaniards made their crossing anyway, and the warriors retreated without putting up a fight. De Soto set out with an advance party of cavalry and came late at night to the main town of Chickasaw. All the people had fled. The rest of the army came in—the next day, presumably—and the Spaniards settled into Chickasaw for the winter.

From the chroniclers we have this information about the Chickasaws' main town: it was small, only about twenty houses; it was palisaded; it sat on a high ridge of land (Garcilaso says the ridge ran north and south); below it were savannahs (open land) where the inhabitants lived in dispersed homesteads, as in the land of Mabila. Nearby were some related people, tributaries of Chickasaw, who were called the Sacchumas. They were no more than twelve miles distant, as Charlie infers from things that happened in relation to them. To the north about one day's travel (fifteen miles) were the Alimamus, whom the army encountered when they left Chickasaw the following spring. After the Alimamus there was no one for eight days, until they reached the Mississippi delta.

This was the information we had to work with in locating the land of the Chickasaws in 1540. The U.S. De Soto Commission put the location at Tupelo, where the Chickasaws lived in the eighteenth century. Archaeology, however, has since shown that the Chickasaws moved into that area after the time of De Soto. There is no archaeological evidence of an occupation there for the early sixteenth century. The pottery for the De Soto period in this part of Mississippi is a variant of the same Moundville III pottery that was being made by the peoples of Apafalaya and Tascaluza in Alabama. This Chickasaw variant is called Sorrels phase.

We worked mainly with Richard Marshall, an older archaeologist who has a wide knowledge of all Mississippi archaeology, but especially of the Starkville area. We also talked to two younger archaeologists, Janet Rafferty, who knows the Tupelo area farther north, and Jim Atkinson, who has done much archaeological surveying for the Tenn-Tom project. And most delightfully of all, we found ourselves with another of those local people who have taught themselves enough archaeology to hold their own with professionals, at least so far as their home turf is concerned. This was Rufus Ward, Jr., a young lawyer from West Point, the small town we had come through the day before on our way from Columbus to Starkville. Rufus is the genuine article, a Mississippi boy born and bred, with reddish blond hair, a slight build, and a powerful intellect—quick and sharp the way a good lawyer has to be. He has an amazing amount of knowledge about the archaeology and history of the area. He came bearing large-scale maps made by the original land surveyors when Mississippi was being settled in the early nineteenth century. He had photocopied them at the county courthouses. They showed vegetation as it was at the time and the trails and roads that were then in use.

Dick Marshall also had maps spread out for us, including a large aerial photo. Charlie added his map to the pile and we spent the morning standing around, considering one thing and then another, looking at it this way and that. The concentrations of Sorrels-phase sites in the Starkville area and the surrounding region make a general fit for De Soto's Chickasaw, though we could see that we were not going to get the precision here that we felt we had at Apafalaya. This is more like what we had for Apalachee and Mabila, where dispersed settlement makes it hard to determine where the capitals were. These Mississippi archaeologists knew of only one town of any size in the entire region, and that was at Lyons Bluff, northeast of Starkville. It has about fifteen to twenty houses, is palisaded, and is on a bluff overlooking a creek bottom that was full of dispersed homesteads. It fits the descriptions and is of the right time period, but no Spanish artifacts have been found there. But then, only a part of the site has been excavated.

In the afternoon we went out to take a look at it. Six of us piled into a long-cab truck: Dick Marshall driving; Charlie and I in the front seat; Rufus Ward, Jim Atkinson, and Jim's wife, Terry, in the back. It was a day of blue sky and cool air. Dick was concerned about the farm road going into the site. In summer, he said, they would wait three days after a rain before they tried to drive those roads. Here it was winter, and it had only been two days since it had rained. From his concern, I knew that in this black prairie we were dealing with a different kind of mud from any I was used to.

As it turned out, the road was too muddy to risk getting the truck stuck, and so we went in on foot, a pleasant walk of half a mile or so through fields. Considering the fact that there had been two days of sunshine since the rain, the ground was amazingly wet. This soil does not drain. It is quite dense. When it is wet it turns to heavy, sticky mud; when it is dry it becomes stiff and hard to work. Its absolute blackness makes it look very rich. When you look closely you can see that the black is sprinkled through with white flecks, which come from the limestone that underlies it. There is no clay subsoil, just crumbled limestone. It is very strange. In places where the topsoil has eroded away there is nothing left but white, gravelly gullies.

Pine trees do not grow here. Climax forests are oak and hickory primarily. To the east of the Tombigbee, in the hills of Alabama and in most of the southern land through which De Soto had come, the climax forests were mixed hardwoods and pines. At the Tombigbee there is a dramatic break in vegetation. De Soto's chroniclers noted it. Here in Chickasaw, they say, there are many "walnuts" and oaks. There were no hickory trees in Europe, nor pecans, which are a kind of hickory, so the Spaniards, having no word for these trees, called them walnuts, which are close to them in leaf structure. There is a huge native pecan tree standing alone in the field near the mound at the Lyons Bluff site. Never having seen a native pecan before, I searched around in the leaves and found a nut. It was small, only about an inch long. The trees that produce the more familiar larger nuts are hybrids that are grafted onto this native rootstock.

The owner of Lyons Bluff knows it is an important site—which it is regardless of whether De Soto wintered there—and has kept it out of cultivation for the last six years. To further protect it, he keeps the gates of the farm road locked. The site itself is well kept and mowed. There is a lot of wildlife around. In the mud of the farm road we saw tracks of rabbit, deer, raccoon, wild turkey, and the print of a large cat, perhaps a bobcat. The pad was nearly round in shape, about an inch in diameter, and had four little neat round toes above it. The six of us made a rather large crowd as we walked along, and we flushed out a rabbit that Dick Marshall nearly stepped on. In its fright, it took off like a shot and collided head-on with my ankle. Immediately it recovered itself and got free of us, running for the woods, its white tail bright against the land.

It will take more archaeology to find out if Lyon's Bluff was the main town of Chickasaw when De Soto came through. It should become evident if much of the site is excavated. The Chickasaws delivered a serious blow to the army just as De Soto's men were getting ready to break camp in the early spring. All winter Chickasaw warriors had been harassing the Spaniards, making noises all around them at night, keeping them awake and nervous, but not attacking. Then on one of the last nights, when the Spaniards no longer paid attention to those noises, the warriors attacked and burned down the town. Because it was night the horses were of no use to the soldiers, and the Indians did great damage. Much equipment was lost in the fire, as were a great many pigs. A large number of horses were killed. Some Spaniards were killed and wounded. The Chickasaws sustained few casualties, in marked contrast to the Indian debacle at Mabila. It was the worst moment for the army in the entire expedition.

If extensive excavations are done at Lyons Bluff and no Spanish artifacts are found, this cannot be the place we are looking for. The use of Spanish artifacts as evidence is a tricky business. If they fail to show up in a place where De Soto was supposed to have passed through but in which he did not spend much time, it does not mean that the route is wrong. Metal objects and glass beads are all that would survive in the soil after four hundred years, and the Spaniards treasured their metal and did not carelessly throw it about. They needed it, especially for the nails they had to have to build boats. They would melt down other objects if necessary and reforge them into nails. Blue glass beads were given as gifts to Indians, but De Soto was not always on friendly enough terms to be giving them away. Often his policy toward the native peoples was more one of force than of diplomacy. Glass beads and any metal objects lost by the Spaniards could easily have been carried by Indians from one place to another. It may be that they did not normally carry them very far—from one town to another in their polity, most likely—but the possibility always remains that these artifacts could be moved a considerable distance. Thus the presence of an artifact does not mean De Soto was there, nor does the absence of artifacts mean that he was not there—not usually. But at a place like Chickasaw, where the whole army stayed an entire winter and then was burned out, losing much of their equipment, you would have to expect to find evidence of that in the archaeological record.

Dick Marshall will be the one who eventually confirms or rules out Lyons Bluff. He is the primary investigator for the site and has been working there a little at a time for many years. This is "his" site, and I admired him for the way he did not try to champion it as the place where De Soto wintered. He is by no means ready to settle down on that site as the only possibility.

After Lyons Bluff we climbed back into the truck, and Dick drove us out through more countryside, pointing out various Indian sites and features of the land. We talked about the prairie. It is now selling for about eleven hundred dollars an acre, down several hundred dollars from four or five years ago. Earlier in the day John Peterson had told us that farmers around here are selling out. They cannot make a go of it anymore. There are few left who are full-time farmers. They work at city jobs and farm on the weekends—a field of soybeans or a pasture of cattle, nothing complicated. As the small farmer sells out, corporations buy the land.

I asked the group in the truck about that. They agreed. The corporations are soon going to own all the good farm land, Dick Marshall told us. Prudential, for example, is buying up huge tracts of land in the Yazoo Basin—the rich delta of northwestern Mississippi.

"What are they going to do with it?" I asked.

"Farm it for profit for twenty years and then sell it," said Dick. He had actually talked to a Prudential man who had told him this.

"You mean they'll farm it until the land is worn out?" I asked.

"No, it's just that if they sell after twenty years they will get the maximum return on their investment."

Evidently twenty years marks the point of diminishing returns. It is hard to see how farmland will do anything but suffer under such a system, with no one who cares about it for the long term.

We drove east toward the Tombigbee River to look at a crossing place that lies below the mouth of Tibbee Creek. Rufus thinks this lower crossing would be more likely than the higher crossing Charlie was considering, even though the river carries more water here than above the mouth of Tibbee. The reason it would make a better crossing is that high land pinches in close to the river on both sides, which would have meant less swamp to cross. The crossing we had seen a few miles north had an extensive swamp on the eastern side. When the weather was wet, which it was for De Soto, that would be a hard crossing.

The same feature in the land that made this point in the river below Tibbee a good crossing place also made it a good place for the Army Corps of Engineers to put a lock and dam in the Tenn-Tom Waterway. We pulled into the parking lot beside the lock to take a look at what might have been De Soto's crossing place. If that is the place, De Soto would not recognize it now. Even Jim Atkinson, who had surveyed this stretch of the river, was bewildered as he got out of the truck. He turned all around in a circle.

"I can't make sense of it," he said. "I don't recognize anything."

All the land had been moved around, straightened out, built up, squared off. Everything was very neat: gravel and concrete and green grass. The channel of the Tombigbee flowed through the gates of the dam. Under normal conditions the water behind the dam is thirty-four feet higher than the water below. That is how far the boats are raised or lowered in the lock.

The idea behind the Tenn-Tom is to connect the Tombigbee River with the Tennessee River, thus making it possible for barge traffic on the upper Tennessee and Ohio rivers to come down the Tenn-Tom to Mobile instead of going all the way up to Cairo, Illinois and then down the Mississippi River to New Orleans. This required a twenty-seven-mile canal through northern Mississippi to connect the two rivers. That is longer than the Panama Canal. They had to move a lot of dirt, and to get rid of it, they filled every available valley in that section of northern Mississippi—leveled the land. The last lock connecting the canal to the Tennessee is a seventy-five-foot lift.

Boondoggle is the word you hear often in connection with the Tenn-Tom. There is a question whether the barge traffic is going to take up the Tenn-Tom's offer. Some people say the Tombigbee is simply too small to handle any large barge loads, much less the massive ones that come out of the center of the country on the Mississippi. There are places on the Tombigbee, they say, that are too shallow or too narrow, despite all the work the corps has done. The Tenn-Tom has been touted as an economic blessing for Mississippi and Alabama, which may have been true in the construction phase. But now that the work is finished, a barge passing by on the river will not do much for local economies. And in exchange the people have lost the natural beauty of their land and river. Archaeological sites have been destroyed. And a great deal of tax money has been spent. It will be years before anyone knows whether it has been worth it in the long run.

We got back to our motel in time to grab a bite to eat and rest a little before Charlie's lecture. The lecture went well, and afterward there was that lively reception at the home of Jan and John Peterson. Charlie was surrounded by eager questioners for the entire evening. I even took care of a little of the overflow, listening to an amateur historian from several counties to the north plead his case for De Soto's making a more northerly crossing of the Tombigbee. He had just the site for the main town of Chickasaw, a large Mississippian town.

"What time period in Mississippian?" I asked him. "It has to be late. It has to have Moundville III—type ceramics. Does yours have that?"

He did not know what Moundville III was. He had no clear idea of the time depth of the Mississippian period, which in all lasted more than five hundred years. But he felt very wronged by Charlie's interpretation of the route, as if prejudice in favor of the Starkville area was making him ignore the truth. I told him that it did not matter to Charlie where the route was, so long as it fit all the facts. If this man's site had Moundville III ceramics and if the travel time was right from Apafalaya, then it was certainly a contender for Chickasaw and Charlie would look into it. I would tell Charlie about it myself, I assured him. And I did tell him about it this morning. But those counties the man was talking about have no Moundville III ceramics, or Sorrels, as it is called in Mississippi. We went over all of that with the archaeologists yesterday.

As the guests began to thin out, I had an opportunity to stand and chat with John and Jan, whom we have known for years. They have always been, and still are, a handsome couple, vivacious and forward-looking. Their ideals were formed in the civil rights days of their youth, and they still have a conscious dedication to racial harmony in the South. John is from my own hometown in southern Georgia, and he is also one of Charlie's former students. He and Charlie arrived at the University of Georgia at about the same time, Charlie as a new professor fresh from graduate school, John as a Ph.D. candidate. As we stood talking, Jan looked fondly across the room at Charlie, who was conversing animatedly with someone who was asking him questions about De Soto.

"He still has that look about him when he's listening to people's questions," she said. "The way he cocks his head. That twinkle in his eye."

It is true. There is a generous, engaging spirit that comes into Charlie when he is teaching. It is one of his best features. It drains him, though, and by the time the party broke up—some time before eleven o'clock—he was exhausted. But he was pleased, as well, at the interest and enthusiasm he has found here in Mississippi. People had driven in from Ole Miss and the University of Alabama to hear his lecture. He had talked to a young man whose mother owns Commerce Landing, where De Soto may have crossed the Mississippi. He told Charlie that he used to take his girlfriends out there and tell them that was where De Soto built his boats. There has been a long-standing controversy about whether De Soto crossed at Commerce Landing or Clarksdale. This fellow was very excited that Charlie seemed to be coming out in favor of Commerce Landing. He gave us his mother's phone number.

We decided to stay in Starkville another day. Charlie wanted to clear up a few loose ends with the archaeologists and I needed to do the laundry and write. So this morning Charlie went alone to the institute and took a drive with Dick Marshall and Jim and Terry Atkinson to do a little more looking around. They had some interesting conversation. We had been talking with Dick Marshall yesterday about the pre–De Soto decline of Mississippian, and it turns out that Dick, too, has been giving thought to the Little Ice Age. He had some good ideas about it that Charlie hopes he will publish. Dick had also been thinking since yesterday about the problem of how to narrow in on De Soto's Chickasaw. Maybe we should start by taking Garcilaso at his word, he said, and survey all the north–south ridges. It could be done with remote sensing.

Charlie says he feels these Mississippi archaeologists are going to move into action here. We find this almost everywhere we go. To exchange letters at a distance or talk together briefly at a conference does not necessarily draw people into the quest. But to actually go to them and stand with them over the maps, exchanging ideas, trying out different scenarios—that gets them. They can see the possibility of actually finding the route, and they can see how much light would be shed on the archaeological picture if the exact route could be known. From that 1540 baseline they could go backward and forward in time, putting together more and more of the big picture. Charlie keeps talking about the multiplier effect. Matching the De Soto narratives to the archaeology yields an understanding of things that is many times greater than what could be gleaned from those two sources separately. We need archaeology to make sense of De Soto and De Soto to make sense of archaeology—and once they have been joined together, it is amazing how much we can understand.

Memphis, Tennessee
Saturday, December 1

We spent an exhausting day driving through Mississippi. It started out all right. The weather was pleasant, blue sky again and cool air. The countryside was scenic, lots of farms. We went up to West Point, turned west on Mississippi 50 for a few miles and then north on a small paved road—Mississippi 46—heading toward Montpelier and then Houston. We had learned from our Mississippi friends that this was a very old road, and Charlie thinks it might be the way De Soto went north from Chickasaw. In this general area between West Point and Montpelier are creeks that run in deep gorges, which might meet the description the Spaniards gave of a ravine that figures into their story at this point. The Spaniards came upon a fortification, heavily defended, and attacked it, thinking they would find stores of food inside. But when they broke through the wall, they found nothing at all, not even the Indians, who had slipped out a back door and escaped across a ravine. The banks of the ravine were so steep the horses could not follow. The fort seemed to have been constructed for no other purpose than to harass the Spaniards. Jim Atkinson had surveyed in the vicinity of these steep-sided creeks and told Charlie about them. There are Moundville III sites nearby, which would be where the Alimamus, who built the false fort, were living. Friday Jim and Dick took Charlie to see these creeks, and Charlie said they were amazing, ten-foot banks, straight up and down, deep in the black, limey earth.

Beyond the Alimamus came eight days of wilderness in a northwesterly direction before the Spaniards reached Quizquiz in the Mississippi delta. They say nothing of the wilderness land except that there were many wet, pondy places. As always when looking for the oldest roads, we followed the railroad track, taking Mississippi 15 due north through Pontotoc to New Albany. There we picked up U.S. 78, which took us northwest to Holly Springs. There were low hills all the way, with more farms than we had seen in similar areas of Georgia and Alabama—not so much of this farmland has yet been abandoned to timber. Mississippi seems in general to be about ten years behind the times. It certainly makes for a prettier countryside.

We had lunch in Holly Springs. It is an old antebellum cotton town only thirty miles from Memphis, though it seemed not to be much affected by the city. It has a square of stores around a courthouse, and although the square did seem a little spiffier than it might have been had it been farther from Memphis, there did not appear to be much outside traffic moving through. The place where we ate—the City Café, on a corner of the square—was like a set for a movie about rural Mississippi. Our waitress, who seemed a very sweet person, looked like a neatly dressed country woman from the 1940s. There were two hunters at one table, a genteel elderly couple at another, and at another a woman with dyed black hair sitting with a tough-looking, wiry, working man with a pack of cigarettes rolled in the sleeve of his tight-fitting T-shirt. We ate baked chicken, black-eyed peas, turnip greens, and cornbread, and we split a piece of sweet potato pie for dessert.

We were now about as far north as De Soto got when he reached Quizquiz, but we were too far to the east. We had to cut over to the delta. Charlie had figured that they would have followed the driest route, one that went around the headwaters of the major streams. This would have taken them west across De Soto County, and in fact through the county seat of Hernando. (It obviously has long been assumed that Hernando de Soto crossed the Mississippi somewhere in this vicinity.) We did not want to miss Hernando. We would have taken a side trip to visit it even if the route had not gone through there. And as it turns out, the route may not have. There is certainly no well-worn path across that country today. We have never yet made such a difficult journey or been lost so many times as we were in De Soto County, trying to find the town of Hernando. Later we appreciated the humor of it, but at the time we were about to tear our hair out.

It had started out well enough. We took U.S. 78 northwest from Holly Springs to Byhalia, then took Mississippi 309 south. We had two maps. One was a large state outline map that showed topographic features as well as roads and railroads. Despite their large scale, these maps do not always show all the roads that a road map will show, so we also had a road map. According to the maps, we could take 309 south a few miles to Warsaw and there pick up a road that ran west through Ingrams Mill to Cockrum and from there west to Hernando. It looked simple enough. But we were in a part of Mississippi where evidently no one ever goes who does not know where he is going. Not even mapmakers go there. They must get their information second hand, because the maps do not match the roads. There are dirt roads where paved roads are indicated and paved roads where no roads at all appear on the maps. On the maps there are towns of which you see no evidence on the land, not even an old store, and there are prominently named crossroad towns with stores and mills and houses that are not shown on the maps. There are never any signs pointing to the next town. There are no road signs at junctions of state roads. I have heard elderly people tell of how in the old days one always had to stop and ask directions when traveling because the roads were not marked. This is what it was like in eastern De Soto County. We thought we would never find Hernando. In a space of what should have been twenty miles from Warsaw to Hernando, we got lost four times and had to stop each time and ask for directions.

The last stretch before we reached Hernando was on Mississippi 304, a miserable road with half its surface coated with asphalt patches. It was as rough a paved road as I have ever been on. As we got near Hernando, we were exhausted and angry at ourselves for wasting so much time trying to take this route, which we now felt was not the one De Soto took. There was a much stronger road to the south, Mississippi 4. That now seemed a better candidate. Charlie said he at least wanted a picture of the city limits sign of Hernando and that I should be sure to watch for it and stop. We started passing more houses. We knew we were close. Then we saw the sign and started laughing. It was bent and torn, the most beat-up city limits sign we had ever seen. It was barely legible. HERNANDO, it said over the silhouette of a small-town skyline. We got out laughing and took pictures of it. It seemed just right after all we had been through. As we drove on, we kept laughing—it was one of those times when laughter takes over and you cannot stop.

Only if you have ever spent three weeks driving three thousand miles through the South on the trail of Hernando de Soto, completely absorbed for every waking hour in that and nothing else, could you know how delightfully funny it could be to drive through the town of Hernando in De Soto County, Mississippi. Hernando Fish Market,

De Soto Gas Company, Hernando Chain Saw Repair. We took half a dozen pictures, slides for comic relief in future lectures. It will be too bad if it turns out that Hernando did not even come through De Soto County. It may be that the route is through Tate County to the south. There certainly is not a strong east–west road through De Soto County. At least not these days. We will have to solve this part of the route with old maps that show the earliest trails.

Mississippi 304 west from Hernando is a much better road than the same 304 that comes in from the east. We had no trouble getting through the western half of De Soto County. Just past the little town of Eudora, we went down a short, steep hill—and there before us was the Mississippi delta, perfectly flat to the farthest horizon, huge tilled fields of wet, black soil, water standing in the furrows. It was like coming into another country, the same feeling you get when you reach the marshes and beaches along the ocean. We drove a little farther west and then turned south on Mississippi 3 and went about ten miles to the little town of Savage to check out the Coldwater River where Mississippi 4 crosses it. Charlie had earlier thought that this would have been a difficult crossing and that the main trail would have followed the more northerly route to avoid it. But seeing it first hand, it did not look like such a bad crossing, which is a good thing, since the more northerly route did not seem to be working out.

We turned back north again and drove through Prichard to Tunica. This is where sites have been found that Charlie thinks were inhabited by the people of Quizquiz.

I was amazed at the poverty of the delta. Rich land does not necessarily make a prosperous economy. Black people are living in unpainted, falling-down tenant houses that look like scenes from the Depression days. I remember blacks living in houses like that in southern Georgia in the 1950s and 1960s, but you seldom see it there anymore, nor had we seen it in all the rest of the South we had driven through until now. Not that there are no rural people in the greater South living in substandard houses, but usually those houses are painted, usually they are places that poor people in the Third World would feel lucky to live in. But these old tenant houses in the delta are another matter. The children playing in the yards, however, did not look shabby. These are not old-time blacks in raggedy overalls. And when we ate supper in what seemed to be *the* restaurant in Tunica, there were as many black people dining there as there were white people. So some things are better than they were in the old days. But other things are still not so good.

From the restaurant we tried to call the woman who owns Commerce Landing, but she was not home. We drove on up to Memphis, about thirty miles, to find a motel for the night. We will try again to call the Commerce Landing woman, and on Monday we will go back down there to take a look around. We also want to get in touch with Charles McNutt, an archaeologist at Memphis State University. We would like to meet with him, too, on Monday and see what he knows about the Quizquiz area and the route from Holly Springs.

Tomorrow we are going to do Memphis—by ourselves.

CHAPTER SIX

Delta Riches

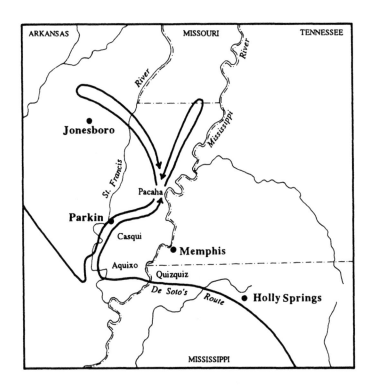

On the day of our arrival {in Casqui}, the Cacique said that inasmuch as he knew the Governor to be a man from the sky, who must necessarily have to go away, he besought him to leave a sign, of which he might ask support in his wars, and his people call upon for rain, of which their fields had great need, as their children were dying of hunger. The Governor commanded that a very tall cross be made of two pines, and told him to return the next day, when he would give him the sign from heaven for which he asked; but that the Chief must believe nothing could be needed if he had a true faith in the cross. He returned the next day, complaining much because we so long delayed giving him the sign he asked and he had good-will to serve and follow us. Thereupon he set up a loud wailing because the compliance was not immediate, which caused us all to weep, witnessing such devotion and earnestness in his entreaties. The Governor told him to bring all his people back in the evening, and that we would go with them to his town and take thither the sign he had asked. He came in the afternoon with them, and we went in procession to the town, while they followed us. Arriving there, as it is the custom of the Caciques to have near their houses a high hill, made by hand, some having houses placed thereon, we set up the cross on the summit of a mount, and we all went on bended knees, with great humility, to kiss the foot of that cross. The Indians did the same as they saw us do, nor more nor less; then directly they brought a great quantity of cane, making a fence about it; and we returned that night to our camp.

—Luys Hernando de Biedma

West Memphis, Arkansas
Sunday, December 2

We had a wonderful day in Memphis today. We got up early and went to the Peabody Hotel for breakfast. This is the hotel that has ducks swimming in the fountain in the lobby, though the ducks do not come on duty until ten o'clock. So we did not see them at breakfast time, nor had we expected to. We went there to repeat a lovely breakfast we had had in the Peabody two years ago, and we were not disappointed. A basket of pastries comes with the breakfast, and everything is served in a style reminiscent of the way railroad dining cars used to be—white tablecloths, heavy, silver-plated tableware and coffee pot, white dishes with narrow black and brick-red bands around the rims, good coffee and rich cream. We lingered over the coffee and pastries. Our waiter, a young black man—who was not at all like the old-time black waiters on the trains, but a self-confident, middle-class youth—showed us a picture of his fiancée among the other brides-to-be on the society page of the morning paper.

From breakfast we set out for Mud Island, a museum-park in the middle of the Mississippi that we had heard much about because of its half-mile-long, built-to-scale replica of the Mississippi River. On the way I had an unpleasant brush with the law. Mud Island is right there at downtown Memphis, not far from the Peabody. We thought there was a bridge we had to drive over to get to it, and we headed down a street parallel to the river looking for a sign that would tell us to turn left to Mud Island. We found such a sign, but we could not make the turn because of a policeman who was redirecting traffic away from a herd of marathon joggers who were trotting wearily along the street in front of us, straggling out for blocks and blocks. He made us turn right. Now we were going away from the river. One-way streets frustrated us further, but we finally regained a reasonable course. We saw another Mud Island sign. But there was another policeman and more joggers.

We had to wait a long time at the intersection while the runners went by, almost walking, a few at a time. It looked like it would go on forever. And it was obvious we were not going to be allowed to make a left turn down that street either. Finally the policeman waved us across the intersection. I stopped beside him in the middle of the intersection where he was standing and rolled down my window.

"How do we get to . . ."

"Move on," he said brusquely, motioning me ahead.

"But how . . ."

"Get out of here," he said sharply, getting very agitated. "Get out of these people's way!"

I thought he meant the people in the cars behind me. I thought he was refusing to take even a small moment to help me. My adrenalin rushed. I was furious.

"Just tell me . . ."

Charlie started telling me to be quiet and go.

"Go on!" the policeman shouted and actually laid hands on my car, trying to push me out of the intersection. Charlie was telling me to go. I went, but God, I was mad, pure adrenalin. I glared at the policeman in my side mirror.

"Asshole!" I shouted back.

"Shut up!" said Charlie, sliding down in his seat.

And rightly so. I was trembling and only as I drove on did I realize what had been going on back there. It was not the traffic behind me the policeman was worried about but the next wave of joggers bearing down on us. I had forgotten all about the joggers. And I could not believe I had carried on like that with a policeman. They haul you in for failing to obey an officer—and for cursing them. I do not know why I did it, except for the adrenalin rushing. It was very stupid of me. The policeman was not even being abusive or mean, given the circumstances. He was just trying to do a very difficult job, move traffic through a marathon race, and there I was in my stupidity about to foul up the race despite everything he could do.

It took me a while to calm down from that. We finally found another policeman (several blocks away, who could not have known of the incident—otherwise I would not have dared to stop), who told us we had to park our car and walk to Mud Island. So we did.

There is a quarter-mile-long walkway that goes to the park—or you can take a monorail. We walked and had the walkway to ourselves. Down below us more joggers were running by along the river. I stopped and cried for a minute about my fracas with the policeman, and after that I felt better. Though for the rest of the day I still did not like to think about it.

However, Mud Island certainly did put it out of my mind. It was perhaps the best museum experience I have ever had. It was wonderfully effective, with recreated scenes of life on the Mississippi that you could walk into and experience as if you were a part of them. There was everything from the Indians and De Soto through steamboats, the Civil War, levees and floods, and blues music, to Elvis Presley. I loved every bit of

it. We spent three hours there and then another two hours outside walking along that amazing model of the Mississippi, from the headwaters
to the Gulf of Mexico. It is sculpted into the concrete pavement and has
water flowing through it with the depths everywhere to scale. It has the
entire floodplain along the course, all the terraces and old meanders. It
has the towns laid out like city maps. I walked over Paducah, Kentucky,
and Cape Girardeau, Missouri, and Vicksburg, Mississippi, and New
Orleans, where we stood at the site of the Café du Monde and watched
the water flow around that sharp bend, just as we had recently done in
New Orleans itself, when we were there for a professional meeting.

We especially spent a lot of time looking at the De Soto places on
the river. It helped us see what we are going to be running into as we
go looking around the Arkansas side of the river for Indian sites visited
by De Soto. Some will be washed away by the river. Some will not have
the river running by them anymore. The area around the mouth of the
Arkansas River is one of the widest, most meander-filled stretches on
the Mississippi. A lot of De Soto action took place around there. We are
going to be relying on Dan and Phyllis Morse to help us make sense of
it. They are Arkansas archaeologists who have offered to show us around
once we get to the other side.

Since we could see Commerce Landing this way, right there on the
scale model, and since we learned the river had changed considerably
since De Soto's day, we decided to forego driving back down to try to see
it first hand.

After Mud Island, we were exhausted. We went back to the Peabody
and had a drink at a table beside the fountain and watched the ducks.
They are terrific. Mallards. One drake and four lady ducks. They do
more than just swim around. They get out and walk on the edge of
the fountain. And the drake is fully operational as a drake. We watched
him service either two females or one female twice. They do this in the
water. She initiates it. First they face each other and bob their heads up
and down. It looks like an outbreak of silliness until you realize what is
going on. Then he comes alongside her and grabs her by the back of the
neck and mounts her. The poor duck has her head pushed under water
for the duration. But then the duration is quite short and ducks are used
to having their heads under water, and she certainly does seem pleased
with it all when it is over.

We could afford drinks in the Peabody, but we could not afford to stay there. We came over here to West Memphis to find a cheap motel. We drove over on Interstate 40, which crosses the Mississippi River on the Hernando de Soto Bridge.

Memphis, Tennessee
Monday, December 3

We had a rough night last night in the motel in West Memphis. We were very tired. I had finished my writing and was ready to go to sleep, but Charlie did not want to turn off the television. He had slipped into a kind of zombie state and wanted the anesthetizing effect of the tube. We did not argue about it, but the tension level rose. I asked him what we were going to do the next day. Was he going to get in touch with McNutt? I was trying to remind him that we had De Soto work to do and needed to go to sleep. He said he thought maybe we would just go on to the Morses, let Memphis go. And still he watched television. I could tell he was disconnected—exhausted and for some reason discouraged. He was supposed to have called McNutt already, but clearly he could not do that or anything else. I could not see leaving Quizquiz unexplored. It would be the only portion of the route about which we had not consulted with anybody. But I was tired, too, and did not press it. I kept up my unsubtle hints that I wanted the television off, keeping just this side of outright argument. When he finally gave in and turned it off, he was sullen. He tried to look at his De Soto work. He picked up the Arkansas map and stared at it for a long time, but I could tell he was not taking anything in. He was so very tired. Finally he threw it all down and turned out the light.

I asked him what the trouble was. He said he could not see how he was going to be able to do anything more on the route. He did not feel prepared for the western route. He felt overwhelmed by it. He had had no time to go over the western scholars' responses to his proposed route. He did not have the details of the western route in his head the way he had for the eastern route. And he could not imagine getting on top of it at this point.

"Let's get some sleep," I said. "We're tired. This will all seem better in the morning."

And it did. As soon as we had had breakfast, he called McNutt, who directed us to Gerald Smith at Chucalissa, a reconstructed Indian village at a mound site on the south side of Memphis. Charlie called Smith and found that here was someone who had given a lot of thought to De Soto. We set up a meeting with him at Chucalissa at noon. Then Charlie called Dan Morse in Jonesboro, Arkansas, and told him we would be arriving there on Tuesday afternoon. Things were back on track again.

We got to Chucalissa on schedule and met Gerald Smith and his wife, Kay. They live in a little house just a few feet behind the museum. They have been there for sixteen years, since Jerry became director of the museum. Jerry has such an unassuming style that you could easily mistake him for just another employee of the museum, rather than the man in charge. He has lived in Memphis most of his life. As a young man he was interested in archaeology and got involved with the excavations at Chucalissa under Charles Nash. His interest in archaeology became a calling, and he went to graduate school to become a professional. Just as he was finishing his doctoral degree, Nash died, and Jerry, with the necessary credentials newly in hand, was given Nash's job. And there he has been ever since, working and thinking.

He took us to the museum lab and started pulling his work out of the files. His maps and charts were of astounding thoroughness. He had maps of seven Mississippian time periods in the middle Mississippi Valley, each with its phases as he had determined them. He brought out his 1540 map, and he and Charlie leaned over it. Jerry showed him the phases—the social entities—he thought De Soto had passed through. Charlie nodded with each one—that was the same way he had figured it. He had Jerry narrow in on De Soto's Quizquiz, which both he and Jerry thought to be Walls phase. Jerry showed us how he thought De Soto came in along Johnson Creek. The first town was right there as you come out of the bluff onto the delta. No slogging through the delta before reaching it. The possibility of surprising the people of Quizquiz. It fit the narratives.

When we went out to see the sites, however—Jerry drove us there in his Jeep—we could not be sure of the actual sequence of sites. De Soto visited three towns in Quizquiz. The first one he surprised. It was on a river, but not the Mississippi. It could have been an oxbow lake that looked like a river. Water does flow in those when the land is draining. Then a league past that was the second town and a league past that the third, which was on the Mississippi River. The first town in Jerry's scenario, the Irby site, is not on a river. Johnson Creek is just a creek. But the general distribution of sites over a several-mile stretch from the bluffs to the river is right. If all the sites were known and if a topography of the area in 1540 could be reconstructed, a fit might be made. This is a little north of Commerce Landing. And it would bring De Soto right through De Soto County, approximately as we had tried to drive it. But we will still need old maps to locate that trail.

Quizquiz was in the delta, and as we drove around on the backroads with Jerry, I became more familiar with the kind of country the delta is. The river dominates everything there—it has made the land. All the delta is flat, flat, flat. But then you learn there are degrees of flatness. There are high places—natural levees—and low places—backwater swamps. The native peoples lived and farmed on the natural levees. The backwater swamps, which today have been cleared and drained and put under cultivation, were in the old days covered with cypress and gum trees.

There are patches of natural levee all through the delta along old channels of the river. They are formed when the river floods. As the river overflows its banks, the water slows its speed. The faster the water flows, the more particulate matter it holds, so when it overflows and slows down, the suspended particles of earth start falling out. First the heavy ones—sand—and last the fine particles of clay. There is more of the initial deposit than of the final one. Natural levees are highest on the side that bordered the old channel. There is a lot of sand in the soil there and it is easy to work with a hoe and is well drained. As the levee slopes down away from the old river channel, the soil gets heavier and heavier with clay until you are down in a backwater swamp.

So wherever you see a high spot in the delta, aboriginal people probably lived there. The problem for archaeologists is that farmers do not want high and low places in their fields. Low places are the problem. The land drains so poorly that a very slight dip in the land will put a large part of a field under water after it rains. Therefore much of the delta has been "land-leveled." They come in with heavy machinery and knock off the high spots to use as fill for the low spots. Now you have true flatness—a flatness that even looks flat to Jerry Smith. Most of the delta, he told us, has been leveled to a 2 percent grade, just enough to let the water drain off into ditches. That certainly makes a mess of the archaeology. And to top it off, the farmer comes in with a chisel plow that reaches down five feet into the soil to break up the hardpan. So the stratigraphy goes topsy-turvy.

However, despite all this there are still sites left. Many have people living on them today—the same high places that were good for pre-historic houses are still good for houses. And not every natural levee in an open field has been land-leveled. Jerry showed us six or seven sites yesterday.

We talked about the farms in the delta. I asked him if they were mostly in private hands or owned by corporations. Most were private, he said, but corporations are starting to buy them. Delta land comes in big pieces—ten thousand acres or more. The going price is about two thousand dollars an acre, although as a rule you cannot just go out and buy yourself some delta. You inherit it, or marry it. Or you might get a chance to buy it at a tax auction, if you have that kind of money. Twenty million dollars or so would set you up on a delta farm. One site we looked at was an operation that until recently was owned by the Hunts of tomato-catsup fame. It had its own huge gin, which was in production—it is that time of year—though not many people were working there, maybe five or six cars and trucks parked outside. The fields stretched on and on, but there were few houses—three or four old tenant houses and about that many newer brick homes, modest in size, nice houses with neat yards and late-model cars in the driveways.

These farms are truly industrial, said Jerry. Each one is like a factory. The owners treat their employees fairly well, but they have little use for anyone else, especially for archaeologists poking around. This was experience talking. Jerry had faced people who had guns in their hands as they told him to stay off their land.

These big farms have precious few employees compared to the old days, so they can well afford to give them a decent living. Memphis now is full of people in their fifties and older who were forced off the land by mechanization in the 1940s and 1950s. Most of them knew nothing except farming.

Before we left to go out looking at sites with Jerry, we phoned David Dye, who is an archaeologist at Memphis State University. (Jerry is also affiliated with Memphis State.) Dye is a young scholar, strong and upcoming. We met him several years ago and have seen him since at meetings, and Charlie has corresponded with him about a few things. He invited us all to his house for dinner and offered Charlie and me a bed for the night. Of course we took him up on it. So when we finished driving around with Jerry, we all went over to David's house.

David's wife, Deborah, gave us a splendid meal—amazing that she could throw it together on such short notice. We had a lovely relaxed evening with them. Now it is almost midnight. The Smiths have gone home. The dishes are washed. I am in our room writing, and I can hear Charlie and David in the living room talking—the young and the senior scholar talking like old friends, David seeking advice and Charlie freely giving it, talking about the progress of a career, how you are pulled this way and that in the beginning, how you try to do too much, how you have to learn to say no, how you have to focus.

Charlie has agreed to give his De Soto lecture to one of David's classes tomorrow. That frees David from a lecture preparation—a small enough repayment for the kind hospitality.

Jonesboro, Arkansas
Tuesday, December 4

This morning I read back over the narratives about Quizquiz and realized that Elvas, who is the only one to mention that the early Quizquiz town was near a river, mentions only two towns in all. Ranjel mentions three. Elvas tends to condense things. So the Walls-phase sites do not have to be ruled out just because the first town (the Irby site) is not near a river. The second town, by Lake Cormorant Bayou, could have been the one where they encountered the Indians who threatened them on the bank of a river and then gave it up.

Before Charlie gave his lecture, we looked at David Dye's maps at Memphis State. He has been working on an elaborate reconstruction of the meander belt below Memphis for the sixteenth century. The only good alternative to having De Soto come in on Johnson Creek to Walls phase is to have him come in just north of Coldwater River, where there was an old road, and go to the Commerce or Hollywood area. But that would require crossing a very swampy section of the delta and some oxbow lakes. We also tried a more northerly approach to the Walls phase, the next creek above Johnson, but the sequence of sites did not work out so well. We finally concluded that Jerry Smith's Johnson Creek solution looked pretty good.

Jerry came to hear the lecture, as did several faculty members of the anthropology department and various other students and interested people. Not a bad little crowd for such an impromptu affair. This is the paper Charlie gave at the Southern Historical Association meetings in

Louisville last month, in which he and Chester and Marvin presented the crux of their De Soto work to the historians. Charlie worked day and night all summer long to finish the preliminary work on the western route so the whole route could be presented in this paper. It was a bit formal for a small group like the one this morning, but he pulled it off well. There were a lot of questions, and several people lingered afterwards to talk about it.

We then went to lunch with David and Deborah, Jerry, and Charles McNutt at a barbeque place, said by David to be the best in Memphis, though Charles McNutt said there was another place that had the best *ribs*. They are very enthusiastic about barbeque in Memphis. There is a barbeque restaurant on almost every block.

We left Memphis feeling that we had gotten a handle on Quizquiz. David and Jerry were both talking about following up on the questions that had been raised—zeroing in on the sites and looking for roads on old maps. Everywhere we go, people are so amazingly helpful.

We drove into Arkansas and headed northwest toward Jonesboro, home of Arkansas State University, where Dan Morse is the entire anthropology department. It was about a sixty-mile drive, most of it through the flat (land-leveled) land of the flood plain. As we got closer to Jonesboro the land seemed to rise just a little, so that water was no longer standing in the fields, and now there was cotton everywhere and fields that went right up to the very yards of the houses at the edges of the towns. The sky was heavy with a threatening winter storm—snow or sleet, the weatherman said this morning. Cotton pickers were in the fields—mechanical cotton pickers, not people, except for the drivers. You could see there was an air of haste, of needing to get the crop in before the fields become too wet with winter rains. We stopped in a restaurant that was full of farmers talking about the weather. Charlie and I went in with a big map and two books of De Soto chronicles and notebooks and papers, and we spent an hour or so reading and getting ready to start working on Arkansas. I know that as soon as we left, there must have been at least one person in there who said to somebody else, "Who in the hell was that?" Probably everybody did.

We were kindly received by Dan and Phyllis Morse when we got here to Jonesboro. They had long ago offered to put us up on this leg of the trip. Charlie had corresponded with them in the past, but we have only just met them in the last couple of months—at an archaeology conference in Mississippi. They are good, kindly, and enthusiastic people. They have three sons—Danny, Johnny, and Bobby—two in college and one a senior in high school, all living here at home. We had a rich conversation in their living room over wine, with a fire in the fireplace. I want to write about it, but at this moment I am too tired to do it justice.

Jonesboro
Wednesday morning, December 5

The rain has started. It is seven in the morning and it is cold and wet outside. A few people are stirring in the house. This would be a good day to work with maps, but I think Dan is anxious to take us out to see the sites. This area that we are in, he says, is the richest archaeological region in North America. He wants us to see how dense the population was in the protohistoric period. You have to actually get out on the land and see it with your eyes to absorb it, he says.

This is the richest archaeological region in North America, and he and Phyllis are the *only* archaeologists in northeastern Arkansas—and the only ones who have ever been here. Moreover, they have had to operate with almost no money. Dan seems to be somewhat shocked that the course of his career has been, and will be, run out in an underfunded university in one of the poorest states in the country. But this is where the archaeology has needed to be done, and this is where he has stayed. Phyllis is professionally trained but does not have a regular job in archaeology. In fact, she has developed an interesting sideline—buying and selling antiques, with a specialty in old tools. She and Dan travel on weekends to big flea markets around the South, particularly to one in Nashville.

Dan and Phyllis both went to graduate school at the University of Michigan and studied under Jimmy Griffin, who is now the grand old man of southeastern archaeology. Phyllis did not quite finish her doctoral degree: she brought up three sons in lieu of writing a dissertation. In their early days they worked in Tennessee. Dan knew Richard Polhemus when Richard was still a child. They also worked in Georgia for a while. They were at the Etowah site working on Mound B with Lewis Larson while Art Kelly, the patriarch of Georgia archaeology, was working on Mound A. This was in the late 1950s. Southeastern archaeology (and Georgia archaeology in particular) was still in its infancy. One weekend when their superiors were not around, Dan and Phyllis got together with Frank Schnell, then a student at the University of Georgia, and drew up the first consistent system for numbering sites in the state of Georgia. Until then every archaeologist used his own numbering system, and in fact they did not even like to tell each other about their sites, each guarding his own territory without much spirit of intellectual exchange. All southern archaeology was shorthanded in those days. Art Kelly *was* the anthropology department at the University of Georgia. He was one of the WPA archaeologists, like Kneberg and Lewis and Charles Fairbanks, but was less effective than many. He was fond of drink, excavated haphazardly, and shot from the hip when interpreting his data. But he was a marvelous storyteller and had a wonderful memory for details. People were fond of him and he always had a devoted following of students and shovel-bums. The community of archaeologists throughout the South was closer then. It must have been exciting for the young ones like Dan and Phyllis to be in there with this older generation, the pioneers who had already become legends. Even today the stories about them keep going around.

Good archaeology in the Southeast has only begun to exist on a significant scale in the last twenty years, and still it is terribly undermanned and underfunded for the amount of work that needs to be done. I asked Dan how he thought the Southeast compared to other parts of the country. The Southeast, he said, is the most exciting place to be for a North American archaeologist. The archaeological record is richer—there were more complex prehistoric societies here than anywhere else. The Southwest is rich, but there they have been doing sophisticated archaeology for years—sophisticated by old standards—and there is much good material already written and venerable schools of theory and methods well established, so that before anything new can be said, an archaeologist of today always has to address the large body of work that has gone before. It has a straitjacketing effect. In the Southeast almost everything that has gone before is highly preliminary and in some cases outright inept. Here is the richest of all archaeological records and plenty of room in which to operate.

What about the Midwest, I asked him?

There you have something of the same thing as in the Southwest, he said, though to a lesser degree. The grand old men are there to be contended with. You have to fight your way out of the old methods and interpretations. Before Dan came to Arkansas, he was at Idaho. In the Northwest, he said, you have to be an environmental archaeologist or you will have nothing to do. The aboriginal Native Americans there got no further than the hunting and gathering stage of society—ten thousand years of hunting and gathering—and so there is not much you can say about them except how they responded to different aspects of the environment. California is more interesting because of the dense population—a lot of little hunting-and-gathering groups living in close proximity to each other. But that is another place where the earliest and best archaeology grew up. California is second in that regard after the Southwest, and there again you have to contend every step of the way with what has already been written. The Southeast, Dan says, is where the most exciting archaeological work will be done for the rest of the century.

And the Mississippi Valley is the richest of the rich in terms of the archaeological data. Yet it is appallingly impoverished in terms of the number of good archaeologists working here and the funding available. In the past most good archaeology in the Southeast has been done by two northern schools—Harvard and Michigan—and both have concentrated on the Mississippi Valley: Harvard on the lower valley, and Michigan on the middle valley. But here in place—in Arkansas, Tennessee, and Mississippi—are the Morses, Jerry Smith, and David Dye, among others, struggling alone against hoards of treasure seekers who are destroying hundreds of sites every year by digging for pots that sell for anywhere from fifty dollars for plain ones to twenty thousand dollars or more for fancy ones. It is an underground industry here. People make good money from pot hunting. North American antiquities are avidly sought by collectors all over the world. The prices have risen 20 percent a year since World War II. A plain pot that sells for fifty dollars in Arkansas will bring five hundred dollars at auction in New York City.

Jonesboro
Wednesday night, December 5

There are two inches of snow on the ground and a casing of ice on everything. This is an unusually early winter storm for northeast Arkansas, they say. It did not slow us down today because we spent the whole day with maps. Tomorrow we are supposed to go look at sites, but the forecast is for a high temperature of only thirty degrees, so we will not be able to set out until at least around noon.

This morning we went to Dan's lab on campus to work with the maps. We made some progress, but it was hard going. This is a very complicated region, archaeologically. There is such a mess with the meandering Mississippi River and the density of population. It seems it would be impossible to figure out exactly where the crossing was made. Not only would it be very difficult to reconstruct the channel as it was in 1540, but it may also be impossible to find the sites De Soto visited at Aquixo, which was the first polity he came to on this side of the river and of which all traces may have been washed away by the shifting channel. At any rate, there are no sites for Aquixo exactly where we need them, though Dan says that area has not been surveyed. I got very frustrated while we were working on all this today. I felt like giving up.

However, the Parkin archaeological phase looks good for Casqui, and the Nodena phase looks good for Pacaha. There again, though, Charlie wanted a good wet place to separate the two chiefdoms, but there are too many candidates and no clear frontrunner. There is too much in this area. Too many sites. Too many swamps. It is hard to nail anything down.

Jonesboro
Thursday morning, December 6

This morning the sun is shining, but there still is ice on everything. The question is whether the roads will clear off enough for us to go out to look at sites. I think we can see a lot even if we have to stay on the main roads. The Parkin site is actually in a town, or on the edge of one. And for the rest—Aquixo, the rest of Casqui, and Pacaha—there are sites everywhere, plenty to be seen from the highways. All these sites, and Dan and Phyllis alone take care of them. They are like the sheriff and his deputy in the old westerns, standing alone for justice against the hoards of rustlers. Except here reality prevails and the rustlers, with their greed and vastly superior numbers, have the upper hand. The pothunters are the ones who dig the sites—with probes and backhoes. They can afford to spend what money it takes—as much as a quarter of a million dollars in pots can be pulled out of a single protohistoric site, and there are hundreds of sites. Dan and Phyllis, on the other hand, have *no* money for excavations. They have done quite a lot with the little support they have received.

Dan looks the part of the good guy in a modern-day western. He wears boots, jeans, plaid flannel shirts, a denim jacket lined with sheepskin and a slightly beaten up cowboy hat. His primary affiliation is with the Arkansas Archaeological Survey, which has an archaeologist stationed in each of the different regions of the state. The Survey is under the administration of the University of Arkansas at Fayetteville, while Arkansas State University, at Jonesboro, provides Dan's facilities and a small portion of his salary, for which he does a limited amount of teaching. His facilities are not glamorous. They are part of a large hangarlike building that houses the physical plant (maintenance department) of the university. It is hangarlike because it was built as a hangar by the military during World War II. Dan has a long hallway along one side of the building. On one side of the hall are continuous floor-to-ceiling shelves of boxed artifacts. On the other side are doors to his office, labs, and a classroom. He is virtually a one-man show. He has a part-time secretary, and when she is gone he has to run to the office to answer the phones. If he hears someone in the hall, he goes to see who it is, since no one else has any business being there. (Today the intruder was one of his sons.) This year for the first time in eighteen years he has a graduate assistant.

Despite his underfunded situation, Dan Morse is one of the most respected archaeologists in the Southeast. He has done pioneering work in several different areas. His bent is toward scientific experimentation. (His father was a medical doctor.) Dan was one of the first to use random squares in excavation, a method of taking a controlled random sample of a site when a more extensive excavation is not feasible. He supervised a student who did important work on the use of shell tempering in prehistoric pottery. He dug an important Dalton site—a cemetery ten thousand years old—and recovered an astounding wealth of stone tools, and in his analysis he added much to a general understanding of the manufacture and use of stone tools. He and Phyllis have pieced together the development of native societies in the middle Mississippi Valley, particularly the rise of the Mississippian chiefdoms. In the time between the U.S. De Soto Commission in the 1930s and this present project, Dan and Phyllis were the only ones to piece together a significant portion of De Soto's route.

The sun is warming things up. The ice is melting. We should be able to go out today without much trouble.

Jonesboro
Friday morning, December 7

We went out just before noon yesterday—Dan and Phyllis in the front seat of a red Arkansas State van, Charlie and I in the back seat. It was roomy, with lots of windows all around. Our first order of business was to go to the Parkin site, which Dan wanted us to see if we saw nothing else in northeastern Arkansas. Parkin is down near Memphis, about twenty miles west of the Mississippi River. We think it was the main town of Casqui. When De Soto left Quizquiz and crossed the Mississippi, he was looking for Pacaha, the great chiefdom to which Quizquiz was subject. He came first to Aquixo just across the river from Quizquiz. It was also subject to Pacaha. Then he set out for Pacaha. But on the way he went to Casqui, a chiefdom that was at war with Pacaha. Pacaha was up the Mississippi River from Aquixo, and Casqui was on the way, more or less, but on a separate river—the River of Casqui, as the Spaniards called it. This can only have been the St. Francis River, which parallels the Mississippi about twenty-five miles to the west. The Parkin phase is found along the banks of the St. Francis, and the Parkin site itself is on the edge of the town of Parkin, just below the confluence of the St. Francis and the Tyronza rivers.

Parkin is the best-preserved site in northeastern Arkansas, and Dan and Phyllis have been working for years to bring it under public protection. They almost had it once—a HUD grant of one and a half million dollars to relocate the black community that is on top of the site and turn the site into a park. But the fellow in charge of the project embezzled half the funds and absconded, and the project was canceled. There is still some hope, they told us as we drove south from Jonesboro. There is a banker in town whom they had found cooperative and enthusiastic when Phyllis was working on the site (under a small grant, not enough to excavate), and this fellow was pushing for a city park. So something might happen yet.

It was nearly one o'clock when we got to Parkin, and I suggested that we eat first, then go look at the site. But for Dan that would have been like eating breakfast before opening your Christmas presents. He insisted we go to the site first.

"So long as we don't *forget* to eat," I said.

So Dan turned off the main drag to take us to the Parkin site. As we approached it, we saw an entire little community, complete with a church, standing on an elevated place in the wide field beside the river. Dan compared the Parkin site to the tells in the Middle East, the ancient cities that have been raised up from the desert floor by the centuries-long accumulation of the debris of human life. Almost all the sites in northeastern Arkansas were once on raised areas like this, but most have been worn down by modern farming. Parkin had this community on top of it, and that is what has saved it.

Driving up onto it was a nice feeling, not so different from going up onto a mesa to a Pueblo village in the Southwest, though this was not nearly so high. We were perhaps ten feet above the valley floor. There was once a deep moat around the site. There used to be a sawmill nearby, and the mill used the moat as a place to dump sawdust. The little community was once called Sawdust Hill. There is a large mound on the site, between the church and the river. It is somewhat misshapen from years of pot-hunting, but it is unusual for still having a fair amount of height—almost twenty feet, not counting the height of the tell itself. We climbed up and stood on top of it. This is where De Soto erected a huge cross after the chief of Casqui asked him for some sign of his divine power. The people of Casqui needed rain badly, and evidently it rained the day after the cross was raised. The warriors of Casqui then went with De Soto to make war against Pacaha, their enemy.

It was because of the enmity between Casqui and Pacaha that the tell was built up. The people of the Parkin phase lived in nucleated settlements, within palisaded walls and moats. This was not true of their ancestors a few hundred years earlier, who had lived in farmsteads scattered through the fields. Before Phyllis did her work at Parkin, these scattered farmsteads were believed to be the settlement pattern through all of Mississippian time. But when Phyllis surveyed the fields around the Parkin site to find the homesteads, she was unable to locate them. Finally she realized that there were none to be found. The people were not living out there. They were afraid to. They were all inside the palisade. Settlement in the Parkin phase was nucleated. And when she and Dan looked further, they found this to be true of the entire middle Mississippi Valley in northeastern Arkansas. These people were at war. With whom?

It is the De Soto documents that clarify it. This is how Dan and Phyllis got interested in reconstructing the route. From De Soto we know that Quizquiz and Aquixo were subject to Pacaha. Casqui was at war with Pacaha—which means it was resisting subjugation. Quizquiz and Aquixo are two parts of what archaeologists call the Walls phase, though Dan and Phyllis think the Walls phase should be divided by the Mississippi River—Walls on the east side, something else on the west, since it is improbable that there was a single polity on both sides, although they may have been allied and evidently were. Parkin phase along the St. Francis shares some traits with Walls phase but is quite different from it, more different than Walls is from Nodena phase, which is north of it up the Mississippi on the western side. We think Nodena is Pacaha.

While we were eating lunch at a barbeque place in the town of Parkin, Dan and Phyllis learned that their ally the banker has died in the last year. That made them feel discouraged about the possibility of saving the site. For me, the state of the town of Parkin itself was enough to be discouraging. It is a very small town, and many of the storefronts are empty and boarded up. The crippled farm economy is obviously taking its toll on this town. It is hard to imagine the taxpayers coming up with any money for a city park. If the Parkin site is to be saved, it will have to be with state or federal money. And it should be saved. It is the last reasonably intact protohistoric site in the middle Mississippi Valley, an area where the Indian culture was so rich that it boggles the mind: a dense population, fine technology, complex political and social structure. And here is a site where, because of the De Soto chronicles, we know the name of the chiefdom and its relation to others around it. And we know De Soto was here with a thousand members of his expedition and that he erected a cross on this very mound.

As we stood on the mound at Parkin looking down on the black community that covers the site, I could not help but feel that just by being here this neighborhood has protected the site, and that so long as it remains, the site will continue to be fairly safe. But the houses are old, and the town of Parkin is drying up. This passive protection will not last much longer.

We drove from Parkin southeast to find Aquixo near where we think the crossing was. This was driving the route backward. We looked for the bad swamp De Soto crossed when going from Aquixo to Casqui and saw there was no shortage of low, swampy land. There were many stretches where clumps of trees were growing, which meant boggy land that is still too low to drain sufficiently for farming even after all the draining and clearing that has been done. And there were rice fields, which mean heavy clay soils, which mean former backswamp. They grow rice around here by driving heavy machinery back and forth over the fields to create an artificial hardpan. Then they build levees around the fields and pump water into them and the hardpan keeps the water from draining away.

Aquixo itself was something of a problem, since the quad map in Dan's site files—a large-scale map on which all known sites had been plotted—did not show sites where we needed them. When we were in Memphis we had been under the impression that there were sites where we thought Aquixo was, but we had not paid much attention, thinking we would deal with the western side of the river when we got over here with Dan and Phyllis. However, while this area south of West Memphis is technically in their territory, it is somewhat out of their range, and they know less about it than they do about the area farther north.

Dan was puzzled about the absence of sites. It seemed to him that there should be some. There was nothing about the land that would make it unsuitable. We went driving around looking, and all of a sudden he and Phyllis were both pointing to a rise in the land that had on top of it the house and outbuildings of a prosperous farm.

"That has to be a site," they said. "Look at the size of it. Why don't we have it on the quad map?"

We drove up to it and pulled into the driveway. When they saw the owner's name on the mailbox, they recognized it. This was a site that had been known for years. They had simply forgotten about it. That meant there was an error on the quad map. A whole section of sites had been left off by whoever had transferred the sites from the old county maps Dan had found in use when he first came to Arkansas. So we found Aquixo just where we wanted it. For me that was the high point of the day. I was not at all happy with our crossing before that. Aquixo had to be there or the crossing would not work. Which meant that Casqui and Pacaha were not necessarily right either, nor Quizquiz back on the other side.

So now we had Aquixo and Casqui. We were confident of Nodena phase for Pacaha, but Charlie wanted to see the land between Casqui and Pacaha. There was a body of water the Spaniards had to cross where the people of Casqui built a bridge by attaching it to trees growing in the swamp. There were some possible candidates for the watery place—Big Creek and Buck Lake, specifically. But this is country where, before all the draining and modification of the land and streams and swamps took place, there were wet, swampy places everywhere. You can take your pick. I tend to give up in the face of such a complicated geographical picture, but Charlie feels confident that he can look at the maps and the landscape of today and actually figure it out. Maybe he can. We did not quite do it yesterday.

However, as the sun was going down, we visited an interesting site on the banks of the Mississippi. It is a candidate for the main town of Pacaha. I found the setting of the site more interesting than the site itself. To get to it we had to drive through a delta plantation complete with a cotton gin, a community of tenant houses, a general store no longer in operation, and a Big House—a brick mansion still being lived in. The levee of the Mississippi River cuts through the site itself, which is one of the reasons why the site is well known. When the levee was built, a lot of pottery was turned up, and it is now in the Pink Palace Museum in Memphis.

We drove up onto the levee—something Charlie and I have been wanting to do ever since we arrived in the delta (Charlie got out and took a picture)—then down the other side through more of the site until the road reached a gate that was full of signs warning us to turn back unless we were "members of the club." Dan turned around without any hesitation.

"We don't want to go in there," he said.

"That's right," said Phyllis. "There's no law in there."

We agreed it was a good idea to turn back, but we did not understand what they were talking about. They explained. The meandering of the Mississippi River has left little pieces of Tennessee on the Arkansas side of the river, and vice versa. This is such a place, a piece of Tennessee, subject to Tennessee law but inaccessible to Tennessee authorities.

People take over these pieces of land as "clubs" to do what they want on them, unhampered by hunting laws or gambling and liquor laws or who knows what else. The dark tone Dan and Phyllis were using, implying murder and mayhem, was perhaps an exaggeration. But it does indeed seem that it would be unwise to wander into such territory uninvited. Unless, that is, you are the law from the other side of the river. They do make raids now and then.

We were running out of daylight anyway, and we had seen what there was to see of the site. We turned around and drove back over the levee, out through the plantation, and headed home to Jonesboro. The sky was clear and the sunset beautiful against the flat horizon. There was still a little snow on the ground. It was dark by the time we got back.

Today we leave the Morses and head west across Arkansas.

Newport, Arkansas
Friday evening, December 7

Today is Pearl Harbor Day. That clicks nothing in my memory, but it does in Charlie's. He was eight years old and was listening to Gene Autry on the radio when the news came through. I asked him if he realized at the time that something big was happening. He said he did because it was the first time he had ever heard a radio show interrupted.

This morning while we were at breakfast at the Morses, Charlie proposed a revised route for taking De Soto from Casqui to Pacaha. It is through essentially the same territory, but Charlie is still working on getting the water crossing in the right place. He suggested that the crossing was at Buck Lake and that they then followed the levee ridge south of the drainage that is now Big Creek and that runs east and west and connects with Lake Wapanocca. That would make the Bradley site, near Turrell, the main town. The advantage of this route is that most of it would run across high land and thus would fit the narratives, which do not mention any swamp after that one crossing.

Dan and Phyllis and Charlie and I tossed this around. We were rested and our minds were fresh. Dan did not like the idea of having the main town so close to the southern end of the chiefdom. And the Pecan Point site, which he favored for the main town, was rich in head pots, the supreme Nodena-phase vessel. The vessel of chiefs, presumably. We talked about where chiefs' towns might be located in expanding chiefdoms. Safe in the center or aggressively out on the cutting edge? We mentioned Coosa in the center of his territory and Tascaluza encountered first at his northeastern edge. Might the chief of Pacaha have come to the Bradley site to meet De Soto if that was his gateway town? Phyllis pointed out that the bones of his ancestors were said to be in pots, that they were portable. Might the capital have moved into new territory as it was annexed? I liked that idea and pointed out that Bradley would be central if you counted Aquixo and Quizquiz as Pacaha's territory. I could see the chief moving his capital there to be closer to his newly conquered territories. But Dan made the point that in fact the Bradley site is one of the oldest Nodena sites—its stratigraphy the deepest. I laughed and said that I could use that, then, to argue that, being so old, it must have been the capital—whatever the evidence, I could make it fit my argument. It was clear we were not getting far in determining where the capital was, but we were having some good conversation about the nature of Mississippian chiefdoms.

We talked about the side trip that some of the cavalry took to the northwest, where they ran into hunters living as nomads. Charlie had thought at first that these were non-Mississippian hunter-gatherers, but from Dan he had learned that in the area around Hoxie, Arkansas, where Charlie thought these nomads lived, there is evidence of late Mississippian hunting groups camping on abandoned early and middle Mississippian sites, which fits just fine.

We talked about what was going on with those hunting camps. Were they hunting to take meat and skins back to the people in the Mississippi Valley? Were they specialized hunters bringing the meat back to the chiefs only, who then redistributed it, perhaps only to the chiefly lineage? Or could a group of people from the valley go out on a hunt and bring back meat and skins for themselves? Had deer been hunted to extinction in the Mississippi Valley? Did hunters have to go far away to find any? Charlie kept talking about the fact that the Spaniards were given fish and rabbits by the people in the valley, but no deer. When the Spaniards got to the point of catching their own food during the last winter they were there, they say they learned to snare rabbits but say nothing of hunting deer.

But Dan says there is no evidence of resource depletion. Plenty of deer bone is recovered archaeologically at sites like Zebree, an early Mississippian site he has excavated. There is a lot of fish, too, and he thinks the importance of fish has been underestimated because of a miscalculation by faunal analysts, those archaeologists who specialize in interpreting bone remains. When faunal analysts take a count of the bone remains in an archaeological site and extrapolate the amount of protein being consumed, says Dan, they figure catfish to be the size of modern catfish, which are much smaller than the potentially huge size more often attained in the old days. I asked him if a good faunal analysis had been done on a protohistoric Mississippi Valley site. I wondered if the deer bone count would go down as human population increased. He said none had been done, and that was the great shame, no money for thorough excavations. If they could only do one site the way it should be done.

"The Parkin site," I said.

He and Phyllis nodded vigorously. That is the one, they said—the one that is the most complete. If this one site could be preserved, just this one out of all the richness of the prehistoric past, if this one could be set aside and kept safe, even if it is not excavated for five hundred years. You could hear in that plea their frustration, their years of working alone in the middle of the richest archaeological region of North America, pitted against the greediest, most numerous, most professional pot hunters anywhere in the country except perhaps the Southwest. You could hear the frustration of working as employees of one of the very poorest states in the nation, where there is little public support for archaeology and even less funding. At least in the Southwest there are plenty of archaeologists and there have been for decades.

They talked about how isolated they were, no one but each other to talk to about archaeology. Their closest colleague is David Dye in Memphis, an hour and a half away. Charlie told them that theirs was the best work that has been done previously on De Soto. He felt they had done a good job with the eastern part of the Arkansas route. And working together these last few days we had taken it even further. Charlie and Dan worked well together. They both have powerful minds firmly connected to simple reality. They do not get sidetracked into highblown theory. They keep an earthy connection to the real world of human behavior. And they are not dogmatic about their ideas. They will let go of things that are not working out and listen to new proposals.

We left feeling good about our visit with the Morses and headed back down to the delta near Memphis. When De Soto left Pacaha, he went back south to Casqui (Parkin) and south from there to Quiguate, which was also on the River of Casqui (the St. Francis). When we got to Forrest City, the southern end of the Parkin phase, we took a sidetrip to the east on Arkansas 50 to look again at De Soto's original route from Aquixo to Casqui. Yesterday with the Morses we had investigated a possibility for that route that would have taken De Soto northwest from Horseshoe Lake to Parkin. But then we found what we thought was Aquixo near Simsboro. Someone—I think it was one of the Morses—suggested that instead of the northwest route, De Soto might have gone due west from Simsboro and hit the southern end of Casqui and then gone north on high ground along the St. Francis to Parkin. Charlie liked the idea. It was not only a more sensible way to go, but it also fit the travel time better. When we drove that way today, taking it backward, we could see what good high land Casqui had—the chroniclers had commented on it. Then when the St. Francis levee soil ran out, we drove past a long stretch of low, swampy land—the big swamp they complain of—and then hit the Mississippi River levee soils of Aquixo just the other side of Fifteen Mile Bayou, the water they had to bridge before going through the swamp. It was a good fit. And to think that only two days ago I had such misgivings about Aquixo.

As we were driving down to Forrest City, Charlie read back through the narratives again about the trip from Casqui to Pacaha. He is not sure his new theory is airtight. He thinks Pecan Point is still a good alternate to Bradley for the main town of Pacaha. The idea of going due east to Pacaha along Big Creek is still a good one, but the water crossing may have been of that drainage system itself. If so, that would rule out Bradley. It looks like it could only be nailed down with archaeology in combination with historical reconstruction of the river valley as it was in 1540, if that is possible.

So we have Aquixo, Casqui, and Pacaha. We think Quiguate was the Kent phase down around Mariana near the mouth of the St. Francis. We drove down there, but did not try to find a site for it. The land is so changed there—the mouth of the St. Francis has probably moved. In our aimless wandering we happened into the St. Francis National Forest and found ourselves suddenly in a hilly terrain of forest and farms—a little remnant of high sandstone hills in the middle of the delta. It was a feast for the eyes after all that flatness.

The flatness of the delta had gotten to De Soto, too. He stayed nine days at Quiguate trying to decide where to go next. He was told there were prosperous chiefdoms down the river to the south, but he did not want to go that way. He had become interested in finding a northwest passage to the Pacific. And he wanted to get back into mountains again, where gold and precious minerals might be found. He was surely thinking of the Incas in the mountains along the Pacific. That had worked for him before, in his days with Pizarro, when he was the third in command and all that Inca gold had come into his hands. Most of his share of it had been spent on this expedition. He was getting desperate now.

The Indians of Quiguate told him that there were people eleven days away who hunted buffalo ("a certain cattle") and who could provide interpreters who could lead him all the way to the "South Sea." So the army set out to the northwest and went seven days to Coligua. The narratives speak of swamps on the way, but it is hard to understand exactly what they are talking about until you have driven the country. You have to see it on the maps, too, but the maps alone do not bring home the reality.

All the drainage through the lowlands west of the Mississippi River runs north and south. There is a lot of it, running close together. Each stream has a wide swamp on either side, and between the swamps there are avenues of relatively high ground. To go northwest, you would go north on the high ground beside a swamp for a while and then cross the swamp to the west and go north beside the next swamp, and so on. This is what the chroniclers are describing. It is very clear when you know what the land is like. Ranjel says they crossed a swamp a day for four days. We are not sure exactly how they went. They said they had no trail to follow, though they did have an Indian to guide them who, they said, took them as straight to Coligua as if there had been a wide highway going to it. We do think we know from other evidence that Coligua was near Batesville, so we drove in that direction by going west-northwest from Marianna to Brinkley and then north to Newport, which is as far as we got before dark. The swamps along the way were the worst we have seen—worse than they would have been for De Soto, since he crossed them in August, which is usually dry weather, and we are here in December.

The afternoon was gray and cold. We passed a great many rice fields, more than we have seen so far. Some were under sheets of water from recent precipitation. Others were dry, or mostly dry, and would evidently have to have water pumped into them to flood the rice the way it needs to be flooded during certain stages of its growth.

After we crossed the Cache River north of McCrory, the land began to rise a little. It was still flat, but not so wet and boggy anymore. There was a little bit of roll to it, more like prairie than the drained and cleared swamp we had been driving through. If I had to live in the lowlands of Arkansas, I would rather live in this country south of Newport. Far on the western horizon we could sometimes glimpse the mountains. There were more small farms here than in the land we had come through, and more livestock. Here and there I saw a horse with a shaggy winter coat. It made me want to stop in at one of the farmhouses, pet the horse, and then go inside and drink hot chocolate by a fire.

The further away from the delta we drove, the fewer rundown share-cropper houses we saw. There is still poverty here, but not so much squalor. The delta is a lot like the Third World—a few rich people and a lot of poor people. I am glad to see that not all of Arkansas is going to be like that.

CHAPTER SEVEN

Arkansas Salt

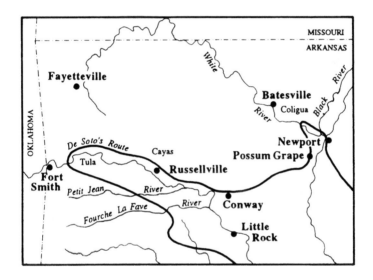

The Governor tarried a month in the province of Cayas. In this time the horses fattened and throve more than they had done at other places in a longer time, in consequence of the large quantity of maize there. The blade of it, I think, is the best fodder that grows. The beasts drank so copiously from the very warm and brackish lake, that they came having their bellies swollen with the leaf when they were brought back from watering. To that spot the Christians had wanted salt: they now made a quantity and took it with them. The Indians carry it into other parts, to exchange for skins and shawls.

The salt is made along a river, which, when the water goes down, leaves it upon the sand. As they cannot gather the salt without a large mixture of sand, it is thrown together into certain baskets they have for their purpose, made large at the mouth and small at the bottom. These are set in the air on a ridge-pole; and water being thrown on, vessels are placed under them wherein it may fall; then, being strained and placed on the fire, it is boiled away, leaving salt at the bottom.

—*A Gentleman of Elvas*

Conway, Arkansas
Saturday, December 8

We have been working steadily on the route without a day's rest since Thanksgiving. But we feel there is still much to do and not much time to do it, so we push on. We got a good night's sleep in Newport and took a leisurely approach to the morning, our compensation for no day off. We were underway by ten o'clock and tried to follow Arkansas 69 to Jacksonport, where 69 crosses the Black River on a ferry. The junction of the Black River with the White River is somewhere in this same vicinity. The Black flows down from the north-northeast and the White comes in from the west-northwest. Once the two rivers have joined, they go on as the White River, which makes a sharp angle just below the junction and flows south (nothing flows from west to east across those lowlands). Batesville (Coligua) is about thirty miles up the White River, northwest from Jacksonport. Ranjel says the army came on one day to the River of Coligua and then on the next day came to it again. The next day after that they reached Coligua. Then when they departed Coligua, they crossed the river again and went on.

Charlie interpreted that to mean that the trail they were following reached the east bank of the White River on one day, then left it and went up the outside of that sharp bend to cross the Black River, which would be when they came to "the river" again, and then went west along the north side of the White River to Batesville. On leaving Coligua they crossed the White near Batesville and went south—down U.S. 167, he thought.

Well, the ferry at Jacksonport was not running because of high water. That snow-and-ice storm has swollen the rivers now. There was a state park on the riverbank at Jacksonport, just a little below the ferry, and we stopped there to look at the Black River. It was very wide. We knew it was in flood and that De Soto had come through in late summer when it would have been at its lowest, but still it was hard to imagine the Spaniards crossing without boats. They had actually made no mention of a crossing, only said they came to a river, and if they had had to stop to build boats, they would have said so.

There was an old riverboat tied to the bank there, part of the park attraction. It looked more authentic than any steamboat I have ever seen. It was painted white and had two black smokestacks, Mark Twain style, but it was not huge like the boats that give tours at New Orleans or Louisville. In its construction it looked like the porch of an old house that had been kept up through the years and repainted many times. This was a sternwheeler, probably used into the 1930s. Charlie can remember steam-powered sternwheelers on the Kentucky River when he was a boy. This boat was about the size those Kentucky River boats would have been—perhaps twice the size of a large houseboat. Seeing it in that setting, tied up to that wooded bank, I felt I was getting the only true glimpse I have ever had of the old riverboat days.

There was also a museum at the park, and we went in to ask someone about the river. We wanted to know if the water level in the summer was low enough to be forded. We were informed by the woman who worked there that indeed it was—it got quite low in the summer, though if you were walking across you might have to swim a stroke or two through the deepest part. She also informed us that this was the White River here at the park. We were just immediately below the junction with the Black.

Well, what about the Black? Can you ford that in summer?

"No," she said. "It's narrower than the White but much deeper. The White is wide but shallow."

That was important information. We thanked her and tried to explain what we were doing. She was unable to take it in. She evidently had never heard of De Soto. She knew about expeditions and Indians and tried to tell us about the French in the eighteenth century and the Indian hunters and the pioneers coming west. We did not press about our Spaniards. We bought two postcards of the riverboat and left.

So, the Black was too deep to ford. A new interpretation: they came to the White River around Newport and forded it, left the river to cut across the inside of the sharp bend and came to it again the next day, where they again forded it just south of Newark, and then the next day went along the north side of the river to Coligua, near or at Batesville. The travel time works out perfectly, about fifteen miles a day.

So we drove that route. Coligua was said to be in a lovely valley of a medium-size river like one in Estremadura, in Spain. It was between two ridges, they said. Batesville fits that description better than any other locality along the western border of the lowlands. Furthermore, it fits the Spaniards' stated purpose, which was to find guides who could lead them northwest to the Pacific. You can follow the White River northwest through the mountains into Missouri.

However, the inhabitants of Coligua told De Soto that there were not many people up that way. They said the population was thin and the weather was cold. There were so many buffalo that people were unable to keep them out of their corn and so were unable to farm. In other words, the army would starve. The best thing for them to do, they said, would be to back up a little and go west-southwest to Cayas—which turned out to be the westernmost Siouan group on the Arkansas River. Beyond Cayas were Caddo groups—buffalo hunters—and beyond the Caddos, the Great Plains. The Spaniards would find more people—and more corn—at Cayas, they were told.

So that is where they went after Coligua. Ranjel says they left on one day and crossed the river again, went another day past mountains and came to Calpista, where the Indians got salt from a spring. Dan Morse had gotten in touch with some Arkansas soil people to find out if there were any salt springs where we need them. He learned that during the Civil War salt had been mined near Bald Knob. The Spaniards could make it there from Coligua in two days of hard travel, and to do it, Charlie had them going directly south from Batesville on U.S. 167.

We set out to go that way. The road climbed up on a ridge, then went along evenly. Just a few miles from Batesville we passed by a range of mountains on our right. Perfect. Charlie got out and took a picture. We went on, but now the road was getting rather hilly. We realized we were not passing by mountains as Ranjel had said but were driving through them. This cannot be right, we said, and got out our maps.

Dan had kept trying to tell us about the old Military Road, which runs northeast–southwest along the western edge of the lowlands. It is now U.S. 67. It crosses the White River at Newport, just below the junction with the Black, and runs on down to Little Rock past the foot of those hills we were on. We knew now that we needed to hook up with that road. The question was, How would a trail have gone to it from Batesville?

We now figured that the Spaniards had left Coligua the same way they had come in, by following along the north side of the river for about fifteen miles—a day's travel—and crossing the river south of Newark. Then on to link up with the Military Road, passing by the mountains that lay to the west—the ones we were still sitting on while we were figuring this out. This worked better. They would be going by the mountains instead of through them.

We now wanted to go east to get off the ridge and get onto U.S. 67. We were at Pleasant Plains, about fifteen miles south of Batesville. We took Arkansas 157 past some attractive hill farms down to the White River valley again, almost to the town of Oil Trough. At this point we took a short cut, or at least it looked like a short cut on the map. Charlie was sure it was the old trail that had once connected Batesville to the Military Road. So just before we got to Oil Trough we turned off on a county road to Thida and Union Hill.

We are probably the only outsiders ever to visit Union Hill, Arkansas, who do not have relatives there. That road was not the old trail. It went up and down hills that no one ever needed to go over who did not live there, and it turned into a gravel road before we found civilization again. We could see on our map that it was going to do that, but just at the place where it did become gravel, the paved road went off to the right, and we followed that, thinking the other was a side road and this the main road with still more pavement to go. When the paved road finally did turn into a dirt road, Charlie assured me that it was doing what it was supposed to do. But I did not like it. We were going west and north instead of south and east. And the road was rougher than a road on a map should be. It was terribly bumpy in places where it had been graded down to bedrock, and it was taking us up and down steep hills where nobody lived.

In these situations it helps for us to remember that we live on an unpaved road in rural Georgia. As long as we keep that in mind, we do not feel we are in a completely alien land when we are lost on the backroads of the Deep South. We would expect to find help if we were in trouble and would not expect mayhem from the local people we might encounter. However, that is not to say that we are as comfortably at home as we would be in a McDonald's on an interstate, where strangers like ourselves are the rule rather than the exception. When this rutted dirt road began a sharp descent to a concrete bridge that had no railing and that crossed a large, flooded stream that was several inches higher than the bridge, and with nothing but steep wooded hills all around us and mountains in front of us, I decided it was time to turn around. After all, we were trying to go south and east out of the mountains, not north and west into them.

"We missed that turn onto the gravel road at Union Hill," I told Charlie, and we turned around and went back to it. The county line just south of Union Hill was the reason for the change in the road surface. We got onto the gravel road and found it much better than the dirt road we had been on earlier. There were more houses and farms along it. But still we had to follow it for ten or fifteen miles, and there were a couple of times we had to choose between two roads with no signs. I tried to set our course by the sun and keep us going either south or east, and finally, when we were about to lose hope, the road turned back to pavement, and then a few miles later we were suddenly at the very rim of the hills. Down below us were the lowlands stretching east as far as we could see. In the distance was the White River in flood, winding along the valley. It was beautiful.

That is the way they would have gone, we said, pointing down into the valley. They would have stayed down there the whole way. Charlie had already studied the map in this regard and now believed that they had followed along Departee Creek from Batesville to the Military Road.

"Just look at the name of the creek," he said. "It is probably the way the French left the Batesville area to go south."

We drove down the steep decline of the hill into the flat country. Our maps said we should be coming to U.S. 67 at a little town called Grand Glaise. It was only with Departee Creek and Grand Glaise that it began to sink into me that Arkansas used to belong to the French. Their colonial history is French instead of English. This is an amazing revelation. Eastern Arkansas looks and feels like the rest of the South, and yet here are these southerners in a country full of French place names, living in a land where Frenchmen once trod. I could grasp this for Louisiana but somehow not for rural Arkansas.

We came to what our map said was Grand Glaise but found no sign of it. What we found instead was Possum Grape. We stopped at a country store—Possum Grape Mercantile—and went in to ask the local people if they had ever heard of any salt springs in that area. Our new way of bringing De Soto out of Batesville makes it not very likely that he got as far as Bald Knob, where we have that firm report of salt. We need some kind of salt around Possum Grape or Bradford, which is a few miles to the south.

First we asked what happened to Grand Glaise. There used to be a post office there, we were told—Old Glaise Post Office. But the government closed it and the building is gone, the last remnant of Grand Glaise. The community is now known as Possum Grape. It seems the French have been ousted.

We explained our mission, although this time we did not mention De Soto or Spaniards, just said we were doing research on an expedition from the old days. Did they know of any salt? One fellow was particularly helpful. He was a well driller in the area and was sophisticated enough to understand what we were after. He had a hook for one hand and used it to point to places on our map. When we mentioned Departee Creek, giving it a slightly French pronunciation, he gave us a puzzled look. Charlie pointed to it on the map.

"You mean Partee Creek," the man said, pronouncing it like "party." The French have definitely lost ground in Arkansas.

No one knew of any salt springs. But there is salt in the area. They told of someone's well up the road that has salt in the bottom of it.

And there is a lot of sulphur around. There are people who have sulphur in their well water and cannot use the water for most things. One old man in overalls assured us his water was so bad he could not cook beans in it—it turned them hard as rocks. You cannot make coffee with that water, someone else told us. It tastes too bad. We do not yet know the connection between sulphur and salt, but we are going to look into it. There *is* a sulphur spring in the area. The problem with finding a salt spring is that the water table has fallen so much that many springs have stopped running. All we can hope for is evidence of salty places that might once have had water flowing through. The well driller said there were places where, in bulldozing up the earth, patches of a certain sandy gravel would be turned up and then nothing would grow there anymore. We also found out there was plenty of blue slate in that area. North of the Arkansas River salt is extracted from blue slate, as we understand it. South of the Arkansas it can be found in running springs.

At this point I was beginning to have real faith in Charlie's idea of bringing De Soto through Batesville. For the last few days I have been skeptical, wearing him out with my doubts at every step, because it seemed to me he had so little to go on—they leave Quiguate on the Mississippi River, go seven days in an unspecified direction, and come to Coligua in a lovely valley between two ridges. It seemed to me it could be anywhere. But if you start looking, that is not so. Actually, a large number of conditions have to be met. He did not have all of it right when we started out, but that is why we are driving the route. You have to see the land with your own eyes to know whether it fits. You can fool yourself using only the maps.

After today I feel confident about Batesville. It works day by day, and it works in the larger picture in that Batesville is one of two gateways to the West. When De Soto left Coligua, he headed directly for Cayas, the second gateway, this one on the Arkansas River instead of the White. We followed close along his trail by taking U.S. 67 southwest past Bald Knob and Searcy to Beebe, where we turned due west on U.S. 64 and followed a corridor through the ridge-and-valley region to Conway. Here we stopped for the night. U.S. 64 is on a strong trail that goes west to Fort Smith, which once was a major staging ground for wagon trains heading out across the Plains. Conway is the first place I have ever been where a significant number of men wear cowboy hats. We are coming to the border between the South and the West. It was the same in

De Soto's day. The change in the native peoples was very great, a change from corn-producing chiefdoms to buffalo-hunting tribes. Eventually the army could no longer operate among them and ended up having to turn back.

We will be dealing with that tomorrow.

Fayetteville, Arkansas
Sunday, December 9

This morning at our motel in Conway we were awakened around five o'clock by people in the next room who got up and off to an early start. It was not that they made a lot of noise, but the walls were paper thin and it was as if everything was happening in our own room, especially their car starting up and pulling out. We snuggled back down for another hour of sleep, but then in a few minutes came sounds from the people on the other side of us—a rapid thump, thump, thump of a bed against the wall behind our heads, and a woman vocalizing, though not in words. I have never so clearly heard another couple making love. We laughed. We had already come to like them. The night before, they had tuned in to a country music show on television and he had sung along with all the golden oldies.

We did get a little more sleep and we were on the road by nine o'clock. Conway, we think, was near the first town of Cayas—Tutil-coya it was called. Charlie believes Cayas corresponds to the Carden Bottoms archaeological phase, which, as he understands it, runs along the Arkansas River more or less from Conway to Russellville. If this is Cayas, these should be the last of the Siouan-speaking people with connections back to the Mississippi Valley. Beyond lay the Caddos.

We took U.S. 64 out of Conway. Just to the west of town we turned down a side road and went south a mile or so to see the Arkansas River at Cadron Settlement, a park now, once a frontier outpost. They have reconstructed the blockhouse that was built there in the late eighteenth century to protect the frontiersmen from attacks by the Osages, who hunted in the Ozark Mountains north of the river. It is an impressive structure on a low bluff overlooking the river. This was our first look at the Arkansas, and we were disappointed to see it so visibly altered by the Army Corps of Engineers. It has a lock-and-dam system to make it navigable, and it is noticeably impounded.

Cadron Creek runs into the river at Cadron Settlement, and there are also a number of springs there. Cadron Springs they are called. A historical marker told us that the springs were the reason this was a good place to live, because the water of the Arkansas River and Cadron Creek were not potable. Too salty, evidently, which is hard to imagine. We have to find out more about these Western rivers.

We were the only ones at the park, and we enjoyed poking around. But finally we got back in the car and drove on down U.S. 64 to Morrilton. Here we dipped down to the river again, this time to a little park where Point Remove Creek comes in. All these parks have been built by the Corps of Engineers. There was nobody at this one, either. Charlie took a picture of the creek. A marker there told us that around 1810 the Cherokees were given land that lay between the Arkansas and White rivers in northwest Arkansas. Their eastern boundary ran from here at this spot to Batesville on the White River, where we were yesterday. These were Cherokees who moved west voluntarily from the mountains of Georgia, North Carolina, and Tennessee. They could see that forced relocation was coming and elected to move on their own. But even so, they were allowed to stay in Arkansas for only ten or twenty years, then were pushed on into Oklahoma with the others from back east.

We left the park and got back on Highway 64 and went a few miles down the road to the little town of Blackwell. Just past Blackwell we started looking for a side road that would turn off to the right and take us back to a swampy place called Goose Pond. We were looking for salt. When De Soto's army was in Cayas, they found that the Indians extracted salt from a certain kind of soil. A party of horsemen rode out to one of the places where they were doing this, and the horses drank some of the brackish water, which made their bellies swell.

It is because of this salt that most people have put Cayas south of the Arkansas River, which is where most of the salt is. However, when Dan Morse looked into it with the soil people, he did find salt in two locations north of the Arkansas: one near Bald Knob, south of Possum Grape; and the other here, just north of Blackwell.

We had a wonderful time finding out about this salt. It is a good story, but I am too tired to tell it now. We are at Hester Davis's house in Fayetteville, which is where the University of Arkansas is located. Hester is the assistant director of the Arkansas Archaeological Survey. Tomorrow we will talk to Mike Hoffman at the university about the archaeology of this area. I will try to get up early and write about the rest of what we did today before another day overtakes me. Right now I have to go to bed.

Fayetteville
Monday morning, December 10

Six hours of sleep. I could use more, but that will have to do. The road we took from Highway 64 to the salt place was a gravel road. We had a quad map Dan had given us, so we knew exactly where we were going. It would be wonderful to have enough room in our car to carry a complete set of quads for the entire route. These are quadrangle maps made by the U.S. Geological Survey, and a map the size of a regular state road map covers an area only about ten miles square. Every little road is shown, every house, church, and barn. The only way to get lost is for the roads to have changed, and then you will not get very lost. On this quad Dan had marked as a "salt locality" a large area that took in a swamp and some adjoining high land on the north side of Point Remove Creek. On the south side and down the creek a little way was the notation "Indian material." Goose Pond was a swampy place immediately across the creek from the indicated salt area. There were roads and houses on this side of the creek, and we could see where the swamp touched the road. So we decided to go there instead of to the other side, which would have been difficult to reach, reasoning that if there was salt on one side of the creek, there would probably be salt on the other.

We followed along gravel roads for two or three miles through the Sunday morning stillness. It was pretty country with woods and pasture—small cattle farms. We came to the spot we were looking for, where a tip of the swamp came out to the road, flowed through a small culvert, and petered out just on the other side. It was like the point of a star coming out from a round, swampy pond—though Goose Pond was more a swamp than a pond. We parked our car on the edge of the road—there was no shoulder—and got out. The sky had been completely overcast earlier in the morning, but now the sun was coming out. The air was warm and pleasant, like spring. We wanted to taste the water to see if it was salty but thought it would be unwise to do so. Charlie said he could smell sulphur. I was not sure I could.

A shiny blue van came by, slowing down to get around us. Two men in church clothes were in it—blacks, early middle-aged. They stopped when Charlie hailed them, and Charlie started talking to them about salt through the window of the van. Before long they had turned off their engine and were standing out in the road looking at our quad sheet with us and telling us all about the place. The water in Goose Pond was not salty so far as they knew. Cows drank from it without their bellies swelling like De Soto's horses' had. But there was a lot of bad water around there. Their grandmother had a sulphur well—she drank it, but they themselves could not. And not far from where we were standing, about a hundred yards back up the road, there was an area where there was salt in the ground. In the dry season the top of the ground would actually be white in places—or it used to be. At one time nothing would grow there, but they had been plowing it for years and sowing grass seed on it until finally the grass had taken root.

They walked down the road with us to show us the place. We learned their names. They were Walter and Marcellus Cunningham, two brothers. Walter was in his mid-forties, I would guess, and Marcellus in his early thirties. They owned all the land around us, and their father had owned it before them. We enjoyed talking to them. They were nice fellows and they knew a great deal about the area.

The ground was too wet to have any salt showing white, but we could see the poor patches where the grass was thin. Walter said that as a boy, in summer, when the salt had evaporated out on the dry ground, he and his friends used to get down and lick it to see what it tasted like. It tasted like epsom salts, he said, and laughed to remember having done that.

We explained to them what we were doing. They are some of the few local people we have encountered who were not baffled by it. Walter remembered learning about De Soto in grade school. He told us about the Indian site up the road—a mound and graves. A lot of Indian material used to turn up when it was plowed, and people would pick it up, but now there is not much left of it. It did not seem at all strange to him that we would be here on this road through his farm trying to track down a Spanish expedition that had come traveling through among the native peoples centuries ago. He said he remembered a poem he had learned in the first grade, and he recited it for us—a poignant little verse about this land we now trod having once been home to the Indian. He said he has often thought about that while out working in his fields, that once this was another world where only Indians lived.

We were sorry to leave these guys. We shook hands all around and

Charlie took down their mailing address, promising to send them a copy of his paper on this part of the route when he gets it finished. It could be a year or more, he warned them. They said they would be interested to see it. We got back in our car and returned to U.S. 64 and headed on toward Russellville. Russellville was only about twenty miles away, but we never go anywhere directly. We turned off on a small road—Arkansas 105—and drove down toward the river again. Charlie wanted to see Coon Bayou, which 105 crossed. The Spaniards had slept by a swamp the day before they got to Tanico, the last town of Cayas, and since he thinks Tanico was near Russellville, he thinks Coon Bayou might have been that swamp. And it might have been, though it is not the swamp now that it once was: it has been channelized, and there is a machine-made levee running along one side of it to keep it out of a nearby field. There was a little bit of swamp on the other side, and Charlie took a picture, just for the record.

This road looped on around toward Russellville, so we stayed on it, following right along the river for quite a distance. It was in that stretch that we came to a woodsy place where there was a wrought-iron archway like the ones we have seen at the entries to cemeteries out here in the West. (We started noticing this feature about halfway through Arkansas.) The arch seemed to be there for no particular purpose. There was, however, a historical marker, and we stopped to read it. Galley Rock, an old riverport town established in 1860, was once located near here. When the railroad came through in 1872, the town died out. All that is left, said the marker, is this cemetery on this wooded ridge above the river. Cemetery? We took a closer look and sure enough, there were tombstones scattered all through the woods under the vines and leaves. And even more surprising was what good condition they were in, solid and erect, their names and dates and messages clearly legible. Some of the monuments were quite elaborate. I have never seen a cemetery so completely abandoned, unless it has been a very small one and the markers all but vanished. We poked around a few minutes. The last burials were around the turn of the century.

From there we went on to Russellville and had a good meal at the Old South Restaurant, where evidently most of Russellville, or at least the older set, eats their Sunday dinner. We had chicken and dressing, green beans, carrots, salad, peach cobbler, and coffee, all for less than four dollars each. We studied the people. Not exactly southern anymore.

Partly southern, but a definite midwestern look has crept in. Western midwestern.

Charlie feels that Tanico, the town where De Soto stayed while he was in Cayas, was around Russellville. From here De Soto took a party of cavalry on a jaunt to Tula, a land whose people were enemies with Cayas and spoke a different language. Because of the enmity Cayas had no one who could serve as interpreter. This marked language change has to mean that the people of Tula spoke a Caddoan language. Tula was said to be to the south of Cayas—a two-day journey. We think Cayas was synonymous with Carden Bottoms phase. Archaeologically, Carden Bottoms phase is the last Mississippian phase up the Arkansas River. Its affiliations run east to the Mississippi River. Presumably its people spoke a Siouan language. Immediately to the south of the Carden Bottoms section of the Arkansas are the Petit Jean and Fourche la Fave rivers, which run roughly parallel to the Arkansas—first the Petit Jean (pronounced Petty Gene) and south of that the Fourche la Fave (usually shortened to Fourche and pronounced "Foosh"). They empty into the Arkansas in the Carden Bottoms phase area. On these two rivers were Caddoan-speaking people. The archaeological sites are Caddoan, their affiliations running to the Fort Smith area. Charlie's route fits this break precisely. The only question is, where is Tula? On the Fourche or on the Petit Jean?

We had no idea. Charlie has been in touch with Arkansas archaeologists, who suggested these two rivers as possibilities for Tula and said there were some late sites along them, although very little is known about the area. Almost no surveying has been done. We hope to get more information while we are here in Fayetteville, but first we thought it would be a good idea to drive through parts of the two valleys just to get a feel for the country. So from Russellville we turned south and crossed the Arkansas, then followed Arkansas 7 to Ola and there picked up Arkansas 28 to go through a low gap in the mountains into the Fourche valley.

We hoped for that gap to be a dramatic one—a notch in the mountains would have been nice. When De Soto got to Tula with his band of cavalry, he found himself fighting some people who knew how to do damage to men on horses. They had lances, and they used them as pikes, standing firm before the charge of a horse and impaling the horse or its rider. They were the only native group the Spaniards had encountered on this expedition who knew how to do that. Charlie believes it was because they were used to hunting buffalo. The Spaniards say they were buffalo hunters. The cavalry fought its way out of that situation and hightailed it back to Cayas. They rode hard and were particularly worried about getting through a narrow place in the mountains where they would be more vulnerable to Indian attack. After going through that pass they were back in the river valley of Cayas. This was why we wanted a constricted pass at Ola. As it turned out, it *was* a pass from one valley to the next, and there was some constriction, but it was not dramatic. It will do if nothing better turns up, but we would feel more confident with something narrower.

When we got into the Fourche la Fave valley we felt we were in a different kind of country. It seemed more western than southern. There were no tilled fields anymore, only pasture—range for cattle. There were more pines than hardwoods. The streambeds were gravelly, and the water was clear. There were no grain silos, just hay barns. We had gone from farms to ranches. I am not sure where the change took place—back around Russellville somewhere. It was the same as the Mississippian-Caddo break. You could imagine buffalo in this country.

We drove as far as Briggsville and turned down a small paved road to take a look at the river. We were the only ones around, no other cars on the road. The highway crosses the river on a one-lane bridge. A larger bridge is being built beside it, so the area was a little messed up right around the construction. But a few yards downstream from that was a low, concrete, damlike structure that crossed the river in a curve instead of a straight line. It ran right out from the bank, about a foot above the water, and was wide enough for a car to drive across, though it was broken in the middle and the river poured through. Whatever it was, we walked out onto it, to the middle of the channel, and with our backs to the bridges we could look downstream into the natural wildness of the area. It was very pretty. Something about it was definitely western, but we had a hard time saying what it was. The more arid vegetation, perhaps. And the gravel along the banks. But even more, something clean and crisp. I could have stayed there a long time, but the afternoon was getting late and we had to hurry on. We were supposed to be in Fayetteville by six o'clock.

We backtracked a little and crossed through the mountains at a different place—still looking for a narrow pass. This road took us to

Danville. On the map it had looked like a good possibility for the pass, but when we tried it, we knew it was not right. It was too high and steep, too much up and over the mountains instead of through them. The Spaniards would not have gone that way.

From Danville we drove west up the Petit Jean valley and then northwest to Ozark—ranch country all the way, not a tilled field to be seen. This is one of the reasons this area is so poorly known archaeologically. It is only when a field is tilled that potsherds are turned up in it. An archaeological survey in a large area where no fields are tilled will yield little. The only place anything at all can be found is along the banks of the streams, where the action of the water is eroding sites and artifacts are washing out.

The sky had gone from completely overcast and drizzling in the morning, when we had started out from Conway, to sparkling clear in the late afternoon. The air was unseasonably warm. At sunset, as we were driving along U.S. 64 west of Ozark, we came around a ridge and there below us was the Arkansas Valley—we could see almost to Fort Smith, thirty miles away. The sun had just dropped below a ridge of mountains on the horizon, and the sky above was the rosiest I have ever seen, the clearest of clear. Charlie started singing "Home on the Range."

A few minutes later we reached U.S. 71, which runs north into the Ozark Mountains to Fayetteville. It was getting dark. We stopped and fortified ourselves with a hamburger and then drove the last forty-five miles over winding roads through mountain scenery we could not see. Tomorrow we will go out by the same road in daylight.

Fayetteville is in the heart of the Ozarks. There is a spirit here that I recognize from back home in the Appalachians: an emphasis on folk culture and crafts, a strong presence of the sort of people who want to be self-sufficient and free of the trammels of civilization. The university adds an academic and cultural element. In all, a pleasing place.

Fayetteville
Monday night, December 10

We met today with Mike Hoffman, an archaeologist in the anthropology department here. He is the one who first suggested to Charlie that Tula might be on either the Petit Jean or the Fourche la Fave river. Charlie in his first attempt at this part of the route had put Tula at Fort Smith, which is up the Arkansas River from Cayas. But when he sent that version to the Arkansas archaeologists, he was told that the archaeology at Fort Smith did not fit, nor did the archaeology for the area to the south that he had suggested for Quipana. The reason Charlie had put Tula at Fort Smith was that one of the chroniclers said it was upstream from Cayas. It was Mike Hoffman who suggested that upstream could be up either the Petit Jean or the Fourche, since both empty into the Arkansas River in Cayas territory. That also fits better with one of the other chroniclers, who says Tula was to the south. Charlie had overlooked that little detail.

We spent the better part of the day trying to nail Tula down to one of those two rivers. There is a site in the Fourche la Fave valley, just a little upstream from where we were yesterday, that has late Caddoan material in it, which would be of the right time period. We looked at some of it in the museum collections. The collections themselves were astounding. They are housed in what used to be the stacks of an old library. In one huge room, on shelves that were once bookshelves, were aisle after aisle of prehistoric pots from Arkansas—beautiful, elaborate pots. Mississippi Valley red-and-white pots, effigy pots with all kinds of animal, human, and monster forms sculpted into them, and engraved Caddoan pots. It was amazing to see them in such number and to realize the immense archaeological wealth of Arkansas.

So there is a mound site on the Fourche that appears to be a late Caddoan site. There is little else that is firm on either the Fourche or the Petit Jean. There are some early reports of sites on the Petit Jean, but nothing to indicate when they were occupied. There is one site that may have had some late material, but that is uncertain. This area is what some of the archaeologists around here call the Black Hole of Arkansas—the least-known region in the state. It is to be hoped that Charlie's interest in it will be infectious and that someone will go to work on it and find out what is there.

After we had searched the site files for everything that could possibly be helpful to us, we reached the point of simply staring at the map, unable to take it any further. All we can say at this point is that Tula was either on the Fourche or the Petit Jean. We began to look at what comes next—Quipana. Quipana was southeast of Tula, and it took the Spaniards four days to get there. Ann Early, who works for the Arkansas Archaeological Survey and with whom we will be meeting later this week, has suggested that Quipana might be on the Ouachita River, which is in her area. Charlie thinks that is a good idea. However, looking at the straight-line distance from either of our Tulas to the Ouachita, it was hard to see how it could have taken four days to get there, even over the worst kind of mountainous terrain. Just eyeballing it, it looked like about a two-day trip—three at most.

There are times when I lose all faith in Charlie's route. Lots of times. Every time we enter a new segment of it, in fact. There has not been any leg of the route that has not at one time or another looked to me as if it were not working and as if its problems were insurmountable. Many times I have thought that if I were the one doing it, I would quit. I do not know how Charlie began to know that he could figure out De Soto's route. It is not just that he believes that he can, he *knows* he can. He did not know it at first. It was only as he and Chester and Marvin worked together in the beginning on the Pardo route and began to feel confident of their solution that he realized that De Soto, too, might yield. But even after they had been working on Pardo for two years, there came a day when he reread a part of one of the Pardo documents and thought he had found something that undermined their entire reconstruction of the route. It was awful. He lost all faith in it. We went out that night and had dinner at an Italian restaurant, and he got drunk. He does not usually do that, not really drunk, but he did that night. The next day he got up and tried starting over from scratch, taking Pardo the only other way he conceivably could have gone, the way everyone else had always tried to take him—up the Savannah River instead of the Wateree. But that simply did not work at all. Instead of one inconsistency, he had dozens. So by the end of the day he had Pardo back on the route where he and Chester and Marvin had put him before. And because his loss of faith had been so total, and because he had tried so wholeheartedly to take the route another way and had seen how many problems the wrong solution presents, he ever after had a much firmer belief that these routes can actually be reconstructed. Not all can be retraced equally well. He does not think Luna can be nailed down as precisely as Pardo and De Soto because there is not enough of the right kind of information available in the Luna documents. But he knows they have solved the Pardo route, and he knows they can solve De Soto. He knows because he has been working on it for five years and understands the parameters. He knows there are geographical and archaeological constraints. He learns the geographical ones from the maps and from driving around and looking. He learns the archaeological ones from the literature and even more from talking to those archaeologists who know most about their regions. In archaeology there is so much that has never been written up. Archaeologists have it in their heads and in their site files.

Charlie knows there is only one route that will work from beginning to end. There might be segments that are vague—like whether Tula is on the Fourche or the Petit Jean—but that is not a large area in which to be off the mark. Quipana works in the Ouachita valley no matter which Tula we use. And we do know now that Quipana does work there. Charlie found the solution today while we were staring at the maps and I was thinking we would never figure out Arkansas and that if it took them four days to get to Quipana, maybe Quipana was over in eastern Oklahoma. I suggested that.

"The narratives say it's southeast of Tula," Charlie answered sullenly. It wears him out to have me always challenging him, but I cannot accept a part of the route just because he says it is where it is. My mind insists on asking any question, voicing any doubt that comes to it.

I did not see then how it was all going to work. Tula and Quipana were too close together. Charlie could see that, too, and yet he knew they had to be where they were; the archaeology and all the itinerary and geography up until now said it had to be true. I stopped looking at the map. I was tired and wanted to quit for the day.

"How *would* they have gotten through those mountains?" asked Charlie, narrowing in on the rugged range that separates the Fourche valley from the Ouachita valley. He started tracing the roads with his finger, following them through the contour lines on the map. All the short roads were too high and steep. Then he found a longer one. It followed a low passage all the way through, along the valley of a stream.

"That's the way I drive through those mountains to go to Arkadelphia," said Mike Hoffman.

We got the quad sheet for that area and studied it in more detail. A nice narrow passage running lengthwise through the mountains instead of going straight across, which was up and over. And to get to this passage the Spaniards would have had to go a day or more to the west, then cut back to the east as they picked up the pass. It looked like about a four-day trip from Tula.

The pass came out through some steep mountains into the Ouachita valley. Quipana was said to be at the base of steep mountains. But we had been told that the concentration of sites in that area was under Lake Ouachita, which is a few miles downriver from the mouth of the pass.

"Could there be any late sites up here close to the mountains?" Charlie asked.

Mike consulted the files and found a late Caddoan site right where we needed it. The first town of Quipana. The day after visiting that town, they left the mountains, according to Ranjel. Charlie had earlier interpreted that to mean they left Quipana, but now he could see that it simply meant that they moved out from the mountains they had been coming through for four days and entered the wide Ouachita valley.

Everything is looking good. I have regained my belief that we will solve the route in Arkansas. This is the De Soto state. Those Spaniards went everywhere in Arkansas except up here into the Ozarks around Fayetteville, though back to the east they did prod into the Ozarks at Batesville.

At three-thirty Charlie gave his De Soto route lecture to the anthropologists on campus. It was well attended and the question-and-answer period ran on for forty minutes—stretching out the entire session to nearly two hours. He winds himself up for these performances and gives it all he has, delivering the material with a contagious enthusiasm.

Afterward we had dinner at Hester's house with several other people, two of whom work for the Arkansas Archaeological Survey. This is a nice group in Fayetteville. They are close, more connected than professional colleagues usually are. I think this is more true of the Survey than of the anthropology department itself, and I think it is true of the Survey statewide. George Sabo, who was one of the dinner guests, is the Survey archaeologist for the Fayetteville region. Dan is the one for the Jonesboro region. Tomorrow we go back east to Pine Bluff to meet with John House, who has the station for the southeastern part of the state. Then back west on Friday to Arkadelphia to talk to Ann Early, who handles the south central region. Hester is the assistant director of the whole business. I am starting to have great admiration for Arkansas archaeology. They are underfunded and have very much work to do and face terrible odds against pot hunters. But they are trying hard with what they have to preserve as much of the archaeological heritage of the state as they can manage to do. Arkansans of the future will sing their praises.

CHAPTER EIGHT

Hot Springs Hotels

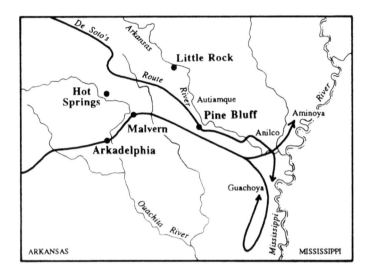

The Governor, conscious that the hour approached in which he should depart this life, commanded that all the King's officers should be called before him, the captains and the principal personages, to whom he made a speech. He said that he was about to go into the presence of God, to give account of all his past life; and since He had been pleased to take him away at such a time, he, His most unworthy servant, rendered Him hearty thanks. He confessed his deep obligations to them all. . . . He begged that they would pray for him, that through mercy he might be pardoned his sins, and his soul received in glory. . . . He asked that they would be pleased to elect a principal and able person to be governor, one with whom they should all be satisfied . . . : that this would greatly satisfy him and moderate the anxiety of leaving them in a country, they knew not where.

Baltasar de Gallegos responded in behalf of all, consoling him with remarks on the shortness of the life of this world, attended as it was by so many toils and afflictions, saying that whom God earliest called away, He showed particular favor; with many other things appropriate to such an occasion; . . . that as respected the election of a governor, . . . whomsoever his Excellency should name to command, him they would obey. Thereupon the Governor nominated Luys Moscoso de Alvarado. . . .

The next day, the twenty-first of May, departed this life the magnanimous, the virtuous, the intrepid Captain, Don Hernando de Soto, Governor of Cuba and Adelantado of Florida. He was advanced by fortune, in the way she is wont to lead others, that he might fall the greater depth: he died in a land, and at a time, that could afford him little comfort in his illness, when the danger of being no more heard from stared his companions in the face, each one himself having need of sympathy, which was the cause why they neither gave him their companionship nor visited him, as otherwise they would have done.

—*A Gentleman of Elvas*

Pine Bluff, Arkansas
Tuesday, December 11

Leaving Fayetteville at eight o'clock this morning, we drove down from the mountains and picked up Interstate 40 to go back east to Pine Bluff to meet with John House. We are cutting back and forth now to different parts of the De Soto route. Our drive today was not on the route, though we did backtrack over the area from Russellville to Conway that we had driven through before on other roads. That was the land of Cayas, the Carden Bottoms archaeological phase. One puzzle about Carden Bottoms is that it has Caddoan pots in it, though they are very much in the minority. That is the kind of pottery the people of Tula made, and it implies some kind of exchange between the two groups. There are, on the other hand, no Mississippian ceramics, which would include Carden Bottoms, found at Caddoan sites. This is a one-way exchange that might be interpreted as Carden Bottoms stealing women from the Caddos, since women are usually the ones who make the pottery. But the people of Cayas told De Soto that Tula was their enemy, that they had no dealings with them, and that there was no one in Cayas who could speak their language. That does not sound like they had any Caddoan women living among them. And it certainly rules out trade between the two groups. So where did the Caddoan pots come from? It has me worried. If it cannot be explained, then it raises a question about the identification of Carden Bottoms with Cayas. Everything else, though, seems to fit.

The land of Cayas extends along the Arkansas River almost to Little Rock. Around Little Rock and below are the people of Autiamque. De Soto came to Autiamque from the southwest on his way back east from Tula. We will deal with the Tula-to-Autiamque part of the route when we meet with Ann Early. Autiamque itself is in John House's territory, as is everything on down the Arkansas to the Mississippi and also most of the provinces along the Mississippi.

We did not stop to look at the land of Autiamque. We will do that later. We turned south on U.S. 65 and went straight to Pine Bluff, trying to get there before the afternoon was gone. The trip from Fayetteville took more than five hours. Charlie spent most of that time writing letters to David Dye and Gerald Smith, Dan Morse, and Mike Hoffman to recapitulate the progress he had made with them on the route and to set forth the remaining questions. He also entered the new findings into his written version of this segment of the route. He worked very well, and this will keep us from having to take out an entire day for that tomorrow.

Little Rock is on a bluff at the edge of the flat Arkansas lowlands, which stretch out to the east for more than a hundred miles to the Mississippi. Pine Bluff is similarly located, about forty miles to the south. The road to it is through pine woods, no farms to speak of. We arrived there in good time, made our connection with John House, and put in a full afternoon of work with him on De Soto. So full, I am too tired to write about it tonight. It will have to wait until tomorrow.

Hot Springs, Arkansas
Thursday, December 13

Thank God De Soto's army came to Hot Springs—or near it, anyway. We were exhausted when we pulled in here yesterday; we haven't had a day off since Thanksgiving. We checked into the fine old Arlington Hotel for two nights. Today is for resting and catching up. This is a perfect place to do it. De Soto would have loved the Arlington Hotel.

We had a wonderful day and a half with John House in Pine Bluff. We got there about two o'clock Tuesday afternoon and found his office and lab on the campus of the local branch of the University of Arkansas. It used to be a black teachers' college and the enrollment is still predominantly black, though there is a white enrollment of about 20 percent.

John House is white. Hester had told us a little about his background—that he was from the Ozarks, not far from Fayetteville; that he had participated in his first dig with Arkansas archaeologists when he was fourteen; that he had studied archaeology at Fayetteville in the late 1960s, had been an antiwar activist, and had refused to take the required five hours of ROTC. He was the first person in Arkansas to take that stand. He turned away from academia for a few years but then came back and was awarded his A.B. degree, the ROTC requirement having been dropped. He has worked in archaeology ever since and is held in high esteem by his colleagues, though he has not been to graduate school at all. His Arkansas colleagues consider him to be as professional as if he had his doctorate, but without the degree he cannot command the salary he deserves. Thus, at their urging, he is planning to go to graduate school next fall. He will return to his job with the Survey when he is finished. Hearing all this about him, I thought I would probably like him. When I met him, I knew I would. He looked like his story—beard, wire-rimmed glasses, work shirt, and blue jeans.

We spent several hours with the maps. De Soto did a lot of coming and going through John's territory. First, before De Soto left the Mississippi River, while still on that leg of the journey we had investigated with Dan and Phyllis, he had come south of Casqui (Parkin phase) to Quiguate (Kent phase). John's most recent work has been with Kent. Then De Soto left the Mississippi and John's territory and went northwest to Coligua, and then southwest to Cayas and Tula. From Tula he came back east through Quipana, in the Ouachita valley, to Autiamque, which was on the Arkansas River just below Little Rock. Now they were back in John's territory. They spent the winter in Autiamque—their third winter—and in the spring they went down the Arkansas valley, passing through several towns and coming to the great town of Anilco at the mouth of the river. Below the mouth of the Arkansas, on the banks of the Mississippi, was the chiefdom of Guachoya, who was an enemy of Anilco. After spending some time at Anilco, De Soto went to Guachoya, and to impress the people there with his military might, he took some of the Guachoya warriors back with him to Anilco, where he slaughtered a great many people. This was shocking even to the chroniclers. The strain of the failing expedition was making De Soto desperate—perhaps even somewhat demented.

From Guachoya he sent a party of cavalry to the south to find out about the sea. He had it in mind to build boats which he would send to Cuba and Mexico to let it be known he was still alive and to bring back supplies. But the horsemen became discouraged by the delta swamps. In several days of effort they were able to cover only fourteen leagues. They were told by the local people that there were no large populations down that way, except for the chiefdom of Quigualtam on the opposite side of the river.

At this point De Soto seems to have despaired. He had tried going north and west and had run out of dense native populations. Nor were there any large societies to the south except more river chiefdoms like the ones he had already found. There were not going to be any Aztecs or Incas in La Florida. His expedition was a failure, and that was more than he could bear. He fell ill and took to his bed. The chroniclers speak of his despondency. As his condition worsened, his captains came to bid him farewell, and within a few weeks he was dead. His men put his body into the Mississippi River to keep the Indians from digging it up and desecrating it.

His lieutenant, Luis de Moscoso, assumed command and decided that the army would try to get back to Mexico by going overland. This is what took them past Hot Springs. They got well into Texas but finally ran out of any native population at all except some very poor hunters and gatherers. They gave up and came back once more to the Mississippi—first to Anilco, the town where the slaughter had taken place. Not surprisingly, the people of Anilco were in disarray and had not planted corn for that year. So the Spaniards went to another province, Aminoya, slogging through terrible swamp to get there. Aminoya was on the banks of the Mississippi, upriver from the mouth of the Arkansas. They stayed there through the fourth and final winter and on into the following summer while they built six brigantines to carry them down the river and around the Gulf Coast to Mexico. During that last winter, there was a great flood of the Mississippi River, and as the water rose they had to build rafts to save themselves. All the land was inundated, they said, except Anilco, which was now an island.

We went over all of this with John House. When John heard Charlie say that Anilco was above flood level, his face lit up. The site that Charlie thought was Anilco, and that John had agreed was a good candidate, is on a piece of high land that never floods. The French built their first colonial town there—the Arkansas Post. As an island in the flood, it would have been a very large one, John said. Ten miles long. Charlie said that was all right. Anilco was said to be the most populous town in all of La Florida. It would have been a large place.

John felt that Charlie's route from Little Rock down the Arkansas was reasonable archaeologically. There is definitely sixteenth-century population all along the river. There are some known sites that might key in with De Soto's towns, but John was reluctant to push that sort of thing too far. Not enough surveying has been done to make definitive statements about the sixteenth-century archaeological picture. There is a lack of chronological control in the Arkansas valley. Most of the late sites are lumped together under the Quapaw phase without regard for whether they date to the sixteenth, seventeenth, or eighteenth century.

When the French were here in the seventeenth and eighteenth centuries, there were Quapaw people living on the Arkansas. They were Siouan-speaking. Archaeologists have assumed that earlier generations of these same Quapaw people lived on the Arkansas in protohistoric times. John House is not so sure. It looks very similar to the situation on the Little Tennessee River, where most archaeologists assumed that the Dallas-phase people of prehistoric times were the ancestors of the Overhill Cherokees who lived there in historic times, when in fact they were the ancestors of the Creeks.

John House says that he likes Charlie's route very much and that it is making him think about his archaeological territory in a new way. He had never considered the possibility that all these chiefdoms De Soto encountered were on the lower Arkansas River. The old U.S. De Soto Commission route had placed them on the lower Ouachita, down in Louisiana. That interpretation had always puzzled him, however, since there are not the populous societies down there that there are further north, and Anilco, after all, was said to be the most populous chiefdom encountered on the whole expedition. To him it makes much more sense that the army would have returned to his part of the Mississippi Valley.

It is here, where Charlie uses the Arkansas for the River of Cayas and Swanton uses the Ouachita, that Charlie's route makes one of its largest divergences from the old U.S. De Soto Commission route. The other place was back east in that loop that goes through South Carolina, North Carolina, and Tennessee. For the rest of the route, Charlie's route and the old route cover roughly the same territory, although, except for the Florida portion, the old route has all the chiefdoms in the wrong places, out of sync. Here on the western side of the Mississippi, there are only two choices for the River of Cayas, only two major rivers flowing into the Mississippi from the interior. Elvas says specifically—and more than once—that both Autiamque and Anilco are on the River of Cayas. And of course, Cayas is on that river, too. Swanton puts both Cayas and Tula in the Ouachita Mountains, using the Ouachita for his River of Cayas. He puts Cayas around Hot Springs because of that reference to a warm, brackish swamp—the one from which the horses drank and got swollen bellies—the one Charlie places in Walter and Marcellus Cunningham's neighborhood. De Soto was in Cayas in September. The Arkansas River valley is the hottest place in Arkansas. Any still, shallow water would be warm.

If Cayas had been at Hot Springs, it would have been deep in Caddoan country, according to the archaeology. And Swanton's Tula is also in Caddoan country. Yet we know there was a dramatic break in language between Cayas and Tula. This means they cannot have been in the same archaeological province. But if Cayas is on the Arkansas, as Charlie believes, then this fits the great archaeological and linguistic division between the Mississippian and the Caddoan peoples. And, as John House pointed out, it also fits the archaeological picture at the mouth of the river, where De Soto encountered such dense populations.

So it works. When John told us that Charlie's Anilco site never floods, it gave me a rush. I felt for the first time that the route is just about sewn up. I have made this entire trip with the constantly recurring dread that some nasty fact is going to raise its head and invalidate everything we have done. But in that moment I got a glimmer that we might be home free. Of course, right after that we ran into difficulties with the locations of Guachoya, the place where De Soto died, and Aminoya, the place where the army spent the last winter and built their boats. Ever the skeptic, my doubts surged up again. It was only by studying the map and seeing the ridiculousness of the Ouachita River alternative that I calmed down again. The River of Cayas has to be the Arkansas. That means Aminoya and Guachoya were somewhere near the mouth of it. But both were on the Mississippi, and it is possible that the towns closest to the river, the ones in which the Spaniards stayed, have been washed away by the shifting channel. We can only make approximate statements about them.

There is still one more chance for us to be undone, and that is in regard to the travel time down the river from the mouth of the Arkansas to the Gulf of Mexico. Charlie's route has them going twice as far as Swanton's route did. We have to look into this. We hope to stop by Vicksburg on the way home and talk to Roger Saucier, who works for the Army Corps of Engineers and is *the* man in reconstructing past conditions of the river.

Yesterday we went out with John House to drive the route down along the Arkansas River to Anilco—the great town that never flooded, the one where the slaughter took place—and to Guachoya. We went in a pickup truck belonging to the Survey, John driving. The sky was overcast with such heavy clouds that they threatened to open up at any minute. It had rained a little in the night. The air was warm and stormy-feeling.

During the hour's drive from Pine Bluff to Anilco, we talked pleasantly with John. He liked the idea of the lower course of the Arkansas being peopled with separate political entities instead of one big homogenous group of so-called Quapaws. He talked about the work that needs to be done to develop a chronology for the sites so that phases can be differentiated and named. We chewed over the possibility that these distinct polities may have had an umbrella, tribute-collecting chief over them, though the chroniclers did not mention this.

Soon after leaving Pine Bluff, we were out of the pine woods and into the delta again. Flat land, big farms. John kept commenting on how much cotton had been planted this year, much more than in recent years. In the last decade or so, soybeans began to take the place of most of the cotton. But this year there is cotton everywhere. We passed gin after gin with big, wire-mesh trailers of picked cotton lined up waiting to be ginned, the gins running, lint spewing into the air and coating the nearby trees like snow. It seemed that a person could get brown lung disease, the affliction of cotton mill workers, just by living near one of these gins.

"The health of people in the delta must be a real problem," I said.

John agreed. He said he would not live in the delta. The pesticides they have been pouring on that land are like a time bomb. Already the cancer rates for the counties in the delta are higher than anywhere else in Arkansas.

We also passed acres of rice fields. Each field had a pump for bringing up underground water to flood it.

"What is that doing to the water table?" I asked John.

"Taking it down, down, down," he said.

It seemed to me unwise to grow rice under those conditions. He agreed but said the farmers have little choice. They have huge payments to make on their land, and if they fail to make them, they lose their farms. They think only a year or two in advance. They cannot afford to look at the future and at what they are doing to the land. Someday, though, they will have to look.

The site that we think was Anilco is an unusually well preserved site for this part of the country. This is because the person who owns it realizes its importance and has made a determined effort to keep the pot hunters out. There is a huge mound on the site, about thirty-five feet high, with trees growing on it. We climbed to the top of it, a steep climb. It is always an experience to stand on top of an Indian mound.

There is nothing else that gives such a feeling of having entered the aboriginal Native American world. Up on that high place that they built,
looking down as their chief men and priests would have looked down,
one can imagine the village and the fields below. We could see through
the woods to the old channel of the river, now a bayou. The trees on the
mound were large, with an old cedar on the highest part. There were
birds everywhere. Just as I was thinking how beautiful it all was, Charlie
recalled De Soto coming up with the warriors from Guachoya and sack-
ing the place, slaughtering men, women, and children. God. That was
just as vivid from that mound as the peaceful village and cornfields had
been a few minutes before. What a nightmare that expedition was for
the native peoples of the South. It was the beginning of the end of all
this, the end of the chiefdoms. Within a few decades no more mounds
were being built—anywhere.

We climbed down from the mound and walked a short distance up a
little wooded road to one edge of the site. It is deer-hunting season and
we felt a bit wary, since this is an area where deer hunters come. Though
if there had been any around, they probably would have been farther
back in the woods. There were, however, fresh deer tracks right there in
the road where we were walking. None of us had on anything red. My
white shirt was our best hope for being recognized as humans, though
I kept thinking about that white flash of a deer's tail as it bounds away
through the woods.

As we were walking along, we suddenly heard John curse under his
breath. Looking around to see what the trouble was, we saw him poking
with his foot at a little spot of freshly turned earth, about a foot and a
half in diameter. Charlie and I had walked by it without noticing it.

"Pot hunters?" asked Charlie.

"That's right," said John. Then he saw another spot a little closer to
the woods. Charlie found a third one.

"How do they know where to dig?" I asked.

"They use probes," John explained. They poke into the earth, and if
they feel something that might be a pot, they dig down to see. If you
find pieces of human bone in the turned-up earth they leave behind,
you know they found a grave and probably a pot. Most whole pots in
the ground were buried there by the Indians in the graves of their loved
ones. John said it had been a long time since he had seen a pot hunter's
hole on this site. The people who watch over the place do a good job.

They do let deer hunters in, though, and this person obviously passed himself off as one and probably even did some hunting while he was back here. The holes had been dug since the last rain, some time in the past week.

Having seen about all there was to see of the site, we got into the truck and headed out.

"Think of the incentive for those pot hunters," I said. "Here a fellow comes hunting deer. Is he going to be satisfied bringing home a deer, or is he going to take a few minutes with a probe and a shovel and maybe take home a prehistoric pot he can sell for five hundred dollars?"

John said it is for that reason that he does not harbor personal animosity toward pot hunters any more than he does toward farmers who land-level and deep-plow the fields with the sites in them. There is an impersonal economic force at work there. He reserves his contempt and condemnation for the wealthy people who collect the pots, who pay the huge sums to the pot hunters, calling themselves art connoisseurs and sponsoring exhibits of private collections, as if they were doing society a service instead of being the ones primarily responsible for the wholesale destruction of our archaeological heritage. They often fancy themselves experts in Indian history, said John, and come to scholarly meetings. They are bold and confident and full of hair-brained answers to questions archaeologists know cannot yet be answered because there has not been enough data collected. And if these wealthy collectors keep on fostering the destruction of sites, there will be many questions that will never be answered.

We stopped by the modest farmhouse of the people who watch over the site, and Charlie and I waited while John went to the door and told them of the pot hunter's holes. He knows they cannot keep everybody out, but he wants them to try their best.

Leaving the Anilco area, we drove farther south to look at the area we think might be Guachoya. This is below the mouth of the Arkansas on a network of bayous a mile or two west of the Mississippi. There is a concentration here of small sites on the high land around the bayous. Charlie is not sure that Guachoya would have been a place of small scattered sites—it seemed to have been a larger, more nucleated chiefdom than that. But it could be that there were some larger towns along the river that have now been washed away.

Since we were so close to the river, John drove on over to take a look at it. There was a road that went over the levee to a large grain-storage facility on the riverbank, where grain is loaded onto barges. We parked a little to one side of the granary on a paved area at the edge of the river. After getting out of the truck, we stood there for a while and watched the water. The sky was still overcast, but it had not yet rained. The river rolled along with amazing swiftness. There was a barge going by. It was somewhere around here that De Soto died. His men took his body out in a boat at night, secretly so the Indians would not know, and dumped it, weighted with sand, into the river—where, we presume, the catfish ate it. It was hard to feel sorry about it.

We got into the truck and headed back to Pine Bluff, more than an hour away. We were tired, but we still talked a little. I like John House. He is young and full of enthusiasm for the work there is to be done in Arkansas. He is a very clear thinker. He understands what needs to be done and in what order. The big sites like Anilco and Parkin do not have to be excavated right now, he says. So long as we preserve them, we can wait a hundred years to dig them. What we need to work on now are the smaller sites before they have all been destroyed by farmers and pot hunters. The archaeological record is being obliterated at an astounding rate, he says—especially here in the Mississippi Valley.

We got back to Pine Bluff about four in the afternoon, said goodbye to John, and set out west to Hot Springs. We were very tired. We had spent the previous night in a motel close by a busy street in which the noise of stop-and-go truck traffic continued all night long. It was an inexpensive motel in which a lot of truckers were staying. The fellow in the room next to ours left his television on until two in the morning. At five the truckers began to leave. They started up their trucks in the parking lot and let them warm up for ten or fifteen minutes before they pulled out. It was hot in our room and we had had to open a window, which made the noise even worse. All in all, we got very little sleep. In addition to that, we were cumulatively weary from so many consecutive days of hard work on the road.

So we were looking forward to Hot Springs as a place to take a break, though we knew nothing at all about it except that it was an old resort town. I told Charlie I wanted to stay in a hotel, not a motel. I wanted a comfortable place to rest.

We stopped at a service station in town and a helpful station attendant recommended the Arlington Hotel.

"It's in the bath-house district," he said.

We only vaguely knew that there *was* a bath-house district. But we followed his directions and drove there. It had gotten dark. We were tired and buzzed out by the lights and the traffic. As we neared Bath House Row a huge building suddenly loomed up in front of us, like a great castle on a mountainside. It was all decked out in Christmas lights. We were astounded.

"What the hell is that?" we muttered. I was afraid it was the Arlington Hotel. It looked like more than we could handle.

Whatever it was, it was not as directly in our path as it had seemed. The street curved and carried us on past it, and also past the bath houses. They were quite a sight, opulent health spas from the early twentieth century standing shoulder to shoulder in what was once a genteel competition for patrons. Strangely enough, they are now part of a national park. And even more strangely, some of them are still in use as bath houses.

At the end of Bath House Row was the Arlington, another great, looming building, though not quite as formidable as the first one had been. But it was intimidating enough, given how stupefyingly weary we were. Charlie, especially, seemed to numb over in the face of it. We did not pull up to the front door. We parked in the street and sat there for a few moments, asking ourselves if we were up to this. I was more game than Charlie was.

"Let's go find out how much it costs," he said. He could envision us dropping a fortune in this place. We went around to the front steps, which were high and wide like the entrance to a palace. The lobby was huge, full of cushioned chairs, a bar on one side and bold, flowery jungle murals on the walls—very chic. Charlie had that distant look in his eyes that he gets when he ceases to function. He had gone on automatic.

"Let's sit down," I said to him. "We need to collect ourselves." So we sat for a minute. Then I went to the desk to inquire about rates. Forty-four dollars. That horrible motel the night before had cost us thirty-one. I reported back to Charlie and we decided to take a room for two nights. I was glad. I was already starting to sink into the comfort of the place. Charlie himself was coming back into focus now, and he handled the registration. We went out to park the car properly and to get our bags. As we came back up the front steps, more relaxed now, he told me what it was that had overwhelmed him. This hotel is a relic of the opulence of the era he grew up in and never was a part of, he a country boy in Kentucky during the Depression years. He had no trouble with a modern hotel in any big city, but this old-time, secluded world of the rich intimidated him. He freely admitted it. And laughed at it. But laughing did not make it go away entirely.

There was more to come. We rested in our room for a few minutes and then went down to eat in the hotel dining room. It was almost empty and had that hushed air that you find in these places. Waiters giving you a little more service than you need. We were doing all right until the strolling musicians came into the room. One man playing a violin, another a guitar. Frank Sinatra–era music. They stopped at the table next to us, and the couple there continued eating uncomfortably while the musicians played at their elbows. We knew they would be coming to us next. And they would ask us what we wanted to hear.

"You'll have to handle this," Charlie muttered.

So I did. I smiled and asked them to choose something for us. They played and I resumed eating my salad. Then I noticed that Charlie was not eating. He had put down his fork and was giving them respectful attention. I thought that was very decent of him and did the same. The musicians warmed to us and I actually found myself enjoying it.

"I sort of got into that," I said to Charlie after they left.

"Not me," he said. "Did you see how stiff I was?"

"But you were charming," I answered.

"That wasn't charm. That was me fighting the urge to get up and leave."

We started laughing. The night before we had been sandwiched between truckers in a crummy motel. And now this luxury that was almost too much for us to handle.

We had a good night's sleep in a comfortable king-size bed, and this morning we woke up happy to be in the Arlington. After a relaxed breakfast, we went out to look at the bath houses and the hot springs. It is truly amazing to see steam rising from a spring and to put your hand in and feel water that is almost too hot to touch. De Soto is all over this place. There is a big boulder in the park called De Soto Rock, and a plaque that says De Soto came here to visit the town of Tanico (which was a town in the province of Cayas). That was what the De Soto Commission said in 1939. The hotel next to the Arlington is the De Soto Hotel. At the visitors' center of the park one can learn all about how the people of Tanico supposedly hosted De Soto by taking him to the hot springs to bathe. And on the outside of a building in downtown

Hot Springs is a mural of De Soto being greeted by the native inhabitants upon his arrival here. A very tidy event in American history, it would seem.

Hot Springs will get to keep De Soto, or at least the De Soto expedition. De Soto himself never made it this far. Luis de Moscoso was in charge when the army passed this way on its attempt to go overland to Mexico. Ranjel's narrative for this period of the expedition is no longer extant, but a summary of his lost text has survived, a few scanty notes. In this there is a mention of hot streams. This comes much later in the expedition than the warm, brackish pond in Cayas that Swanton tried to say was Hot Springs. There is only one place where they could have found the hot streams referred to by Ranjel, and that is right here.

It is a good thing we have this as a firm location on this western part of the route. This entire segment is going to be hard to handle, especially Texas. Charlie made some phone calls tonight to try to find somebody there we can talk to. It looks as if less archaeology is known for eastern Texas than for any place we have been yet. We are going to Arkadelphia tomorrow to see Ann Early. We hope she can help us get a handle on Caddo archaeology.

CHAPTER NINE

Oklahoma Plains

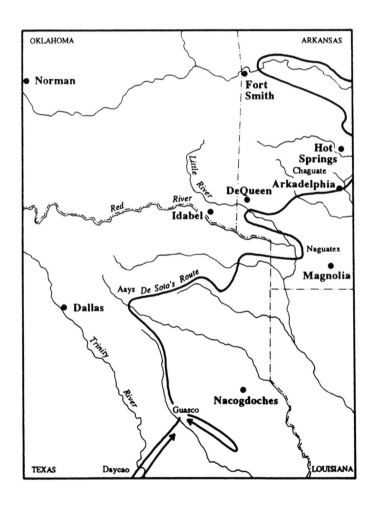

We took another guide, who led us to a Province called Hais {or Aays}, where in seasons, some cattle are wont to herd. . . .

We went from this place and came to the province of Xacatin, which was among some close forests, and was scant of food. Hence the Indians guided us eastward to other small towns, poorly off for food, having said that they would take us where there were other Christians like us, which afterwards proved false. . . . We turned to go southward, with the resolution of either reaching New Spain, or dying. We travelled about six days in a direction south and southwest, when we stopped.

Thence we sent ten men, on swift horses, to travel in eight or nine days as far as possible, and see if any town could be found where we might re-supply ourselves with maize, to enable us to pursue our journey. They went as far as they could go, and came upon some poor people without houses, having wretched huts, into which they withdrew; and they neither planted nor gathered anything, but lived entirely upon flesh and fish. Three or four of them, whose tongue no one we could find understood, were brought back. Reflecting that we had lost our interpreter, that we found nothing to eat, that the maize we brought upon our backs was failing, and it seemed impossible that so many people should be able to cross a country so poor, we determined to return to the town where the Governor Soto died, as it appeared to us there was convenience for building vessels with which we might leave the country.

We returned by the same road we had taken.

—Luys Hernandez de Biedma

Magnolia, Arkansas
Friday, December 14

We left Hot Springs this morning for Arkadelphia, which is to the south, although we began by going north. Charlie wanted to take a look at the route from Quipana to Autiamque. This was a time in the expedition before De Soto died, when the army was heading back to the Mississippi River from Tula. We think Quipana was on the Ouachita River under present-day Lake Ouachita, which is north of Hot Springs. Autiamque, where the army spent the third winter, was just south of Little Rock. We needed to get the army from Quipana to Autiamque without going through Hot Springs, since the chroniclers do not mention the springs at this time. So we investigated possible routes from Lake Ouachita to Benton, which would have taken them north of Hot Springs. No road goes exactly where we think a reasonable trail would have been—down the Saline River—but we could see that the country in general was not too rugged for the trail to have passed through it. We drove through a little town named Kentucky.

At Benton we turned south to Arkadelphia, leaving De Soto to go on to Autiamque without us. At Malvern, about twenty miles south of Benton, we picked up the expedition again as it headed southwest under Moscoso's command, aiming now for Mexico. From Guachoya, where De Soto died, the Spaniards had come up along the Arkansas River to Pine Bluff through settled country, which fits archaeologically, and then across an unpopulated wilderness to Malvern. Even today that area is a barren pine woods.

Now the army entered the land of Chaguate, which Charlie believes runs along the Ouachita River from Malvern to Arkadelphia, roughly. There is a concentration of protohistoric Caddoan sites in this area. In Chaguate the Spaniards found a spring from which the local people were extracting salt. There are prehistoric and historic salt works all around Arkadelphia. This is Ann Early's territory. She is the one who brought this possibility for Chaguate to Charlie's attention. She also suggested Lake Ouachita for Quipana.

Ann is the Survey station archaeologist for this area and has her office and lab on the campus of Henderson State University. She has the most pleasant setup of any station archaeologist we have visited so far. She is in a large white Victorian house, the former home of a wealthy Arkadelphia family. There is a small museum in the front of the house and lab and offices in the back. A fat tomcat lies around on the tables and likes to be petted. We had heard good things about Ann Early, and she did not disappoint us. She is a well-established archaeologist in the middle of a respected career. She is bright and enthusiastic and precise in her judgments. We badly needed her help to get us going on the Caddos, and she was patient in explaining what must have seemed to her some very rudimentary points. I am sure that when we first come into an area, the scholars with whom we talk must think us woefully ignorant, which we are, actually. But the problems with the route help us to organize information fairly quickly, and I do not think it takes us very long to start asking intelligent questions.

We had been told that Ann would know more than anyone about the Fourche and the Petit Jean. She said she knew practically nothing. Which means no one knows. Charlie favors the Fourche as the location of Tula, and she thought that was a reasonable hypothesis. We asked her if she knew about buffalo in that area. The Tula were evidently buffalo hunters, though perhaps not on a large scale. She said there were buffalo around Fort Smith, several days west of our proposed Tula, but she knows of no evidence of buffalo in the Ouachita Mountains. It seems reasonable to us that small numbers of buffalo would have wandered up the river valleys. We are going to pursue this question further as we go along.

Ann says she likes the idea of Tula being the first Caddos the Spaniards encountered, because Garcilaso in his chronicle mentions the body tattoos of the people of Tula. The Caddos historically were remarkable for the degree to which they tattooed themselves. Every European frontiersman who later encountered them and wrote about the experience mentioned the tattooing.

We talked about the problem of the Caddoan pots that are found in Carden Bottoms phase, which was Cayas. Cayas and Tula were said to be enemies, and no one in Cayas could speak Tula's language. Yet here are these Caddoan pots that have been found on Carden Bottoms sites. They clearly imply some kind of relationship between the Carden Bottoms Mississippians and the Caddos. It may be a problem of chronology. The Caddoan pots may be a post–De Soto phenomenon. But we do not know that. What we need, said Ann, is a thorough excavation of a Carden Bottoms–phase site. Among other things.

We left the Tula problem unresolved and moved back to the final leg of the route—the attempt by the survivors to go overland to Mexico. We feel good about placing Chaguate, with its salt springs, at Arkadelphia. After talking to Ann for a while, we began to feel good about locating Naguatex on the Little and Red rivers, just above their confluence around the Oklahoma border. Naguatex was the last truly impressive chiefdom encountered by the army on the expedition. It had military might and plenty of corn. It was a large, flourishing Caddoan society. After Naguatex, as the army went on into Texas, the land became progressively more barren and the Indian societies smaller and poorer until they were no longer even agricultural but only scattered bands of hunters and gatherers.

Texas is going to be hard enough to figure out, but even here in southwestern Arkansas we have problems with the territory between Chaguate and Naguatex. We have to find a little polity called Aguacay that was three days west of Chaguate, and there needs to be some sand there from which salt can be taken, as in Cayas. A day's journey from there must be a salt lake. A day from there we need evidence of a sparsely inhabited area where the army camped in a grove between two mountains. And a day from there we must find a location for Amaye, which was a satellite polity of Naguatex. Naguatex itself was one and a half days farther on through dense population all the way.

We worked on this for quite a while, and Ann came up with a good candidate for Aguacay—a protohistoric site near Murphreesboro. There are salt sources in this general area, but she could not pin any down for us. She suggested we talk to Frank Shambach, the Survey station archaeologist at Magnolia. He also would be the one who would know the sites from Aguacay to Naguatex and might be able to help us on into Texas, at least generally. We talked about the Texas route with Ann, and she was helpful. We are beginning to get a handle on this last leg, though it is still a weak handle. We feel that after we talk to Shambach we will be on fairly firm ground.

We called Frank Shambach and arranged to see him tomorrow morning. At about four in the afternoon we left Ann and drove down here to the town of Magnolia, which is in the Arkansas coastal plain. It is lovely country, a little bit rolling and good for family farms, like the land around Tifton, the town where I grew up in southern Georgia. As soon as we drove into this country with its longleaf pines and familiar landscape, I began to feel nostalgic. It was late afternoon, that time of day when everything looks beautiful to me anyway. I was driving. Charlie was dozing. I was feeling drowsy myself and kept drifting from Arkansas to Georgia, from 1984 to 1964, from middle age to adolescence, no memories, just feelings of being back there in an earlier time, warm and safe and comfortable. It was a pleasant relief, this illusory feeling of no longer being in strange country.

We reached Magnolia just as darkness was falling and found the motel where Frank Shambach had reserved a room for us. It is a comfortable motel. Our room is on the back, away from the road. We should get a good night's sleep. Frank is to meet us here at nine o'clock tomorrow morning. We appreciate his willingness to give us his time on a Saturday.

Charlie learned from him today that he has talked to Hester since we left Fayetteville. He already knows about the changes we have made in the northern part of the Arkansas route.

DeQueen, Arkansas
Saturday, December 15

Today was the best day of the route so far. We had a wonderful session with Frank Shambach. We had met him briefly at an archaeology conference in Mississippi back in September, but I had not remembered who he was until I saw him, and then I remembered him quite well. He read a paper at that conference about a Caddoan site he excavated that seems to have been some kind of skull cemetery—great numbers of skulls with no bodies. He delivered the paper with a wonderful humor, and I was pleased this morning to see that this was the person with whom we were going to be spending part of the day. He is early middle-aged, a chunky man like Charlie—round head; thick, short neck; squinty, smiley eyes. His specialty is Caddo.

He took us to his lab at Southern Arkansas University. David Jean, a knowledgeable amateur who works with Frank, joined us. We started out by reviewing the entire Arkansas route as Charlie now has it worked out. When we got to Cayas and Tula, Frank was very pleased. He said he has been saying for some time that there was a frontier up there on the Arkansas River, a westernmost extent of Lower Mississippi Valley culture (the proper designation for all those Mississippian groups in the delta and up the Arkansas River to Cayas). The language break between Cayas in the Carden Bottoms region and Tula on the Fourche or Petit Jean was perfect. He liked it very much.

But what about the Caddoan pots in Carden Bottoms phase? I asked him. How could they be trading pottery with Tula if they were such enemies that no one among them could even speak Tula's language?

The Caddoan pots are not from Tula, Frank told us. He knows those pots very well and they are from the southern Arkansas area. The people on the Fourche and Petit Jean were affiliated with the Fort Coffee archaeological phase around Fort Smith and westward into Oklahoma. Those people spoke a Caddoan language but they were quite different from the more southern Caddoan-speaking people whose territory was centered on the Red River and extended through southern Arkansas up into the Ouachitas and through the coastal plain up to the delta, where it butted up against the Lower Mississippi Valley cultures. The dividing line in Arkansas between what we might call the Red River Caddos and the Fort Coffee Caddos is the watershed divide in the Ouachita Mountains. Red River Caddos were on the Ouachita River watershed; Fort Coffee Caddos were on the Arkansas River watershed. There would have been a difference in language, but no greater than the difference between English and German. The Fort Coffee Caddos were more like Plains Indians than Southeastern Indians. They were buffalo hunters. The people of Tula were eastern fingers of this culture. Frank felt there was no problem with there being enmity and no communication between Tula and Cayas. Those Caddoan pots were coming up the Arkansas River, not down it. The people of Cayas were probably trading with other Lower Mississippi Valley people who themselves were trading with Caddos from southwestern Arkansas.

At this point I was starting to get very excited. Arkansas, this great morass of archaeological sites and meandering rivers and crisscrossing De Soto routes, was falling into place. I remembered how I had stood over the maps in Dan Morse's lab with this huge mess swimming in my head thinking, "We will *never* figure this out." But we have done it with the help of all these people. Tula was the one problem that was really bothering me. I felt that we did not have it in the right place because of those Caddoan pots in the Carden Bottoms phase. But now we understand Tula, at least broadly. Those Fort Coffee people later became known as the Wichitas.

Frank liked Quipana being in the Lake Ouachita area. He liked Autiamque near Little Rock, and the Mississippi River chiefdoms in John House's territory. As Moscoso assumed command and led the army west, Frank liked the wilderness between Pine Bluff and Malvern, and the location of Chaguate around Arkadelphia. He liked the Murphreesboro area for Aguacay. West of Aguacay we need salt, and he assured us there was plenty, that we were well into the salt region by then.

And he especially liked our placing Naguatex, that last great chiefdom, in the Little River–Red River area at the corners of Arkansas, Oklahoma, and Texas. Naguatex means "salt place" in Caddoan, he told us. That fits the three-corner area perfectly. There is a large Caddoan concentration there which has never been given a phase name. The present-day town of Idabel, Oklahoma, is right in the middle of it.

Frank started telling us about the Red River Caddos. They occupy an ecological zone he calls the Trans-Mississippi South. He looked at me and smiled when he said that, because when I first met him this morning I told him that this area of Arkansas reminded me of Georgia. He had noticed the same thing, he said, when he had come here from the East. This part of Arkansas is like a piece of the old South transplanted to the west side of the river. Many people from the old South settled here, skipping over the more alien land of the lower Mississippi Valley.

These Red River Caddos, then, were the westernmost Southeastern Indians. We asked him how far west this Trans-Mississippi South ecological zone extends. He showed us a map of it that he had drawn. The area went as far west as Idabel and then a broad finger of it extended south-southwest into Texas for nearly two hundred miles.

"That's it!" I said, pointing to that finger. "That's the route into Texas!"

I was really excited now. I felt we had the route and had it all the way. We had thought we might not be able to pinpoint the actual route into Texas. The narratives were so very skimpy, and no one seemed to know the sites. But there it was, a limited zone where Indians still grew corn and had some semblance of Southeastern chiefdom organization. That had to be the way the army went.

The Spaniards said that when they got to Naguatex, the inhabitants told them that if they kept on going due west as they intended, they would come to sandy wastes where no one lived. This would be due west from Idabel, Oklahoma.

"Perfect," said Frank.

So they followed native guides south-southwest (down that last finger of the Trans-Mississippi South), going through thin populations and country that became progressively more arid and miserable.

"Perfect," said Frank.

We started trying to determine where the towns they named would have been. We were now out of Frank's area of expertise, but he certainly knew more about the possibilities than we did. We came up with some good ideas that made us hopeful about that final part of the route.

I got high as a kite in this session with Frank Shambach today. I loved seeing how much it pleased him as the route that Charlie laid out fell into place with the archaeology as Frank understands it. It fits what he knows about Caddos. It fits the land. He says he likes the general feel of it.

We finished about noon. Before we left, we walked with him from the Survey lab to his office in another building. I was struck by the apparent prosperity of the Arkansas Southern campus compared to other campuses we have visited in the state. The same is true of the town of Magnolia itself. Neither the town nor the campus is large, but both seem economically healthy. I asked Frank about the economic base of the area.

"Oil," he said.

It turns out that this part of Arkansas is the very place where oil was first discovered in the late nineteenth century. From here they went on to find it in Texas and Oklahoma. The town of El Dorado, not far from Magnolia, is the center of the initial boom, although the first well that was actually drilled was near a little town called Smackover. We asked where that name came from. Frank said it was the Arkansas pronunciation of a French placename, Chemin Couvert. Smackover.

We wondered how Frank had ended up in Magnolia, so far from New York state, where he grew up. Through Harvard, he said. Harvard has been working for decades on the archaeology of the lower Mississippi Valley. They filled the valley with their graduate students, and when there were no more jobs in the valley, the spillover spread to the uplands. So Frank became a Caddo specialist, leaving the Mississippi Valley behind. He has been in Magnolia for fifteen years, long enough to call it home. He likes it there.

We left Magnolia and drove back up to Arkadelphia to pick up the route again. The sky was blue with wispy clouds. The sun was unusually warm, the temperature well up in the seventies. I felt like dancing or singing. I kept grinning at Charlie and patting him on the shoulder. He had found the route. I knew it now. He had actually done it.

We spent the rest of the afternoon driving the route from Chaguate (Arkadelphia) to Amaye, which was a suburb of Naguatex, that last great Caddoan chiefdom the Spaniards encountered before going down into Texas. We speculate that Amaye was near Lockesburg in the southwestern corner of Arkansas. We know it was somewhere in that vicinity. On the way, we took a look at the Little Missouri River near Murphreesboro, which we think was the territory of Aguacay. One of the little towns we drove through in this area was named Delight.

We were unsure of the route from Aguacay to Amaye. The army made three stops along the way: at a small town subject to Aguacay near a "salt lake" or seep; at an uninhabited place between two mountains; and at a small town called Pato. The more we puzzled over it, the more we began to feel that the route made an arc to the north. This would best fit the travel time, and there was an old road that went that way. It was part gravel, though, and as it was getting late, we decided to stay on the paved roads. Even at that, the state highway we were following— Arkansas 26—was as poor and narrow as a backroad. The entire way from Arkadelphia had been through hills, and the hills grew rougher as we went west. We came into the town of De Queen, population forty-five hundred, by the back way. We could not find the section of town that had motels, so we stopped at a jiffy mart to ask. This is not a part of Arkansas that many people visit, and the residents of De Queen seem to lack practice at giving directions. They did manage to point us more or less toward the Palace Motel, and after a few wrong turns we found it. In the motel restaurant we saw that we were back in cowboy-hat country. Oklahoma is just a few miles away.

But before we go there, we are going to turn back into Arkansas one more time and pick up a leg of the route we have not yet managed to cover—the Tula-to-Quipana route through that long pass in the Ouachita Mountains.

McAlester, Oklahoma
Sunday, December 16

We are finally finished with Arkansas. We were there almost two weeks. We have probably seen more of that state than have many people who have lived there all their lives. If any state can claim to be the De Soto state, it is Arkansas. Two of the four years of the expedition were spent there. Until now no one has known this. The Swanton route had the Arkansas portion of the expedition divided between Arkansas and

Louisiana. But in Charlie's version Louisiana gets only the downriver exit at the very end of the expedition. Oklahoma gets a few days of the expedition in its extreme southeastern corner. I am glad it does. We have been told there is a De Soto mural at the capitol in Tulsa. It would be too bad if they had to paint over it, or whatever it is you do when history is changed out from under you.

Caddo Gap, Arkansas, is going to have to face that problem. This morning we left De Queen and took U.S. 70 northeast toward Hot Springs. A few miles from De Queen we went through the town of Dierks and checked around that part of the country for a possible location of a place where the Spaniards camped between two mountains on the second night before reaching Amaye, on the outskirts of Naguatex. From Dierks we went to Caddo Gap, following U.S. 70 northeast to Glenwood, then taking Arkansas 8 through the gap. This is one of the most famous De Soto spots in Arkansas. It is supposed to be that narrow gap through which the band of cavalry fled back to Cayas from Tula. The Swanton commission located Cayas at Hot Springs, which is about thirty miles northeast of Caddo Gap. The commission located Tula right at the gap, on the north side of it where an archaeological site is located. Therefore, naturally enough, De Soto's band of cavalry came into Tula from the northeast without needing to pass through the gap. In order to bring the gap into play, Swanton declared that when the army fled, they went south through the gap and then circled around the mountain to get back to Cayas.

Besides the fact that this is a distortion of the chronicles, the archaeology does not bear it out. There is indeed a Caddoan archaeological site at Caddo Gap, but it is only a farmstead or two, not enough to have been Tula. Furthermore, the protohistoric sites of the Hot Springs area are also Caddoan, so this does not work for the dramatic linguistic break between Cayas and Tula.

At Caddo Gap there is a large statue of an Indian with his arms raised to the heavens. There are four separate historical plaques planted around it. Two of them have to do with De Soto and Tula. According to the inscribed information, the statue was erected in 1980 to replace an old one that had deteriorated badly with time. Names are given of prominent local citizens and state officeholders who aided the refurbishment of the monument. These people are not likely to be enthusiastic about the new

De Soto route, which does not come very close to Caddo Gap. Some will probably cling to the old route as an "alternate hypothesis."

Having passed through Caddo Gap ourselves, from the south, we were now coming into Quipana territory near Lake Ouachita. Quipana was the next place De Soto went after Cayas and Tula, as he headed back east to Autiamque, near Little Rock, where the army spent the third winter. The major concentration of sites in the Quipana area is under the lake. We did not even bother to go to within sight of the lake. What we really wanted to see was the pass through the mountains from Tula to Quipana. This was the part of the route we had worked on with Mike Hoffman in Fayetteville, when we had nearly despaired because the chronicles gave it more travel time than we could make sense of, until we discovered this long passage through the mountains. We wanted to see whether the first towns of Quipana were truly at the base of steep mountains, and whether it would seem upon coming farther into Quipana that one was leaving the mountains behind. All this was related in the narratives. We would be experiencing it backward, but that was good enough.

We went first to the little present-day town of Oden near the mouth of the pass. We knew from what we had learned in Fayetteville that there was a protohistoric site nearby. Oden was at the base of steep mountains, as we had hoped. And the valley did open up from there so that you had a true sense of coming out of a narrow mountain corridor.

We drove along U.S. 270 through the pass, which follows Brushy Creek up one side of the watershed and Mill Creek down the other. The pass is not at all steep. It is comfortably wide, but there is a high wall of mountains fairly close by on each side. After twenty-three miles we came to Y City, so called because the road forks there through a further gap to the north and another to the west. We took the one to the north and came out into the valley of the Fourche la Fave River, the land of Tula. To see more of Tula, we turned off on Arkansas 28 and went east along the valley for ten or fifteen miles. It is pretty country around there, enclosed by mountains, most of the land in pasture with grazing cattle. The trees give the land a western look. There are shortleaf pines and cedars and a small, gnarly oak that keeps its leaves after they have turned brown. It seems to be the same tree we saw in the sand hills of South Carolina, where it still had its bright red autumn foliage.

When we felt we had seen enough of Tula, we turned back to U.S. 71 and went north on it a few miles to Waldron, where there are known protohistoric Caddoan sites. Charlie felt this was another contender for Tula that should be looked into, though he still favors the Fourche valley. He could see on the map that just north of Waldron there was a pass through the mountains to the Petit Jean valley. We drove through that pass to see whether it might do for the pass through which De Soto had retreated after the battle at Tula. But it was even wider than the pass at Ola, the first one we had investigated a week ago. Charlie felt that the pass at Waldron was not the one. He still holds Ola as a possibility, but he is putting his money now on the pass at Danville. We had driven through that one, too, last Sunday and had felt it could not be the one because it was so steep. We had thought it must be a recent road. But last week at the Survey office at Pine Bluff we were shown a nineteenth-century map of Arkansas that had a road following that same route through the mountains to Danville. So maybe there was an old trail that followed along the edge of the stream bed, too narrow perhaps for a modern road, which would have been cut into the mountain above the stream.

When we got to the other side of the Waldron pass, we were finished with De Soto in Arkansas. Our next task is to talk to Don Wyckoff in Norman, Oklahoma. He knows more about Caddos than anyone and is the archaeologist who has worked with the Red River Caddos around Idabel, where Charlie thinks Naguatex was. So we turned west on Arkansas 28 and drove into Oklahoma. We felt we were still in Tula country, or at least in Fort Coffee country. The vegetation stayed largely the same until we got to Heavener, Oklahoma, about fifteen miles west of the state line. Then suddenly things changed again. The pine trees dropped out almost completely, which made the country look bleaker. Now there were only cedars and those scrubby oaks and another kind of deciduous tree with fine, feathery branches whose leaves have fallen. I have no idea what kind of tree it is. I noticed it back in Arkansas, too.

We were excited to be in Oklahoma. It is the first time that I myself have ever driven into the West. We have been to the Southwest, but we flew there and did not get to feel the transition. We sang a few lines of "Oklahoma," and Charlie did his Gabby Hayes act, talking through his nose about life on the trail and calling me Roy. About twenty miles east of McAlester we saw our first cowboy—an honest-to-god cowboy sitting on a horse in a corral talking to someone who was leaning on a fence. We know he was a cowboy because he was on a horse and wore a cowboy hat, red shirt, and chaps. And of course he was in a corral on a ranch, and there were cows around that do not look like the ones back home—they have longer horns, just as they are supposed to. Charlie did not get as good a look at him as I did and disputed whether there were chaps, but we were both sure he was a cowboy. We laughed and said we should go back and take his picture. But we did not.

We began to understand the reason for cowboy hats as we drove west into the late afternoon sun. This sun is much brighter than the sun back east. It hurts to have it in your eyes. The sky was clear all day today and the weather was warm with a touch of coolness in it. It rained hard last night while we slept. We have been blessed with good weather on this trip. The only rain we have had to contend with was at Moundville, and that just for a few hours. The snowstorm at Jonesboro could have been a problem, but we were working with maps that day, and so it was not. It seems there has been a lot going well for us, all in all. I thank whatever powers that be.

Norman, Oklahoma
Monday, December 17

We are not in the South anymore. People around here do not speak southern. They do not look southern. We are told that people in eastern Oklahoma still have a bit of southern culture and speech, but this is not eastern Oklahoma. We are in the Great Plains, though only by a few miles—less than ten. The big geographic division here is between the hills and the Plains. As we came west from McAlester, the land got rough and scrubby, low hills, no more cedars, just that little scrub oak, not much cattle, a few small pastures here and there. What they do have in those hills is oil wells, though from the look of things people are not doing as well from that as they formerly did.

It was a surprise to come into the Plains. I was not expecting it. I had been told that Norman, which is a suburb of Oklahoma City, is at the edge of the Plains, but I thought it was just into the hills rather than just into the Plains. We had come over a low hill and were starting down the other side, and I was noticing that cedars were back and a few pines, and that there were pastures, and that the hills were flattening, when all of a sudden out in front of us it was really flat, and we could see far into the horizon. The Great Plains! I was thrilled. I had wanted to see the Plains. I had wanted to drive to the edge of the Southeast and beyond to the other side. I had wanted to feel the natural boundaries.

Nacogdoches, Texas
Tuesday, December 18

We have followed the Spaniards down here on their last attempt to get back to Mexico by land, and here is where they stopped—the one remaining extension of the Southeast ends here in eastern Texas. Yesterday in Norman we spent several hours with Don Wyckoff getting a better grip on the western frontier. Most of it is Caddoan. The Tula were Caddoan speakers, but of a different culture than these Caddos here in Texas. This, however, was not the case two or three hundred years before De Soto. In that earlier era all the Caddos from just west of Fort Smith south to the Red River were basically the same. That was when the famous Spiro archaeological site, near Fort Smith, was in its heyday. But the people around Spiro—the Fort Coffee Caddos—seem to have drifted off on a cultural path of their own. They stopped making the elaborately engraved pottery of the Spiro era and stuck to plainer ware. According to Wyckoff, there were environmental changes going on at the same time. A prolonged warm, dry period of several hundred years turned woodland (and farmland) into prairie, and the buffalo came into the area, reaching their peak just about the time of De Soto. The Fort Coffee Caddos turned more and more to buffalo hunting as the herds in their area increased, and by the time of De Soto they were hunting buffalo in a big way. The people of Tula whom De Soto encountered were an eastern finger of this culture stretching up the Fourche and Petit Jean along those lovely valley prairies. Perhaps all of the Fort Coffee phase was known as Tula by the people of Cayas. The Fort Coffee people were still farmers, still southerners to some extent, but they were partly westerners, too—like the people of western Arkansas and eastern Oklahoma today.

The Red River Caddos were more southern in their culture than Fort Coffee was, though they were hunting some buffalo as well as deer. Not far to the west of them were prairies where buffalo herds could be found. But the Red River Caddos were solidly hooked into the aboriginal southern culture. Much of their land looks exactly like Georgia, we discovered today as we drove around in it. The Caddos on the Red River and in southwestern Arkansas were farming on a large scale. They were making handsome engraved pots and trading them along with salt to the lower Mississippi Valley. The core of their population was on the Red River.

Don Wyckoff felt that the Little River–Red River area fit the chroniclers' description of Naguatex very well. There were plenty of late sites in the area, he said. The first river the Spaniards came to, which the local people told them was fordable at certain places at certain times, would not be inconsistent with the Little River. The second river they came to less than a day's march away and found flooded would have to be the Red, he agreed. The Spaniards were surprised to find it in flood because it had not rained in that area for a month. This has to mean that the river extended up into another weather system, again suggesting the Red, which is a very long river. And Don pointed out what seemed to me to be the clincher, and that was that water backing up from the Great Raft on the Red River would have come all the way up to this area. The Great Raft was a huge logjam, unthinkably huge, that blocked up the Red River for centuries. It was located in Louisiana and made a real mess in the drainage system behind it. It interrupted navigation and made a huge morass of swamps that caused people traveling east and west across that part of the country to make a large detour around it. Water backing up from the Great Raft fits the Spaniards' description of the situation exactly. They had to wait *eight* days for the water to go down before they could cross. Until Don suggested the Great Raft, I had had a difficult time imagining how the river could have stayed up so long, since it was summer and probably had been swollen by summer storms, which might be expected to raise the river for a day or two and then pass on by. Furthermore, the Spaniards themselves were puzzled by the phenomenon. They said they thought at first that the water was coming in from the sea, that it was a tidal river, but the local inhabitants insisted that the water always flowed from the upstream direction. And furthermore, these people could tell them nothing at all about the sea, which indicated to the Spaniards that the sea could not be close enough to be affecting the river.

We drove down to Naguatex—the Little River–Red River area—from Norman this morning. We left early, at five-thirty. We had spent the night with Emmanuel Drechsel and his wife, Haunani, friends who lived in Athens several years ago when Emmanuel (Manny) was a faculty member with Charlie at the university. He is a linguist who specializes in southeastern Indian languages. Manny is from Switzerland. Haunani is Hawaiian. She grew up on the big island of Hawaii, which is not the main island. Her grandfather was a farmer and raised taros, the starchy roots that are the traditional native staple crop.

Being with Haunani and Manny gave me a heightened sense of the lands that lie beyond the Southeast. Last night we sat around the table in their kitchen and ate real Swiss cookies, homemade for Christmas by Manny's mother and shipped halfway around the world. These are not like American cookies—not simple chocolate chip or oatmeal or sugar cookies. These have elaborate ingredients and exquisite shapes and subtle flavors that you cannot quite put your finger on. I tried to restrain myself from eating too many, imagining Manny's dismay as these two greedheads from Georgia consumed the little portion of Switzerland that had been sent to him so lovingly by his mother. But Haunani urged me on, informing me that Manny would be going home for the holidays and could get plenty more at the source. So I had another. And another. This morning Haunani sent us off with food for the road: croissant sandwiches, fresh fruit and cheese, carrot sticks, and far more of Manny's cookies than she should have given us. We sang her praises all the way to Texas.

Norman is in the center of Oklahoma, and the land of Naguatex is in the southeastern corner. It was a long drive through more of that desolate hill country. I had always heard that eastern Oklahoma is green, that it is not very much different from the South, and that the southeastern Indians who were settled there during Removal in the 1830s were not exiled into a country so terribly different from the one they had known. I will never believe that again. I can just imagine those poor people as they came west from Arkansas. Already their burden was terrible, their homes taken from them, their land left behind, so many of their number dead from the forced march. And then to see the country they were coming into, the trees thinning out and getting smaller, the dry grasslands, the stark mountains. They must have worried especially about their corn crops—how would they feed themselves in a land like this? They were southerners, and they were being pushed just beyond the edge of southern land. Eastern Oklahoma today is full of Indian place-names transplanted from the South. The Creeks and Cherokees are the elite among Oklahoma Indians, Manny told us. They are the ones most likely to be found in positions of power and wealth. On their arrival in Oklahoma the southern Indians were known as the Five Civilized Tribes, in contrast to the other groups of less acculturated Native Americans. The Indians of the Old South had been in contact with Europeans for centuries longer than some of the other native peoples to the west of them. But the perception that they were more civilized than the others may also have been due to the fact that their pre-Columbian societies had risen to such a complex level of development. Perhaps they really *were* more civilized, intrinsically, in the depths of themselves.

When we got down to the Red River, we were suddenly in the South again. This area is the same coastal plain we found around Magnolia in southern Arkansas and the same coastal plain that occurs in other southern states around the Gulf. We checked out the Little River north of Idabel and found it suitably large to be fordable only at certain times and in certain places—probably not in a rainy December like this one. There was high water everywhere we went today. From the Little River we drove south to the Red River, and I was surprised at the great flood plain of the Red—a wide meander zone, flat for miles and miles just like the Mississippi delta. The river itself is very large. And it is red. Much of the soil and rock in this part of the country is a deep brownish red— from the Triassic geological era.

Once south of the river we were in Texas. We drove south on U.S. 259 to Nacogdoches, a stretch of about 160 miles. We were trying to more or less follow the trail of the Spaniards from Naguatex to Guasco, which was the last corn-producing society they encountered. Beyond that they found nothing but poor country and populations of scattered hunters and gatherers. The Spaniards described the journey from Naguatex to Guasco as being through country that was progressively more sterile and thinly peopled—although Guasco itself was well populated and corn-rich compared to the other places they passed along the way. In many of those places, they said, the Indians hid their corn by burying it, and the Spaniards, weary from a day's march, had to go out and find it in the scrub and dig it up.

This gave us a certain expectation about what the land was going to look like, and what we found did not match up at all. The country looked like home to us, hilly, with green fields and pine forests. The roads were good, the economy seemed strong. We could not keep in mind that this was Texas. It looked like the part of Georgia that lies within a hundred miles of Atlanta—the modern, prosperous South.

We did not try to pinpoint any of the provinces the Spaniards visited on this stretch. We knew we did not know where they were. We were going to Nacogdoches to talk to Jim Corbin, an archaeologist at Stephen F. Austin State University. Shambach and Wyckoff had told us that he would be someone who could help us. Charlie called him yesterday and found out he is planning to leave town tomorrow, so we got up very early in order to get down here in time to see him this afternoon. It was a four-hundred-mile drive from Norman.

Jim Corbin was one of the few people we came to cold—maybe the only one. Several months ago Charlie sent a preliminary route to everyone he thought could help him on the western route, but he had only a very sketchy route for Texas and did not feel he had it anywhere close enough to present it to Texas archaeologists for serious consideration. Nor did he know any archaeologists in Texas to present it to. He knows only the archaeologists who work in the heart of the Southeast. This area of eastern Texas is getting so close to the far boundary of the Southeast that it tends to tip off into another sphere altogether—Caddoan archaeology or Texas archaeology or southwestern archaeology. There is a real gulf.

So Charlie had not been in touch with anyone from Texas. Furthermore, he thought at first the route went more directly west from Naguatex, so that when he did begin to contact people, it was archaeologists who knew the Waco, Dallas, and Austin areas farther to the west. He struck out there. The questions he was asking did not make sense to people, which in a way is nice. When the route is wrong, it fails to click with the archaeologists. Then Saturday with Shambach we figured out that the route went south from Naguatex. That put it in Jim Corbin's territory. The contact Charlie made with him yesterday was only through his secretary, so Corbin had no idea what to expect of us. People who trace routes of early explorers are often amateur scholars who tend to have fixed and rather wild ideas. You can have your day ruined by a person like that, particularly if you are busy trying to get ready to leave town the next day.

Jim Corbin was very polite when he met us in his office and was graciously willing to give us some of his time. He is a handsome man with a dark beard, in his late thirties, perhaps. He knew we had driven a long way to see him, but I could tell he wanted to get this business over with as quickly as possible. He was not familiar with the De Soto narratives except in a general way and had certainly never attempted to fit them to his part of Texas. He was trying to be of what help he could, but he was not really engaging with the problem. The place-names interested him. They sounded like the native groups from his area. He had not known they were in the De Soto documents. He thought they probably did fit the general area we had driven through. But I did not think he would help us nail down the route more precisely. We had caught him at a bad time and had given him no preparation. Here for the first time we had come to someone who was not going to get on board with us.

But just as I was beginning to make little moves and hints for Charlie to wrap it up and let this fellow get on with his own business, Jim Corbin began to click. It was a group of people called the Aays that did it. The Spaniards had come down from Naguatex through several towns, then went through a buffer zone and came upon the Aays, who had never heard of them, which meant they were socially separate from the other people the Spaniards had encountered and were not in their communication network. After leaving the Aays the Spaniards went through several other towns and provinces before coming to Guasco, the last one.

That makes sense for the Aays, Corbin told us several times. Each time he said it, he was more engaged. In the eighteenth century, when the Spaniards had missions in this area, the Aays were with the Caddos, but the Caddos always said the Aays were not true Caddos. They were living farther south at this later time, but Corbin thought it made sense that in 1542 they would have been a separate people in a different place from their later location. He liked the general area where Charlie had located them. And he liked the area for Guasco, the last town on the route. There is a river valley there, he said, with a large flood plain that in later times had a large Native American population. And it would in fact be the last place for a truly agricultural society before the arable land ran out.

And so before we knew it, Corbin was into it as completely as all the other archaeologists we have talked to along the way. It was making sense to him. We talked about the possibility that the Spaniards came down a trail on the western edge of this population zone instead of down the middle as Charlie and I had driven it. We asked him if that would make it seem more as if the land was getting sterile and thinly peopled.

"Yes, it would," he said. He told us that there was post-oak prairie on the western edge of that pine woodland and even some black prairie.

"Prairie?" I said. "Would there be buffalo there?"

"Yes," he answered.

The Spaniards said the Aays lived where there were buffalo. Now we were getting somewhere. Jim pulled out a map of Texas vegetation and showed us the post-oak strip that ran between woodlands to the east of it and prairie to the west. A trail would pass more easily through post-oak country than through the denser woods, he said. And there is a place where a finger of prairie intrudes into the post oaks. It falls just where Charlie had marked on his own map one of the possible locations for the Aays. He had based it on distance traveled, with no knowledge of the geography at all.

While the Spaniards were in Guasco, the last town before turning back, they heard rumors from the inhabitants that other Spaniards had been seen coming into the land and leaving again. Corbin said that this country is right for rumors of Spaniards, since the Indians here had ties directly south to the Gulf, which is where Cabeza de Vaca and his shipwrecked companions went wandering across the Texas coastlands less than ten years before De Soto. Cabeza de Vaca made some forays north into the interior and came very close to this Caddoan area. It turns out that Corbin has done work in the past with Cabeza de Vaca, trying to fit his narrative to the Indians of the coast the way Charlie is doing with De Soto for the interior. Corbin also works with eighteenth- and nineteenth-century documents for eastern Texas and believes that if you work long enough with these sources, trying to fit them to maps and archaeology, you will eventually begin to read them correctly and find that they do make sense.

So here, where I thought we were striking out, was someone more sympathetic to what we were doing than almost anyone we have encountered yet. By the time we left him, we were feeling very good about the Texas route. Corbin seemed to believe that it was valid, at least generally. We did not get the towns nailed down, but there seems little doubt about the limits of the area. Geography constrains it. It all feels right. At this point we have a true sense of having finished the route. We still have to go look at the Guasco area and follow Moscoso and his men from there out into the wilderness on their last desperate push toward Mexico. After reaching a river the Indians called Daycao, they gave it up and turned around and went all the way back to the Mississippi River, where they spent the last winter building boats in which to try to make it out by going down the river to the Gulf of Mexico.

We still have to check out some things about the trip down the Mississippi. But tonight we feel that we have finished the job. It worked out better than we had hoped.

We went out and had a good meal at a Mexican restaurant. We could not get anything alcoholic to drink without first paying six dollars to be members of the restaurants's "club," because of the beverage laws. We could not even buy a beer. The waitress shrugged apologetically.

"That's the way it is in east Texas," she said.

We toasted the end of the route with our glasses of water.

We saw a bald eagle today. We were in Naguatex, driving over a long causeway at the edge of a reservoir just north of the Red River. The reservoir is not a continuous lake but a flooded area that is probably dry in summer. There were patches of dry land and a lot of trees standing in the water. We saw a couple of ducks fly by. Then a flock of smaller birds, probably blackbirds, flew up from a swampy area. And near that flock a large bird rose up. I thought at first it was a heron because of its long wings and the way they dipped as it flew. But the neck and body were not right for a heron. We watched as it came close enough for us to see its coloring—black with a white head and a white tail.

"That's an eagle!" we both cried. "An eagle!"

I stopped the car and was going to make a U-turn to go back for another look.

"Just wait right here," said Charlie. "He's coming by us."

Having crossed over the causeway in back of us, it had turned and was flying in our direction, on Charlie's side. Charlie rolled down his window and we both leaned over and watched as it flew by, almost level with the car, about forty feet away. When it had gotten ahead of us, it wheeled away and flew into the distance and alighted in the top of a tree. We could still see the white of its head and tail. We would have stayed and watched it longer, but a car was coming up behind us and we had to move on.

Neither of us has ever before seen a bald eagle in the wild. It is possible we never will again.

CHAPTER TEN

Mississippi River Currents

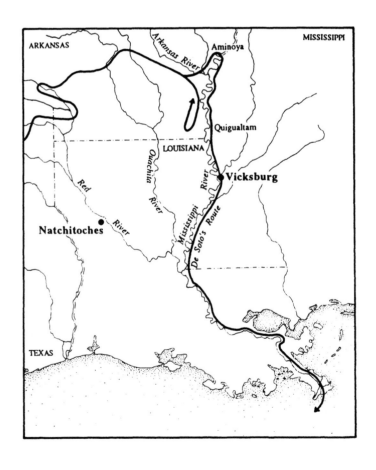

The Castilians, in their desire to leave that land, for the days were becoming to them as years, did not pause for a moment in their work on the caravels. The majority of those who labored at the forges and in the carpentries were very noble cavaliers who had never imagined themselves doing such jobs. . . . Now our Spaniards made seven caravels, but not having an adequate supply of nails to construct decks that would shelter them completely, they covered in each of them only a part of the poop and the prow where they could place ship stores. In the center they carried some loose boards which provided a floor, and by removing one of these boards they were able to drain the water collected. . . .

This group of Spaniards and Indians {servants} set sail as the sun was sinking on the very day of the Apostles—a day so celebrated and joyous for the whole of Christendom, although for our Castilians a sad and lamentable one because . . . they were abandoning the fruit of the numerous hardships they had experienced in that land, and were forfeiting the . . . reward for the magnificent and heroic deeds they had accomplished. . . . Each brigantine carried seven oars to the side, and at these oars, all persons aboard, without exception unless it were the commanders, took turns rowing their hours.

On the second day there began to appear in pursuit a most magnificent fleet of . . . canoes, . . . among which . . . some were observed of such unusually large size as to cause our people to marvel. The command ships and others like them were so immense that they supported twenty-five oarsmen on each side, and in addition, held twenty-five or thirty warriors placed successively from poop to prow. Thus many of these canoes had a capacity for seventy-five or eighty passengers with each of them placed in such a manner as to be able to fight without obstructing the others. . . . But though so large, these vessels were made of only one piece of wood. Hence one may see what very handsome trees are to be found in that land.

In order for all to row simultaneously and in rhythm, the Indians compose various songs of different tunes, the length or brevity of

which depends upon the haste or slowness with which they are mov-
ing. . . . There is still another curious detail to relate concerning the
canoes. . . . This is that each individually came tinted within and
without even to the oars with a single color, such as . . . blue, yellow,
white, red, green, scarlet, purple, black or some other hue. . . .
Furthermore, the oarsmen . . . and the warriors even to the feathers
and skeins of thread worn around their heads, and their bows and
arrows—all were tinted with a single color. . . . thus had they
been bands of cavaliers who . . . wished to hold a tournament of
canes, they could not have sallied forth with more exquisiteness than
they now achieved in their canoes, for since these boats were numerous
and of so many colors and in such an arrangement as they observed,
and since the river was very broad and they could spread out in all
directions without breaking rank, they made a magnificent spectacle
to behold.

—Garcilaso de la Vega

Vicksburg, Mississippi
Thursday, December 20

We have done what the Spaniards did—we went to the Trinity River in
Texas and then turned around and came back to the Mississippi. Only
they went back to Aminoya, where they spent the last winter, and we
have come to a place considerably downriver—and we have crossed to
the eastern side. Tomorrow we have an appointment with Roger Saucier
at the Army Corps of Engineers Headquarters here in Vicksburg. We
want to see what we can find out about the channel of the Mississippi in
1540, particularly up around the mouth of the Arkansas River, where
so many De Soto–related sites were located. Roger Saucier is *the* man on
the historical geography of the river. He also knows archaeology.

We spent most of yesterday in eastern Texas. We left Nacogdoches
about nine o'clock in the morning and drove west on Texas 21 through
Alto to Weches, where we turned off on a side road and took a look
at the verdant flood plain of San Pedro Creek. This is where we think
Guasco was, the last corn-producing province the Spaniards could find
on their attempted trek to Mexico. Texas 21 follows the Camino Real,
the Spanish road of colonial times. In the early 1700s there were Spanish
missions along this road. There is also, on the Neches River, a large

Caddoan mound site that had its heyday around A.D. 1200. It was probably not occupied when the De Soto expedition came through. Texas has a small state park on the site with a marvelous interpretive museum telling all about Caddoan life. On the grounds outside they have built a tall, magnificent, beehive-shaped Caddoan house, using the same materials the Caddos would have used. Walking into it, we were awed by the grandeur of its towering, domelike ceiling. It had a pleasing grassy smell from the bundles of thatch with which it was covered, like shingles, from the peak of the roof to the ground. There is no break between roof and walls. The floor is twenty to thirty feet in diameter, and the peak of the roof is at least twenty feet high. There are lofts in that great cathedral space above. The idea is much the same as a modern A-frame, though with a circular floor plan. The native people whom the Spaniards encountered from southwestern Arkansas down into Texas were living in houses like this. They had brush arbors for outside shelter in the summer—long, rectangular, open sheds.

San Pedro Creek is to the west of the Neches River. The flood plains here are very rich. When later Spaniards came into east Texas in the early eighteenth century, this was where the largest concentration of Indians lived. The De Soto expedition found more corn in Guasco than they had found anywhere else since leaving Naguatex. But they also found that they had come to the end of the trail. The people of Guasco told them that there were no more rich provinces to the west or southwest. They said that several days' journey to the west was the River of Daycao, where they sometimes went to hunt deer, and they sometimes saw people on the far side of the river, but they did not know who they were.

The Spaniards made a desperate resolve to push on—they would reach Mexico or die, they said. They loaded up all the corn they could carry from Guasco and set out. One of the narratives says they went six days, the other says ten. We are going with the six days, because we are fairly certain that the Trinity River was the River of Daycao. We drove to the Trinity, going through Crockett, Texas, which was founded in 1837 and named for Davy Crockett, who had passed through there the year before on his way to the Alamo. We had lunch in the downtown cafe in Crockett, and the people there were as Old South as any we have seen on the entire trip. The town and cafe made me think of Holly Springs, Mississippi. There was that same feeling that time had passed this place by, that the people were still linked to the past in a real and authentic way. The only obvious difference between Crockett and Holly Springs was that some of the people in Crockett wore cowboy hats.

The Spaniards described the stretch from Guasco to the Trinity River as wilderness, and it is true that not far from Guasco the land begins to change. But it did not change into what I expected to see. I expected mesquite and sagebrush, maybe a few cacti and cow skulls. What we found instead was low, open, rolling land that looked very much like central Florida. Cattle ranches. It was not arid like Oklahoma, although the soil was sandy and the trees were post oaks. There was a lot of grass and shrubby growth, much of it still green. And it was warm like Florida. Some of the shrub was yaupon holly, which grows all around the southern coast and from which the Native Americans made a tea similar to maté, a South American tea popular even to this day. They called it black drink and drank it ceremonially from big conchshell cups. Charlie serves it on the last day of class to the students who have taken his course on the southeastern Indians.

The Trinity is a big river. The water was up and the current swift. We were still unsure if this was the River of Daycao. The distance from Guasco seemed short for the travel time: about forty-eight miles, eight miles a day for a six-day trip. In the first year or two of the expedition the army would often travel twelve to fifteen miles a day. Consistently since we crossed the Mississippi we have found them going less far in a day, and this especially seems to be true after De Soto died and the army headed out west under Moscoso. By the time they got to Texas, it was summer, and the heat in that very hot part of the country must have also slowed them down. In Naguatex they say they camped away from the river in a grove of trees because of the extreme heat. They also mention at that time setting up a camp at midday, which suggests that the heat was shortening their marching time.

So eight miles a day might well have been it, though when we got to the Trinity River, we had not yet pieced together this understanding about the heat and the shortened travel days. The next river, the Navasota, was thirty miles farther west. An eighty-mile trek in six days would be more like it, we thought. The Brazos was another twenty or more miles beyond that, but we thought that to be too far. We had only intended to drive to the Trinity, but now we felt we had to take a look at the Navasota, just to see what it looked like. We both were tired, but on we went. It was a balmy day, with scattered clouds. The temperature was in the seventies. The Florida-like aspect of the land gave us a fun-in-the-sun feeling. We drove on to the Navasota and found it a puny little river, even in flood. We knew it could not be the River of Daycao. It was inconceivable that the people of Guasco would come all the way to this swampy little river to hunt deer. The Trinity was beginning to seem like the right place, the true end of the overland route. We drove on across the Navasota and looked for a place to turn around. There was a picnic area not a mile from the river. We pulled in there. There was yaupon holly growing all around, full of red berries—some people call it Christmas berry bush. We took each other's picture in front of it to mark the end of our search. Then we got in the car and started back, feeling exhilarated to be heading east, leaving the De Soto route behind.

The place where we turned around was about a hundred miles northeast of Austin. Going back we cut south some twenty miles to Huntsville, which is seventy miles or so north of Houston, and then we headed east toward Louisiana. The reason for taking the more southern route was to drive through the Big Thicket area of Texas. We had always heard about the Big Thicket and did not want to come this close to it without seeing it. It is supposed to be one of the most impenetrable wildernesses in America. I have heard that there may be some ivory-billed woodpeckers still living in the Big Thicket. These are huge birds and need correspondingly huge dead trees for their survival. Because timber almost everywhere is now cut on a regular basis, there are few forests left where trees get big, grow old, and die. So the ivory-bill is almost extinct.

Driving through the Big Thicket on a federal highway (U.S. 190), we did not expect impenetrable wilderness. We hoped, though, that we could tell something about the area by going past the edge of it. Had we had the time we would have turned off on some of the side roads and explored it more deeply—and we also would have stopped at the Alabama-Coushatta Indian reservation to take a look at their museum. But time was in short supply. As it was, we noted that the land we passed through was thickly wooded, though not extraordinarily so. Much land had been clear cut. Everything we saw had been timbered in the last few decades—there were no old forests. I think the Big Thicket proper is a swampy area that has been difficult to get in and out of for timbering purposes. The Alabama-Coushatta Indians obviously were able to hang on here because of the inaccessibility of the region. They are Muskogean-speaking people whose ancestors once lived in Alabama and Tennessee. Coushatta is the same word as Koasati, which is the same as Coste, the people De Soto encountered somewhere around Bussell Island in the mouth of the Little Tennessee River south of Knoxville. All the people in the upper Tennessee Valley evidently spoke the Koasati language, according to Robert Rankin, a linguist at the University of Kansas who has been working with Charlie on the place names of the Pardo and De Soto routes. There are other Coushattas still living in equally inaccessible parts of Louisiana. They are the most conservative Indians in the present-day Southeast. All the children speak Koasati as their first language.

We tried last night to make it to Natchitoches, Louisiana, but it got dark and we were exhausted, so we stopped fifty miles short at Leesville, Louisiana. This morning we got up and drove on into Natchitoches and called Pete Gregory, an archaeologist at Northwestern State University, who came to meet us and led us to his office and lab on the campus.

Nacodoches and *Natchitoches* are the same word spelled differently, the first one a Spanish rendering and the second one French. Both are attempts to spell the name of an Indian group—an eighteenth-century conglomerate of these same Caddoan people encountered by the De Soto expedition in the area from the Red River to San Pedro Creek. *Naguatex* in the chronicles is another form of the same word. The Texas town is pronounced "Nack-a-*doe*-chis." The Louisiana town is "*Nack*-a-dish." Both pronunciations make the names impossible to spell, but this is especially true of the Louisiana version. I still cannot spell it without help.

Pete Gregory is an unassuming, easygoing man whose scholarship is widely respected. His enthusiasm for his subject matter is contagious. He knows the archaeology of the Louisiana Caddos. He also knows a lot about all Caddoan archaeology and the general archaeology of Arkansas and eastern Texas. His expertise and greatest love, however, are the fascinating eighteenth and nineteenth centuries in his region, where the French and Spanish were nose to nose and the foundation was laid for the rich ethnic diversity of the Natchitoches area. Natchitoches is the oldest French town in Louisiana—older than New Orleans. It is on the banks of the Red River. The French came up the river and set up a trading post there, offering European goods to the Indians in exchange for horses, salt, and Indian slaves. From this French presence came the French Creoles who still live in the area today. They are a mixture of French, black, and Indian. There is also a small population of people who are a mixture of Spanish and Indian, the result of a Spanish fort and mission that was established just a few miles west of Natchitoches in an attempt to keep the French from coming farther west into Texas. Then there is the predominant Anglo population, which came in from the Carolinas and Georgia to grow cotton in the early nineteenth century, and the black population, originally brought in as slaves for the cotton plantations. All this rich historical texture can still be seen in this not so very large town. It is a lovely place, and we regretted not having several days to spend there.

We got most of this historical background from Pete before we settled down with the De Soto maps. But finally we had to get to work. We laid out the map with the Arkansas route, and Charlie started going over it. There was nothing specific we wanted from Pete, just his reaction to this whole western route, since he knows the archaeology of the area, and also because he had shown himself to be somewhat on the dubious side in his reaction to Charlie's first version of the western route. Pete has spent some time trying to reconcile Louisiana archaeology with Swanton's route, and he had concluded that the De Soto narratives are too vague for anything more than playing around with the route. He felt that at best archaeology might offer some way to test different hypotheses about the route at specific sites, as for instance at Charlie's and Swanton's respective Anilcos.

But by the time Charlie was halfway through his new version of the Arkansas route, Pete was with him, nodding his head. Two other faculty members had wandered into the lab and became absorbed in the work with us. One man was from northern Texas just south of the Red River in the Naguatex region. He started helping us think about the route south to Guasco, whether it would have been due south or a little more to the west—the same question we had considered with Jim Corbin, and essentially the same conclusion, which was that we lean toward the more western route, though we cannot yet be sure. We also talked a long time about whether the River of Daycao was the Trinity or the Brazos, which is the next river after the Navasota and is large enough to be a contender, though the distance to it is probably too far. Again, everyone felt it was the Trinity. Charlie is beginning to feel fairly firm on that, though there is still need for archaeological confirmation.

It was a good session. Pete Gregory seemed to like the route all the way. It removes De Soto from Louisiana, but he had no problem with that. Now he does not have to fool with it anymore, he said. When we were talking about Charlie's Anilco being on a site above floodlevel, he nodded with approval. Swanton put Anilco at Jonesville, Louisiana, and that had bothered Pete. The Spaniards said Anilco stayed dry during that huge flood they endured, but Jonesville always goes under in a flood.

This is what we keep hearing from people, that certain parts of Swanton's route in their own territories had never seemed right to them. And at the same time their eyes light up and their heads nod when they hear the details of Charlie's route.

There is still much work to be done on the route to nail it down precisely at every point along the way. Charlie does not care to take it that far himself. He wants the work to be done by the archaeologists in their own territories. They are the ones who can best handle the problems. By going out and talking to so many of them and getting them excited and involved, the job is more likely to be carried through.

When we finished going over the route, Pete took us to lunch at a fine Creole restaurant, Lazyone's, of national renown. I had the most delicious red beans and rice I have ever tasted. I always knew they could be that good. After lunch Pete gave us a tour of the town. We loved it all: the food, the architecture, the lovely Creole people we saw on the streets. We wanted to stay longer and see more, but we had to move on to Vicksburg.

We left Natchitoches and drove northeast on backroads through timber country, passing logging truck after logging truck, until we came to the town of Monroe in northern Louisiana. Here was Interstate 20, which would take us to Vicksburg and then all the way home to Georgia. When we drove onto the expressway, I knew the time for seeing the country was over. It was like getting onto a train and being sealed off from the world outside. We were soon down in the delta again—all that flatness out there. But it was not the same experience as before. We zipped along—four lanes, cars and diesel trucks, green signs, billboards, golden arches. Just as it got dark we crossed the Mississippi into Vicksburg.

We see Roger Saucier at eight o'clock tomorrow morning. Then we are going home. This is our last night in a motel. Glory.

Athens, Georgia
Saturday, December 22

Home. We got in last night around ten-thirty, having driven straight from Vicksburg on I-20 through heavy Christmas traffic, past two bad wrecks, and through thirty minutes of a creeping traffic jam caused by road construction near Birmingham, Alabama. We saw nothing but expressway, billboards, and corridors of pine trees.

We got up early in Vicksburg and arrived at the Corps of Engineers Waterways Experiment Station just after eight o'clock. We had to stop at a little booth at the entrance, just like an army base, and that puzzled me for a minute until I remembered it is the *Army* Corps of Engineers. This *is* an army base. We told the man at the booth that we had an appointment with Roger Saucier, and he seemed to have been informed beforehand that we would be coming. He said they wanted us to check in at the public affairs office, where we would be given a map and shown where to find Saucier. The experiment station encompasses a large area with a number of buildings on it. It felt a little strange to be in a research establishment where they keep such close control over people's comings and goings. This was a much different atmosphere from the college campuses we had been visiting.

And Roger Saucier is a different sort of man from the archaeologists with whom we had been dealing. Saucier is a geologist working among engineers. He is a military-looking man, a man of precision and rigor. Archaeologists, on the other hand, are a fairly laid-back crew. They often have beards. They seldom wear ties, and when they have to wear a sport coat, it is usually made of corduroy. They deal with a body of data that is anything but precise. Their *methods* are precise, but when it comes to interpreting the data, there is room in archaeology for imagination and creative leaps. Those who can employ that element in a controlled sort of way are the best archaeologists. They would not necessarily make the best consultants for engineers. For that you want someone like Roger Saucier.

Saucier has worked a lot with reconstructing past conditions of the Mississippi River. This turns out to be very hard to do, and he told us that most of the success they have had is based not on geology but on archaeology. They can date old channels of the river by the dates of the archaeological sites they find around them. If they have a levee ridge with an archaeological site on it dating back to A.D. 600, then they know the river channel that formed that levee ridge is at least that old. At least I think that is basically how it works.

Saucier was willing to try to be of help to us on the route, but he warned us at the outset that his knowledge was probably more general than the specific knowledge we were hoping for. Charlie went through the route around the Mississippi for him, and Saucier said he thought the different parts of it made sense geographically. That is, if the Spaniards came into the delta in April and mention no swamps, it makes sense that they were coming in just south of Memphis, where the delta is narrow. Things like that. He also pointed out several times the variability of the land according to season: that the delta would not be very swampy at all in late summer, for instance. These bits of information were helpful.

As for the river channel as it existed in 1540, he said that the reconstructions that have been done for that time period are fairly accurate, although there is a lot of room for error. To reconstruct even a small segment of the channel any more precisely would take years of work and a huge amount of money. In other words, it cannot be done, not for something like this. And even if the time and money were available, it would still be a difficult if not impossible task.

So we may never know precisely where Aminoya and Guachoya were, nor Pacaha.

Finally we came to the part of the route that we wanted most to try out on him—and also dreaded most—the boat trip down the river from Aminoya to the Gulf of Mexico. Charlie's route requires the boats to go twice as far as Swanton's route requires, in the same amount of time. Sixteen days, the chroniclers say.

"What figure are you using for a day's travel?" asked Saucier. "Twenty miles?"

I started dying right there. Charlie was using a figure of forty to fifty miles. For some reason he only heard Saucier ask what figure he was using and did not hear him say twenty miles. So he proceeded unflapped, asking Saucier if a four-mile-per-hour current would be reasonable.

More like three miles per hour, said Saucier. And in summer maybe only two—and when the river is really low, maybe only one.

This trip was in July.

At this point I knew Charlie was wilting, too. The one thing we had dreaded was doing the whole route and having it come out at a place on the Mississippi where someone who really knew the river would say, "But they could not get down to the Gulf from there in sixteen days." There are only two possibilities for the place on the river from which they started: either at the mouth of the Arkansas, as Charlie had it, or at the mouth of the Ouachita, as Swanton had it.

"This was summer," I told Saucier. "But the river wasn't low. The chroniclers say that at this time of year the river usually is low, but that God saw fit that the water should come up just when they were ready to launch the boats, and so they were able to float them to the river instead of dragging them, which they had been afraid would damage them."

"All right then," said Saucier, nodding. "Three miles per hour. Maybe even four."

There are so many variables, he told us. It is a mistake to think of the current as a steady force from one end of the river to the other. It changes from place to place. In some stretches it moves swiftly, in others it comes almost to a standstill.

"How much would oars add?" asked Charlie. He explained that they had seven oars to a side on each of the seven brigantines.

Saucier was not sure. This is peripheral to his expertise. But he ventured that they might do five miles per hour or even six, though it would be difficult to sustain that day after day.

Charlie told of how the Indians chased them in big war canoes, forcing them to row day and night for several days; and of how everyone took his turn at the oars, even the grandees among them. Saucier could see the possibility of their keeping it up under those circumstances. He could see the possibility of their making it out in the time frame Charlie needed. The variables are so great, he said, that any figure at which one could arrive would have a window so large that Charlie will probably be safe. Saucier seemed to think that if the Spaniards say it took sixteen days to get down the river, and if Charlie's route works in every other respect and brings them to the mouth of the Arkansas River, then they did indeed make it from there to the Gulf in sixteen days.

He was in all very helpful. He said he would track down some references for Charlie on early river travel and would talk to the corps historian to try to find out where Charlie can go for answers to some of the questions he is asking.

We talked for a while about the character of the river. He explained that it is only in fairly recent times that the river has flowed so neatly in one channel. It used to divide its water between different channels that were constantly changing—sometimes 60 percent would go this way, 40 percent that way. Then it would rearrange itself in another manner. We had heard John House talk about this. He had shown Charlie an article about it: "The Forked River."

We left Saucier, feeling good about having taken the route all the way through to the end. If Saucier could accept a rate of three to four miles per hour down the river, then Charlie does not have to worry about a serious challenge on this point. He still intends to do more work on the river trip, but we feel confident that it will all work out—more confident than we had felt before talking to Saucier. This is not to say, however, that we did not already have a certain amount of confidence, just because the rest of the route has been fitting so well. How could the River of Cayas not be the Arkansas? It has to be. Everything fits.

According to both Saucier and Pete Gregory, what the narratives say about there being no big societies south of Guachoya on the west side of the river is consistent with the archaeology. So there is another way the route fits.

The Spaniards set out in their boats from Aminoya, just above the mouth of the Arkansas River. Upon passing by the mouth of the Arkansas, they were attacked by the war fleet of the chiefdom of Quigualtam, which was on the eastern side of the Mississippi. At the end of Quigualtam's territory—around Vicksburg—that fleet turned back, and another came out and started chasing them. In other words, there was another big society on the east side of the river below Quigualtam. After the second fleet turned back, no other war canoes came out to give chase, which means no more big societies. And this, too, is consistent with the archaeology. There are two impressive archaeological phases that coincide with those two river-warrior provinces. And below that there are no other populous societies. So the route holds to the end. It was wonderful to be back in our own house last night.

In our own bed. We both woke up about three o'clock in the morning, and we had both been dreaming the same dream—that we were still back in Texas, still looking for De Soto.

We have been struck by how quiet it is at our house. No traffic noise at all. We are on a rural road where no more than one car an hour goes by during the day, far fewer at night. For six weeks we have been constantly bombarded by noise and movement. Now everything is still.

EPILOGUE

Eight years have passed since we made that journey in search of De Soto. Work on the De Soto expedition, by Charlie and others, has continued to move forward. Not every lead we followed on our trip has panned out. Not every idea was a good one. But the overall route has held.

New ingredients have been added to the De Soto stew: government activities, both state and federal. Florida was the first to set up a state De Soto commission for the purpose of marking a highway route that roughly follows the trail of De Soto's army. Experts were called in, including Charlie. Alternative routes were proposed, argued, and examined. In the end the route that Charlie and Jerry Milanich had worked out was the one that was adopted. Distinctive De Soto Trail markers were placed at frequent intervals along the way, and at less frequent intervals outdoor kiosks were erected to present information at some depth about the expedition and the Native Americans through whose land it passed. Alabama followed Florida, appointing its own De Soto commission, and after bitter wrangling between those who favored Charlie's route and those who wanted to keep the route closer to its old configuration, Charlie's route was adopted and marked—with the expressed understanding that future scholarly discoveries could change it again.

On the federal level a bill was passed in Congress in 1987 directing the National Park Service to investigate the possibility of making De Soto's route a National Historic Trail, like the Lewis and Clark Trail. Charlie was asked to produce a written version of the updated route for use by the Park Service, who then held public meetings in every De Soto state to air the pros and cons of the new route. So much controversy was raised by those who did not want the route moved from its traditional path that the Park Service finally concluded that, in the absence of the kind of firm historical evidence that exists for the exact locations of other National Historic Trails, the De Soto route does not qualify for similar treatment.

At the regional level, several southern governors appointed a De Soto Trail commission with representatives from all the De Soto states for the purpose of coordinating the separate state-level De Soto activities. After examining and debating the "Hudson" route, the commission voted to adopt it. However, some states are more strongly in favor of Charlie's route than others. Arkansas, for example, has lined up very strongly behind it, while Mississippi is divided by two parties who favor different crossings of the Mississippi River, each of which would require a different route across the state to reach it. One crossing is very close to the traditional crossing on the Swanton route, and there are some scholars who support it. The other crossing is the one proposed in Charlie's route.

In truth, the new route is no longer "Charlie's" route, even though it is usually referred to these days as the Hudson route. Many other scholars have become involved in the De Soto problem and have invested much effort in refining the route Charlie initially proposed. The new De Soto route is now the work of a wide consortium of scholars.

In looking back at our journey and thinking about what has happened since, a number of particular developments come to mind. In Florida Marvin Smith finished his Ph.D. Jerry Milanich and Charlie continued their De Soto collaboration and have written a book about the expedition in Florida. Also in Florida, an exciting De Soto event made wire-service news in 1987, when Calvin Jones discovered a very early Spanish site within the city limits of Tallahassee. Subsequent archaeological research at this site—the Governor Martin site—by Jones and Charles Ewen has turned up chain mail, early sixteenth-century Spanish coins, other early Spanish artifacts, and even pig bones. The consensus among archaeologists is that this was very probably the spot where Hernando de Soto spent the winter in Apalachee.

Florida has not only led the rest of the states in marking the trail, but its former governor and now senator, Bob Graham, has spearheaded the effort in Washington to gain National Historic Trail status for the entire route. After the first effort with the Park Service failed to produce the hoped for results, Graham steered another bill through Congress (S.555), which has been approved and signed by President Bush. It authorizes the appointment of a national De Soto commission that will oversee research for the purpose of defining the route and interpreting it to the public. As the national commission is formed and empowered, the regional De Soto Trail commission will phase itself out.

In Georgia, the Marshallville Ferry is no longer in operation, which is too bad. But in that same area there has also been a positive development. John Worth, a new young archaeologist and another of Charlie's former students, has surveyed the banks of the Flint River and located the boundaries of the province of Toa north of Montezuma. Farther along, in South Carolina, the segment of the route we explored through the great wilderness between Ocute and Cofitachequi did not ultimately work out, despite our seeming triumph at the time. The route is now believed to have been farther north, so that neither the North nor the South Fork of the Edisto River figures into it.

In Tennessee the site we visited with Richard Polhemus hoping it was Tanasqui has not fulfilled our hopes. Whether it was in fact the site of Tanasqui and the convincing evidence has yet to be found or whether Tanasqui was located elsewhere is still not known, though Richard remains interested in the problem. We were sad to hear that his father, Jim, succumbed at last to emphysema in 1990.

In Alabama there were years of unrelenting controversy over the locations of Mabila and Apafalaya. The strength of the argument was with Charlie's theory, which puts this part of the route farther to the north than his challengers would like. But without concrete, undeniable evidence to clinch Charlie's locations, his challengers have kept up a vigorous attack against them. Recently, however, a Nueva Cadiz bead—one of those highly diagnostic sixteenth-century trade beads—was found in the general vicinity of Moundville, adding welcome evidence to Charlie's belief that Apafalaya was in the Moundville area. As time has passed and Charlie's route has become generally accepted in the scholarly community, the opposition group in Alabama has grown quiet, though it probably never will concede.

In Mississippi, the marking of the route by the state government has been stymied by the proponents of the traditional idea that the location of De Soto's crossing of the Mississippi was in Coahoma County, near the town of Clarksdale. In the meantime, the more northerly crossing just south of Memphis, in the Walls-phase area—the part of the route we investigated with Jerry Smith—has held and is now accepted by most scholars. It is the excellent fit with what follows in the expedition on the other side of the river that gives strength to this crossing place.

In Arkansas, that golden De Soto state that we came to love so much, good things have continued to happen. Dan and Phyllis Morse, Frank Shambach, and Ann Early have all made significant contributions to confirming and refining the route. Dan and Phyllis have made a strong case for the Bradley site as the capital town of Pacaha. And the Parkin site is now widely accepted as the central town of Casqui. Dan and Phyllis's long campaign to save the Parkin site has finally been rewarded: the state has bought the site and staffed it with a full-time archaeologist, Jeffrey Mitchum, one of Jerry Milanich's former students. Arkansas plans to develop Parkin into a state park and museum. A little farther along the trail, one of Dan's students, Scott Akridge, went looking for the salt location we needed near Possum Grape, and he found one: a reference in a historical document to a Civil War salt works. Its location has been forgotten by local residents and the exact spot has not yet been found, but there is no doubt that there was a moderately productive salt source in that vicinity.

Frank Shambach and Ann Early have been working on the location of Tula and have concluded that instead of being in the Fourche la Fave or the Petit Jean valley, it was probably in the Arkansas River valley near Fort Smith. Charlie had originally proposed that location on the basis of the narratives, before he knew anything about the archaeology. When he was told there were no protohistoric sites in that area, he tried putting Tula on the Fourche or Petit Jean instead. But now Ann and Frank say that the area around Fort Smith has scarcely been surveyed and may yield the needed sixteenth-century sites when more intensive surveying is done. That investigation continues and looks promising.

Since we visited John House, he has been to graduate school at Southern Illinois University to earn his Ph.D. He is now back at Pine Bluff and continues his work there as station archaeologist for the Arkansas Archaeological Survey.

To the west, in the area where Arkansas, Louisiana, and Texas come together, Frank Shambach has made some impressive correlations between a cluster of archaeological phases in that vicinity and the string of polities visited by the De Soto expedition as they attempted their march to Mexico. He has made a strong case for locating Naguatex in southwestern Arkansas, leaving Oklahoma without any De Soto trail at all.

Jim Corbin has also done some work on the route in Texas. The general area we investigated when we were there remains the likely area for the route, though the details have been and continue to be shifted around. More progress has been made at that end of the route, by Frank, Jim, and others, than Charlie had expected would be possible.

As for the two of us, our De Soto trip remains one of the high points of our lives. For Charlie it was an actual living out, in a highly satisfactory way, of his scholarly quest. Years of work had been invested in the De Soto project up to that point, and he had put forth his theories at considerable risk. The threads of evidence for the De Soto route are slender bits that he had woven together painstakingly and that held only because of the overall pattern into which he had fit them. If the pattern had been disrupted very much in any one place, the entire web would have fallen apart. That could still happen, theoretically. But since our trip it has seemed less and less likely. It was almost as if he went out and physically lived the route, breathed it in and out, examined all its parts, and by the end of the journey he had experienced its coherence. The essential truth of it became a part of him rather than just an idea carried around in his head.

For me the trip stands as just about the most fun we have ever had. It had that same quality that vacations have, of leaving home and routine and traveling to new places, but it was a more satisfying experience than that. It was life lived as a quest, totally absorbing, all our attention focused on that which we were experiencing. Especially rich were the encounters with people along the way, some of them sought out, some happened upon. Preparing this journal for publication has brought back the experience over and over again, and I have yet to tire of it. I feel I never will.

FURTHER READING

For those who wish to know more about De Soto and the early Spanish explorers in the southeastern United States, there are several possible approaches. English translations of all the De Soto narratives—the primary documents—have been available for many years in several editions and can be found in libraries. New and better translations have been prepared under the sponsorship of the Alabama De Soto Commission, and these are to be published in two volumes by the University of Alabama Press as *The De Soto Chronicles*. The editors of this work are Lawrence A. Clayton, Vernon J. Knight, Jr., and Edward C. Moore. Of the older editions, all the chronicles except Garcilaso can be found in *Narratives of the Career of Hernando De Soto*, edited by Edward Bourne and published by A. S. Barnes in 1904. Garcilaso's account, *The Florida of the Inca*, was translated by John Varner and Jeanette Varner and published by the University of Texas Press in 1951. Almost a historical document itself, the 1939 publication of the Swanton route is still available from the Smithsonian Institution Press in Washington, D.C. Entitled *Final Report of the United States De Soto Commission*, it was edited by John R. Swanton.

Most of the recent scholarship on De Soto and the other Spanish explorers is only now beginning to move from articles in scholarly journals into book form. Charles Hudson's work on Juan Pardo's explorations was published by the Smithsonian Institution Press in 1990. Entitled *The Expeditions of Juan Pardo, 1566–1568*, it presents a thorough treatment of the Pardo expeditions and includes a new translation of the Pardo documents by Paul Hoffman, a historian at Louisiana State University. The De Soto expedition in Florida is examined in detail in *Hernando de Soto and the Indians of Florida* (Florida, 1993), coauthored by Jerald Milanich and Charles Hudson. *The Forgotten Centuries* (Georgia, 1994) is a collection of articles by a number of scholars about the

Southeast in the sixteenth and seventeenth centuries. Edited by Charles Hudson and Carmen Chaves Tesser, it includes an article by Hudson that lays out the entire De Soto route in some detail from beginning to end.

A more readable, less technical book about Spanish exploration in the southeastern United States, and also in the Caribbean, is *First Encounters*, written by scholars for the general public and edited by Jerald Milanich and Susan Milbrath. Richly illustrated, it was published by the University of Florida Press in 1989.

The first draft of Charles Hudson's definitive book on the De Soto route is almost completed. These things take time. It should be in print by the mid-1990s, God willing.

CPSIA information can be obtained at www.ICGtesting.com
Printed in the USA
BVOW07s1107240813

329322BV00002B/153/P